The South West Coast Path Association is a Registered Charity, number 1163422, and a volunteer led organisation governed by Trustees. It was formed by Philip and Mary Carter in 1973.

There is a volunteer Path Committee made up of Area and Local Reps who walk and survey the Path to ensure funds raised are spent where they are most needed.

Staff members undertake the rest of the work, ensuring that the Business Plan set out by the Trustees is delivered and that volunteers are supported in their endeavours.

If you would like to contact the Association the details are as follows:
South West Coast Path Association Residence 2, Royal William Yard, Plymouth, PL1 3RP
Tel: 01752 896237

Chairman: chair@southwestcoastpath.org.uk
Administration: hello@southwestcoastpath.org.uk

Published by: The South West Coast Path Association
ISBN: 978-0-907055-29-7

© **South West Coast Path Association 2020**
Designed by Ingrid Kendall, Paignton.   Map imagery by Luke Smith.
Printed by Deltor Communications LTD

Cover photography: Great Hangman by Gary Holpin

Welcome

to the Complete Guide to the South West Coast Path.

This Guide is produced by the South West Coast Path Association, the voice and champion of the Path, to celebrate this magical natural beauty that is our Coast Path.

The South West Coast Path is the longest National Trail at 630 miles in length. Starting at Minehead in Somerset it runs along the coastline of Exmoor and North Devon into Cornwall. After running along the south coast of Devon it then follows the Dorset coastline before finally ending at Poole Harbour.

Whether you're looking for an afternoon stroll with friends and family, or you're a long-distance walker looking for a challenge or you just need some escapism or rehabilitation, our glorious Coast Path has something for everyone.

Join the Path at any point and you will discover myths and legends, secret coves linked to infamous smugglers and natural wonders with a wealth of wildlife and geology all topped with spectacular vistas.

The aim of the Association is to look after the Path, protecting it for future generations and promoting it for the enjoyment of everyone. We have a range of supporters helping us to deliver these promises. This includes a membership of well over 7,000 dedicated South West Coast Path lovers from all over the world. A dedicated few have been supporting us since 1973 when the South West Peninsular Coast Path Association was set up – thank you!

Thanks also to the several hundred businesses supporting the Coast Path, through our Business Membership scheme. This offers advertising for businesses, and support for them to promote themselves to visitors of the Path, whilst at the same time helping invest back into the Trail.

The Association is also supported by business sponsors including South West Water who have been supporting the work of the Association since 2014. Also supporting us are Beach Retreats, Forthglade and Devon & Cornwall Holidays who are all Silver Sponsors.

The listings in the walk Sections of this guide, including places to stay, eat and things to do are all our Business Members. To ensure they can continue to support the Path, we ask you to kindly support them.

Thank you, from the team at the South West Coast Path Association

> Thank you! It costs at least £1,400 every year to look after each mile of Coast Path, with the help of our members we are able to protect and promote it for future generations.

CONTENTS

The South West Coast Path

Planning your journey

Follow the Path

Love the Path

Photographs courtesy of: Angie Latham, Sue Searle, James Loveridge, Russell Pike, Ian Brown, Ian Perkins, Lewis M Jefferies, Julian Baird, Tor McIntosh, Andy Fox, Andrew Trenoweth, Robert Price, Donald Pelliccia, Barry Lockwood, Alexander Hall, Daryl Hutchinson, Neil Taylor, Ian Lewis, Virginia Arendt, Vicky Williams, Kerry Roberts, Peter Ford, Ron Bryans, Vickie Moss , Claire Hughes, Jessica Cooper-Dawkins, Peter Edwards, Josef FitzGerald-Patrick, John Bishop, Jason Gillman, Colin Foster, Jeremy Willcocks, Paul Rhodes, Gary Holpin, Rosie Spooner, Gareth Price, Keith Mashiter, Eddie Skinner, Chris Spracklen, Keith Payne, Alistair Mc Garv, Cliff Palmer, Mick Sandford, James Loveridge, Eleonora Pavlovska, Tim Jepson, Jennifer Rowlandson, Annie Spratt, Fiona Keene, Fern Richardson, Alison Webber, Steve Tew, Mal Ogden, Mike Mayor, Kingsley Scott, Wendy Berg, Maria Martin, Roger Hollingswort.

Important – Please Note

A Gift of Time and Nature

I have friends who believe there are no adventures to be had on our long distance paths here in the UK. That our islands don't hold the excitement that can be found in Europe or the Americas and beyond. They've explained this to me as they've packed their bags, preparing to head off to walk the Camino de Santiago, or the Appalachian Trail, or to hike up Machu Picchu. Complaining that the West Highland Way is plagued by midges, Offa's Dyke is just a walk through farmland and the Pennine Way is nothing but bogs and rocks. That our National Trails are just miniature, uninteresting versions of their foreign counterparts.

They argue our walks don't compare with the soaring drama of the Pacific Crest Trail, or the mountainous spectacle of the Tour de Mont Blanc, and continue to stuff their down jackets and blister plasters into their rucksacks. But when I say - what about the South West Coast Path? - they stop packing. What could they possibly say? What is there that compares with the rollercoaster ride that is the 630 mile Trail around the south west of England? It would be easy to say that the South West Coast Path is tame by comparison to all those exotic and foreign paths. How can you compare the adventure of a hike through remote forested mountains, where you're dependant on dried rations for the majority of the Trail, with a walk along the beaches and headlands of home and a cream tea around every corner?

The answer is of course, you can't. There is no long distance walking trail that compares with the SWCP. Nowhere else can you hike 630 uninterrupted miles of coastline, crossing wild headlands for weeks - or months for some of us - with the calls of oystercatchers in your ears and the smell of salt laden air ever present. This path may not have deep dark forests or towering mountains, yet it still evokes adrenaline, excitement and a sense of wonder. A path that rises and falls from sea level to hundreds of feet and back, over and over until the walker reaches the end only to find they have climbed the equivalent of Everest nearly four times.

If I'd realised it was such a tough walk I might not have tackled it. But if I hadn't I'd have missed so much. I would never have crossed the wind-swept cliffs of Exmoor, so high that I almost flew with the gulls. Or swam with them as they drifted motionless and sleeping in calm sheltered waters. I wouldn't have sat in a wet sleeping bag on a foggy hillside and watched the light break over the headlands, as the seals called in the coves below. Or experienced the absolute tranquillity of Fleet Lagoon, or the uncontained, raw power of the elements on the blocky granite cliffs beyond Land's End.

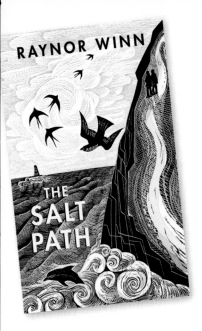

I might never have stood with my face to the Atlantic, nothing between me and Canada other than the wind and raging sea and known the ultimate sense of freedom that comes with such wild exposure.

But more than that, I wouldn't have bitten into a blackberry that held the taste of a ripe purple autumn on the coast. Something that only comes when the sea mist lays a layer of salt on a perfectly ripe fruit and gives us something that chefs can't create and money can't buy. A lightly salted blackberry. Only a walk on the South West Coast Path can give you that – it's a gift of time and nature.

Obviously my friends have already put their passports away, packed their swimming trunks and are heading out for a cream tea on the clifftops as we speak.

Raynor Winn

Pendower Cove

Introduction to the South West Coast Path

Stretching over 630 miles of stunning coastline, the South West Coast Path is one of the world's great long-distance walks. On your journey along the Coast Path you will pass through Exmoor National Park, five Areas of Outstanding Natural Beauty, two UNESCO World Heritage Sites and many more protected landscape, wildlife and heritage areas.

The South West Coast Path is the longest of 16 National Trails crossing England and Wales. As one of the more challenging Trails it has a combined ascent almost four times that of Mount Everest.

You can join the Coast Path in many places and follow the acorn waymarkers to guide you along the spectacular ever-changing vistas that our beautiful coastline offers. Your journey will take you through rocky headlands, ravines, waterfalls and towering cliffs through to sandy beaches and tranquil river estuaries. Travelling along the trail also gives you the opportunity to explore the many villages and towns along the South West coast.

This Guide has been designed as a helpful way to plan your time on the Coast Path. We have included practical information you need to start or continue your adventure, such as tide times and transport information. The Guide splits the Trail into seven sections, with each section including useful information such as ascent, distance, grading and approximate timing for that stretch of the Coast Path. At the end of each of the sections we have listed where to sleep, eat and what to do along that part of the Trail.

Protecting the Path

The South West Coast Path Association is governed by a Board of Trustees with nearly 100 volunteers helping to support this amazing Trail. Our vision is to protect and improve the Coast Path, now and for future generations.

The South West Coast Path National Trail is managed through a Trails Partnership comprising of six highways authorities:

Exmoor National Park Authority; Devon County Council; Cornwall Council; Plymouth City Council; Torbay Council; Dorset County Council along with the National Trust and Natural England, and is coordinated by the South West Coast Path Association.

Making a difference

Your support is crucial to the work we do in protecting and improving the Coast Path. That's why we're very careful how we spend the money supporters like yourselves contribute to the Association.

The Association has a proud history of getting the best value from your support. Following the 2014 storms large numbers of sections of the Coast Path closed. We were able to leverage Association funds to secure partnership funding, which in turn was used to unlock over £1 million worth of funding through the Coastal Communities Fund (CCF). With this money we completed 41 repair and improvement projects in partnership with the National Trust and local councils.

In addition to significant grants, our Path Committee supports many smaller projects along the Coast Path every year; the Association part-funding improvement projects to leverage best value of your support for the Coast Path and its future.

How to help

There are many ways you can help support the Coast Path, from membership to volunteering. If you have a business, you may wish to become a business member or sponsor or just get in touch to see how we can work together. Donations and legacies help us continue Path improvements and can provide a lovely tribute to special people or to commemorate special occasions.

In addition to this Guide visit **www.southwestcoastpath.org.uk** for more inspiration and information about the South West Coast Path, our events and ways to support the Association.

History of the South West Coast Path Association

The Association was formed on 5th May 1973 and registered as a charity in 1974. Inspired by walking the Pennine Way, founding members Philip and Mary Carter wanted to make sure that the Coast Path was just as enjoyable. The plan was for the Charity to promote the Path and lobby for its completion. The South West Coast Path National Trail was opened in stages and officially complete in 1978.

Having succeeded with these initial goals, the South West Way Association (as it was first known) had a long list of improvements for the Path. During the 90s, the Association came of age. Growing standing with local authorities and the National Trust meant that many of these recommended alternate routes and Path improvements were achieved.

More recently, the Association has been championing new and improved access opportunities (including as part of the England Coast Path), and now coordinates the Partnership that looks after this internationally renowned Trial.

The Coast Path has improved significantly since the initial 1970's route, in no small way due to the efforts of Philip, Mary and the many volunteers and handful of staff who have, and still do, work with the Charity. In 2018, the South West Coast Path celebrated its 40th birthday and thanks to the generosity of members, marked the occasion by successfully raising £40,000.

Find out more and read more about our history on our website **www.southwestcoastpath.org.uk**

Membership

If you are already a member, thank you very much for your support. We can't protect and champion the Path without your help.
If you would like to become a member of the Association, and join thousands of others, who are helping us to enable access to this beautiful trail for everyone for always, please join us today or encourage a friend to sign up. Supporting the charity and adding a voice as a member helps us to improve the Path and keep the way open to beautiful coastal places. As a member you give us a voice. With more members we have a stronger voice which helps us to gain more funding for the Path.

Our members are great supporters of the Path, if you would like to join us prices for 2020 are:

Single Membership	**£26.50**
Joint Membership	**£34.50**
Overseas membership	**£34.50**

You can join at **www.southwestcoastpath.org. uk/support-us** or by telephoning **01752 896237**.

Membership benefits include: A copy of the latest Complete Guide, 15% Cotswold Outdoor discount, two editions of our inspirational 'Trailblazing' magazine, monthly enews and exclusive offers across the year. Upon completion of the Path you will also receive a FREE completion certificate and badge.

Funding Path Improvements

- **£25** buys and installs one oak step board
- **£100** buys a stone step
- **£250** covers the cost of buying and installing an oak fingerpost
- **£500** enables us to fund the purchase and installation of an oak gate

Planning Your Walk

You might be planning to walk the whole 630 miles or just taking to the Path for a few hours, half a day or perhaps just a picnic! In any event you are likely to know your capabilities and not need detailed advice. However, it is worth remembering that some lengths of the Coast Path can be quite arduous, with frequent repeated climbs and descents or occasional awkward terrain, and it is not always possible to calculate the time or effort to be taken for a length purely on the distance. The degree of difficulty has to be considered so check in this guide for the grading – easy, moderate, strenuous or severe – of any length you're looking to walk for an idea of what to expect. For example, the time and effort required for a 'severe' length can be twice that for the same distance of an 'easy' section.

Long Distance Walking

If you are looking for advice on a walk along the Coast Path spanning more than a day, there are some helpful points below to ensure you have a safe and memorable time.

Newcomers to the Coast Path

A great way of getting an idea of what coastal walking is about is to take a day walk first. Perhaps start with a length graded 'easy' or 'moderate' in the Guide – start at one end and turn back when still feeling quite fresh to avoid fighting fatigue at the end. Alternatively, walk a section shown as having convenient public transport. If doing this, try to use the public transport at the start and walk back to your base. This avoids having to race the clock to catch a bus at the end of the walk.

While there is little need for special kit on the 'easy' sections – good shoes and a rainproof jacket will probably be enough – once you progress further decent boots and a rucksack for food and drink and other bits and pieces will be needed. And although it is unlikely you will get lost many walkers like to have the appropriate map to keep track of where they are and what is around them.

Long Distance Coast Path Walking

If you have not undertaken walking for more than a day at a time, bear in mind that you will not be able to keep up the same distance day after day as you do in a one-off day walk. The first reason for this is that you will probably be carrying more gear than usual. This may include a change of clothes and overnight kit, all in a bigger rucksack than usual. However, it is possible to overcome this by using Baggage Transfer providers – see page 15 of this Guide or check out website at **www.southwestcoastpath.org.uk**.

Secondly, there is the 'wear' factor – for the first few days especially, it is simply more tiring having to walk each day. And finally, there is the 'interest' factor – the walk is likely to take you through new places and new scenery; there is more to see and you will need more time to look round.

These factors will influence your planning. It is very important not to be too optimistic about what you can achieve each day, especially if booking accommodation ahead. Booking ahead does have the advantage of knowing you have a bed for the night, which can be important in the south west in the summer. On the other hand, it does mean that even if you are tired, have developed blisters and the weather is awful, you have to keep going. Be sure to check the grading in the Guide for the length you will be walking – remember the time and effort for a 'severe' length will be much more than that for the same distance on an 'easy' section.

Some Practical Details

While you will have to carry more gear than usual, think long and hard about every item you think you will need and travel as light as possible. Also remember that rucksacks are very rarely waterproof. A plastic liner, used as an additional inner layer, will prevent arriving at your accommodation after a day in the rain to find that your change of clothes is wet. Another practical point to be aware of is the availability of refreshments. You are recommended to carry water whenever out walking on the coast. Nevertheless, during the summer season, refreshments are quite widely available except for the relatively few remote lengths which are highlighted in the Guide. However, out of the holiday season refreshments can be quite far apart on long stretches of coast and you should take your own food supplies as well as water.

Walking Alone

The most important thing to remember if walking alone is to make sure someone knows your destination and estimated time of arrival. You are most unlikely to get into trouble but it is comforting to know that you will be missed if you don't arrive and that anyone searching for you knows roughly where to look.

Also, make sure you take a mobile phone. It is true that signal coverage is patchy along the coast but it's still worth having one. And if you have a smart phone, there are apps available that enable you to share your progress with family or friends, and so can give a further indication of where you are if you haven't arrived where and when you were expected.

At the Association we have a scheme that enables solo members to meet like-minded individuals wanting to walk the Coast Path, Contact **hello@southwestcoastpath.org.uk** for details.

Be our eyes and ears, as well as feet on the ground.

Please let us know if you spot a problem or want to suggest an improvement to this much-loved National Trail. Local authority and National Trust teams work hard to manage the Path to a high standard and it really helps to have feedback from those using the Path. If you see a broken signpost, think that a way marker may be missing, identify stiles or gates in need of repair, or encounter potholes and excessive mud please use the Report a Problem page on our website **www.southwestcoastpath.org.uk**, contact us on **01752 896237** or email **hello@southwestcoastpath.org.uk** and we'll make sure that the information gets to the right person.

Wembury

Follow the Acorn

The South West Coast Path is one of 16 National Trails. This 'family' of Trails is being added to with completion of the England Coast Path planned for 2020. The South West Coast Path is well signposted and waymarked, using the distinctive National Trail symbol of the acorn.

This acorn is often used alongside coloured arrows or the words 'footpath', 'bridleway' or 'byway' to indicate which public access rights apply to that particular stretch of path.

Yellow arrows indicate a 'Public Footpath' for use by walkers.

Blue arrows are for a 'Public Bridleway' which can be used by walkers, horse riders, and cyclists.

A **red arrow** indicates that the path is a 'Public Byway' which can be used by walkers, horse riders, cyclists, carriage drivers and motorised vehicles.

You may also see a **purple arrow** which marks a 'Public Restricted Byway' where the public have a right of way on foot, horseback, bicycle or horse-drawn carriage.

At some path junctions you will find a waymark post with more than one arrow. The arrow at the top nearest to the acorn symbol indicates the direction of the Coast Path. Below that (separated by a black line) you may find other arrows which indicate the direction of connecting paths.

Alternatively, connecting paths may be marked with arrows on the side of separate posts that don't have the acorn symbol. In most cases the direction indicated by the arrow is obvious - if unsure, they are designed to be read when you are standing looking straight at the arrow.

Waymarker posts along the Coast Path are predominantly made from wood. For some parts of the Trail waymarking more closely reflects particular local environmental characteristics, for example the use of granite waymarks in parts of West Cornwall and Purbeck stone in Dorset.

Please take care when walking the route to follow directional signage on the ground and not just rely on publications. Guide books, leaflets and maps can become out-of-date and so may not show recent changes.

Please also remember that much of the Trail is along cliff-top paths - in places a very high cliff top. Path managers endeavour to keep the Trail safe, but walkers should remember not to stray away from the Path, especially on the seaward side. Cliff edges may be unstable in places.

For some locations, the route description suggests an alternative path away from the officially designated route. Please feel free to use these alternatives as they will be on rights of way or, occasionally, permissive paths maintained by the landowner for use by the public.

The Countryside Code - Respect, Protect, Enjoy

Take nothing but pictures, leave nothing but footprints and kill nothing but time.

- Be safe - plan ahead and be prepared
- Follow advice and local signs
- Protect plants and animals - please take all litter home
- Pick up dog poo and dispose of appropriately
- Leave wildlife, flora and fauna as you find it
- Leave gates and property as you find them.

Looking after our environment

There are lots of ways to protect the Path for future generations, here are some suggestions:

- Use public transport where possible
- Support local shops and services
- Use guidebooks and information
- Keep to the Path to minimise erosion
- Report any problems to the South West Coast Path Association
- Keep dogs under control
- Take care of the Path and of yourself.

Godrevy from Gwithian Towans

Kit list for walking the South West Coast Path

Here is what we recommend you pack if you are walking the South West Coast Path.

Base Layer

A base layer is a good place to start walking outfits. Merino wool is ideal for colder weather as it will keep the heat in, whilst wicking away your sweat.

Spare Insulating Layer

It's always worth having a spare insulation layer, but the conditions you choose to walk in dictate what level of insulation you will need. A light fleece is fine for summer, but British winters demand a down or synthetic insulated jacket.

Waterproofs

Waterproof layers are vital when exploring the Coast Path to ensure you don't get caught out and end up walking in damp clothes. Your waterproofs should be breathable, with ventilation to allow sweat vapour to escape.

Sturdy Footwear

You will need some sturdy walking trainers or boots to take on the sometimes-uneven terrain of the Coast Path in comfort.

First Aid Kit

Whilst you are unlikely to find yourself in danger when walking sensibly on the Coast Path, it never hurts to be prepared. Carry a first aid kit and make sure you know how to use everything in it. Take a torch in case you get caught out after dark, and a whistle is a lightweight way to help attract attention in an emergency. Another handy thing for your kit might be a fold away emergency foil blanket.

Food and water

Keeping hydrated is essential for an enjoyable day on the trail. Aim for at least 2 litres per day, but remember the amount you need to drink is entirely dependent on the length of time you plan to be walking and the temperature. Even if you have planned a lunch stop into your walk, we recommend always keeping a snack with you to keep your energy levels up.

Eye and skin protection

When it is sunny you'll want to block out the bright light with sunglasses so you can fully enjoy the spectacular sea views. Walking when it's warm is great, but it's important to be sun safe, even on overcast days, so pack some sun cream and apply it accordingly.

Map and Compass

Even though the Coast Path is exceptionally well signed, taking a map and compass, and knowing how to use them, is essential on any longer walk. You never know when you might have to change route due to unforeseen circumstances, and a quick look at a map can give you a safe alternative.

Walking poles

Whilst not essential, walking poles can help you move more confidently over difficult terrain and even come in handy should you need to cross a stream or muddy area of the Path.

Mobile phone

You cannot rely on it, as signal is very patchy along many parts of the Coast Path, but it is handy to have a mobile phone with you. To help with any navigation issues, the route of the Coast Path outside of towns is shown on Google Maps, but be aware that using GPS will drain your battery, so it's worth taking a USB power bank as backup.

Safety Advice

It is your responsibility to stay safe whilst out on the South West Coast Path, and to look after others if you are walking as part of a group. Please remember to always keep to the Path, follow the advisory signs and waymarks and stay away from cliff edges. Particular care and attention should be paid to children and dogs, ensure they are kept in sight at all times. It is important to make sure you are well equipped for your walk, and that you take into consideration possible sudden changes in weather when you are packing your kit. Don't forget to check the weather forecast in advance of your trip and take note of when the sun will set, so you know how many hours of sunlight to expect. The Path can get very muddy, especially if you are walking in winter, so take care on particularly steep sections.

We advise you to be mindful of your ability level. Some sections of the South West Coast Path can be very strenuous and/or remote. Always check the difficulty grading in the walk description and for more challenging routes, try and find someone else to walk with you. If you are venturing out alone, we recommend telling a friend or family member exactly where you plan to walk and an approximate time for arrival. In case of an emergency, please dial 999 and ask for the Coastguard.

Weather

The South West Coast Path is more exposed to wind than any other long-distance trail in the UK, so please pay attention to gale forecasts. Along some sections, strong winds can be dangerous, especially when rounding exposed headlands and crossing bridges where a high backpack can act like a sail. Please take particular care on these sections. Wind and rain combined can cause your core temperature to drop significantly. If possible, take a spare layer of clothing with you and opt for waterproof and windproof jackets to protect you against the worst of the elements. It is equally important to shield yourself from harmful UV rays, especially on bright cloudy or breezy days when the risk of sunburn feels lower.

Military Ranges

Two lengths of the South West Coast Path may be affected by the use of military ranges. The use of one, at Tregantle in south east Cornwall only means that a more inland and less picturesque route must be used for a length of some 1.25 miles/2km in Section 46, Portwrinkle-Cremyll (Plymouth Ferry). However, if there is military use of the other, east of Lulworth Cove in Dorset, this means the whole of Section 67 between Lulworth Cove and Kimmeridge Bay will be impossible. Generally the Lulworth ranges are closed to walkers Monday to Friday during school term time and also up to six times a year at weekends. Try to arrange your walk so as not to miss this superb, but tough section.

Information and details for the ranges are included in the relevant Section descriptions and online.

Route Changes

The coast would not look so beautiful and dramatic if it wasn't for cliff and beach erosion. The downside to this is that sometimes cliff falls or landslips close sections of the Coast Path resulting in temporary inland diversions, which can occasionally be quite lengthy. In these instances, always follow signage and information on the ground.

We are also constantly looking for opportunities to improve the route in the few places where it is not as good as it could be. The government's plans to create the England Coast Path around the entire coast of England by 2020 will help with this, and over the next few years we are expecting the route to be changed in places.

Whilst any route changes and diversions are signed, they may make your walk longer so it's worth checking the 'route changes' pages of our website before you set out.

Photography

As you can see from the many photos in this guide, you're going to be walking through beautiful coastal scenery, so a camera is a great way of recording your journey. We love to see your photos, and each year we run a photo competition with the best pictures winning some great prizes including being featured in a South West Coast Path Association calendar. See **www.southwestcoastpath.org.uk** for information on how to enter the competition.

Telephones

Although some telephone boxes are still in use on and around the Coast Path, many have been converted for many different uses, such as libraries, mini cafes, even storage for defibrillators. For those in use as phone boxes still, you should be able to use Switch, Maestro, Delta, Solo and Visa Debit cards. There are still some telephone boxes which will accept BT Phonecards or/and chargecards.

Mobile phones are always useful to have whilst on the Coast Path, but do not rely on them as coverage is not always good. You may also have difficulty in obtaining top-up in some areas. For these reasons, always make sure you have a map and/or detailed walking directions with you.

Cashpoints

ATM machines are widely available along or near the Coast Path. Visit **www.link.co.uk/atmlocator** to find out where they are. With the closure of many stand-alone Post Offices, cash is often available at the small, shop-based Post Offices, regardless of making a purchase and without charge. Overseas visitors will probably find their cashpoint cards very useful. Please note, there are some smaller accommodation providers who are not equipped to take payment via credit/debit card and you may need cash to settle your bill.

Dogs

Most district councils and unitary authorities have dog bans on beaches from 1st May to 31st October. The Association and most of the general public regard this as a sensible measure.

There are several sections of the South West Coast Path that cross beaches and are officially marked as such. These beaches are Croyde Bay in Devon, Harlyn Bay, Constantine, Treyarnon, Perranporth and Penberth slipway in Cornwall, and Studland in Dorset. The routing of the Coast Path (with its designation as a National Trail) across these beaches means that they are public rights of way. A public right of way does carry precedence over seasonal regulations banning dogs, and ultimately, any walker in the process of walking along, but not stopping on these sections of the Path may be accompanied by a dog on a lead.

However we strongly recommend the following:

- ❧ If an alternative route is provided and signposted, that you use it
- ❧ That residents close to dog ban beaches use other walks and do not use the beach path during the ban period
- ❧ That the dog should be on a short (not extendable) lead
- ❧ That your progress should be as unobtrusive as possible to other beach users. To aid this, close attention should be paid to the actual route marked on the map
- ❧ Lastly, but most importantly, all dog mess MUST be removed from the beach

The Association shop has handy poo bag dispensers that attach to a backpack or lead and these can be bought online or by calling **01752 896237**.

Along the Coast Path

Many walk the South West Coast Path with their dogs and all have an enjoyable time and we receive many reports of dogs completing the whole Path. However, we do urge caution because the Path is very high along many sections and it only takes an excited dog to go chasing after a rabbit to cause much grief if it goes over the edge. If your dog is well-trained and you can trust it, then please enjoy your Coast Path walk with your four-legged friend. If it is not and you cannot, then do take great care, particularly on the many sections along the South West Coast Path that have farm livestock grazing.

It is also extremely important that you clean up after your dog. Bag it and bin it wherever you are otherwise you give all dog owners a bad name and can pass on diseases to people and farm animals.

Baggage Transfer

Walking is even more enjoyable when all you have to carry is a light day pack, so why not take advantage of a kit transfer service? Packing becomes much easier when you're not worrying about the weight and you know your overnight bags will be ready and waiting when you arrive at the place you're staying.

Several companies offer this service, moving your bags between overnight stops. All you need to do is arrange on the morning of your departure to leave your luggage with the proprietor of your hotel, B&B or campsite and they will organise for it to be delivered to your next night's accommodation.

There are two luggage transfer companies that proudly support the South West Coast Path Association; Luggage Transfers and WD Transfers. Details of both can be found on our website under 'Baggage Transfers'.

Luggage Transfers are the only luggage transfer specialist covering the whole 630 miles of the South West Coast Path. With over 10 years' experience and over 50 drivers, we continue to support the South West Coast Path Association through voluntary donations from our private walkers. We are now FEEFO Gold award rated and deliver on average 10,000 bags per month which allows us to daisy chain and 'partner up' bookings to reduce our carbon footprint. Your bags are also insured against loss whilst in our driver's care. www.luggagetransfers.co.uk

WD Transfers operate across the West Cornwall section of the South West Coast Path between Padstow and Falmouth. We have over 10 years combined experience transporting luggage for walkers around Cornwall and are the only luggage transfer company solely focussed on this region. We provide point to point baggage transfers for walkers and walking holiday companies alike and are confident that we cannot be beaten for price, reliability and customer service.
www.cornwallluggagetransfer.co.uk

Wheal Coates

Package holidays

Need some help planning your holiday? We recommend contacting one of the walking holiday companies listed in this section who provide complete walking holiday packages along parts of the South West Coast Path. These include guided and self-guided options depending on how you prefer to travel, as well as themed walks from food foraging to wildlife watching.

Walking Holiday Providers

 Absolute Escapes are award-winning specialists in self-guided walking holidays on the South West Coast Path. Packages include carefully selected accommodation, door-to-door bag transfers, and comprehensive information pack with guidebook, map, and recommendations for lunch and dinner each day. They are a leading specialist in walking holidays and offer packages on many long-distance trails in the UK & Ireland. www.absoluteescapes.com/South-West-Coast-Path.html

 **Active England** is an active travel tour company, which takes its guests walking and cycling right through the heart of the British countryside. Experience up-close the stunning scenery of England's South West walking through Dartmoor National Park and the stunning North Devon beaches. Walk along parts of the Cornish Coast Path, visiting the charming seaside towns of St Ives and Padstow. Immerse yourself in the legends of King Arthur and Ross Poldark along the Cornish coast. www.activeenglandtours.com

Encounter Walking Holidays provide walking holidays and short breaks on every section of the Coast Path. They specialise in helping with the requests that others struggle with

or don't want to take on - whether you are a small group looking for the best prices, walking with your dogs, have an unusual itinerary idea or are just arriving from overseas and are new to UK Walking Routes. They provide detailed quotes for walkers with no commitment to book so get in touch with your ideas and questions! www.encounterwalkingholidays.com

 Footpath Holidays is a family owned walking holiday company founded in 1983. Self-guided holidays along the South West Coast; single centre and 'moving on' with accommodation and baggage transfer. Guided group holidays in Devon, Cornwall and Dorset. www.footpath-holidays.com

 Footscape provide walking holidays and short breaks along the famous World Heritage Jurassic Coast. They provide flexibility of choice: where and how much to walk each day, where to stay and precise, foolproof directions. Based in Dorset they constantly update the trails and provide interesting information, bringing the coast to life. Get in touch for a no commitment quote. www.footscape.co.uk

Jurassic Coast Walking offer bespoke walking holidays for individuals, couples or small groups on the beautiful Isle of Purbeck. Walks can be guided, or self-guided and guided walks are led by local writer and photographer Robert Westwood, author of a number of books on the Jurassic Coast, including walking guides for the Jurassic Coast Trust. Robert trained as a geologist and will help you enjoy and appreciate the wonderful history of this beautiful stretch of coastline. www.jurassiccoastwalking.co.uk

Mickledore Travel specialises in self-guided walking and cycling holidays in the UK. They provide a flexible service making the arrangements that suit you, leaving you free to just enjoy your walk. As walkers and cyclists, they aim to provide a service of the highest quality and a holiday to remember. www.mickledore.co.uk

Nearwater Holidays specialise in single based, inn-to-inn trips and bespoke walking holidays along all sections of the South West Coast Path. The walks have been developed with the benefit of local knowledge to ensure the visiting walker has the chance to see a few extra special places that they would otherwise overlook. www.nearwaterwalkingholidays.co.uk

Nomadic Camping Cornwall offer dog friendly, fully supported assistance and camping options for self-guided couples or groups on the SWCP from Newquay on the North Coast to Falmouth on the South Coast. This means that you can walk the Path, carrying only what you need for the day, knowing that a Nordic Tentipi will be set up with everything you need at your next campsite. www.nomadiccampingcornwall.co.uk

Sherpa Expeditions founded in 1973, offer a range of self-guided inn-to-inn walking and cycling tours on their Walkers' Britain programme which has over 25 walking & cycling itineraries to choose from, including routes in the South West. On your travels with them, you will benefit from packages with detailed route notes, maps, pre-departure information and personal service provided. You will stay overnight where available in locally owned and operated B&Bs, hotels and inns to provide you with a charming local experience. www.sherpaexpeditions.co.uk

Walk Kernow Nordic Walking in Cornwall is a fantastic pastime. Not only will you be exercising your whole body with the use of poles, you will also have a few advantages over other walkers on the path such as remaining more upright as you walk and finding it easier to move through more difficult terrain. The poles also make it easier to walk up hills, so your walks become more enjoyable. Walk Kernow provides Beginners Workshops, weekly Nordic Walks and Nordic Walking breaks. www.walkkernow.co.uk

Walk the Trail offer self-guided walking holidays throughout the South West including the South West Coast Path, The Two Moors Way, and The Saints Way along with many other routes across the UK. All holidays include a personalised holiday pack complete with luggage transfers, accommodation location information, maps and guidebooks. Their unique Holiday Finder Tool allows you to choose your start and end locations, giving you greater flexibility to enjoy the Coast Path at a pace to suit you. www.walkthetrail.co.uk

Western Discoveries are the local experts for walking holidays in Cornwall. They are based in West Cornwall and specialise in providing self-led walking holidays along the Cornwall section of the stunning South West Coast Path. Accommodation, luggage transfers, maps, their own detailed route notes and arrival/departure transfers from local transport terminals are all provided with an unparalleled attention to detail. www.westcornwallwalks.co.uk

Single Base Walking Holiday Providers

Bosavern House offers a free drop off and collection service to and from your coastal walk as part of its Walking package which also includes breakfast, a packed lunch and a 3 course home cooked evening meal. Their self-guided walks cover several sections of the South West Coast Path with the advantage of returning to their comfortable bed and breakfast each evening. www.bosavern.com

Led Walks

Meadow View Guided Hikes offers a selection of dates and routes to add depth and knowledge to your walking experience, to avoid walking alone or as a taster/confidence builder. Currently ten public group walks are offered. Bespoke single/multi-day guided walks for private parties on any SWCP section plus cross-country link routes. Led by experienced walk leader, former member of Public Rights of Way team; also volunteer rep for the SWCPA for Mevagissey to Polperro. Self-guided itineraries with public transport options and sourcing accommodation also available. For latest dates and offers, or for a quote on your own idea visit the website. www.meadowviewguidedhikes.co.uk

Explore in Cornwall provides guided multiday, day and half day walks on the South West Coast Path throughout the Cornish and Devon sections of the Trail. All walks are guided by Steve Crummay who has over 30 years' experience of working in Cornwall's most amazing coast and countryside. They provide the very best bespoke walking on the Cornish and Devon sections of the Coast Path and show you the amazing places, wildlife and fascinating heritage that can be encountered on Britain's longest National Trail. www.exploreincornwall.co.uk

Led walks at Fowey

Access to the start of the Path

Access to the start of the Path can be made locally and from outside the region, with a bus service linking Minehead to the mainline railway station at Taunton.

Railways

Few people have the time to complete the entire Path in one go, instead they split it over a number of holidays. The easiest way to arrange this is to start and finish your trip at one of the towns along the Path with a train station, as this saves having to get back to your starting point to retrieve your car.

Please go to the map on the inside front cover and at the start of each section to see the main rail links.

Throughout the year there is a regular service linking London Paddington with Taunton, Exeter St. David's, Newton Abbot, Plymouth and Cornwall. There are also regular services linking Birmingham, the North West, North East and Scotland with Taunton, Exeter St. David's, Plymouth, Cornwall and Bournemouth.

There is also an overnight sleeper service between Paddington and Penzance.

There is a half hourly South West Trains service linking London Waterloo, Woking, Basingstoke and Southampton with Bournemouth, Poole, Wareham (for Swanage), Dorchester (for Bridport and Lyme Regis) and Weymouth for those intending to walk the Dorset end of the Coast Path.

East Devon is also served by South West Trains with an hourly service from London Waterloo to Exeter St David's calling at Woking, Basingstoke and Salisbury to Axminster (for Lyme Regis & Seaton), Honiton (for Sidmouth).

The cost of rail tickets varies considerably depending on when you buy them and what time you travel. For the best deals, avoid travelling at peak times and book in advance. If you need to travel during peak time it can often work out cheaper to buy separate tickets for the same train, splitting them between the peak and off-peak part of your journey.

In addition, with a bit of planning you can make your journey even more special by using one of the heritage steam railways that go to the coast.

To book your tickets to the South West, you can visit:

⊕ **www.thetrainline.com**
🕿 **0871 244 1545/0333 202 2222** 8am to 10pm
⊕ **www.nationalrail.co.uk**
🕿 **03457 484950**
⊕ **www.traveline.info**

Bus Services

For information on buses to the South West:

🕿 **0871 200 2233**
⊕ **www.travelinesw.com**
or to buy tickets go to
⊕ **www.nationalexpress.com**
🕿 **0871 781 8181** or **uk.megabus.com**

For Megabus timetable enquiries call
🕿 **0141 352 4444** open 24 hours a day or
🕿 **0900 1600 900** for booking a ticket from 7am to 10pm.

Tourist Information Centres (TICs) can be very helpful with bus enquiries. For details of all coastal TICs see page 200.

The ferry over the River Teign

Airports

There are airports in or near towns close to the Coast Path. In Path order, they are:

Newquay Airport

Direct services from around the UK, Ireland, Germany, Portugal and Spain and indirect services from around the world.
St Mawgan, Newquay, TR8 4RQ
- 01637 860600
- info@cornwallairportnewquay.com
- www.cornwallairportnewquay.com

Land's End

For flights to the Isles of Scilly: Isles of Scilly Travel, Steamship House, Quay Street, Penzance, TR18 4BZ
- 01736 334220
- sales@islesofscilly-travel.co.uk
- www.islesofscilly-travel.co.uk

Exeter

Exeter International Airport, Exeter, EX5 2BD
- 01392 367433
- www.exeter-airport.co.uk

Bournemouth

Bournemouth Airport Ltd.,
Christchurch, Bournemouth BH23 6SE
- 01202 364000
- www.bournemouthairport.com

Sea Transport

Brittany Ferries provide a ferry link to/from Plymouth, Poole and Portsmouth to the French ports of Roscoff, Cherbourg, Caen, St Malo & Le Havre, as well as to Santander & Bilbao in Spain.
Brittany Ferries, Millbay, Plymouth, Devon, PL1 3EW
- 0330 159 7000
- reservations@brittanyferries.com
- www.brittany-ferries.co.uk

. . . .

The Trip Planning Day By Day Guide pages on our website provide suggestions for how the Path can be completed as a series of day walks, using public transport
www.southwestcoastpath.org.uk

Bus Information

Listed below, in Path order, are details of services and information available from County Councils and local bus operators; it is intended for guidance use only. All information provided is correct at the time of going to print; responsibility for any inaccuracies or changes cannot be accepted by County Councils or bus operators. For up to date bus service information, telephone the relevant numbers given in the following paragraphs.

Somerset

For service 28 from Taunton to Minehead. From Taunton you can get a bus to Lyme Regis or Weymouth changing at Exeter and Axminster.

Local bus operator First Bus:
- 0345 646 0707
- www.firstgroup.com
- 0871 200 2233
- www.travelinesw.com

North Devon

The North Devon coast has a range of bus services which may be of use to coastal walkers. The greatest choice of destinations is from Barnstaple.

Devon & Cornwall's First Buses are useful for those walking between North Devon and North Cornwall.
- www.firstgroup.com

For Traveline timetable enquiries telephone
- 0871 200 2233
- www.travelinesw.com

Alternatively the Devon County Council web site offers Area Bus Timetable Booklets to download:
- www.traveldevon.info/bus/timetables

They advise that previously printed timetables will vary from these digital guides, but that the digital guides are the most up to date.

If you find yourself at a bus stop and want to know when the next bus is coming along, find the eight letter reference number on the stop and text it to 84268. You will receive a reply with the times of the next three buses to come past that stop.

Cornwall

Cornwall Council have a list of current bus routes:

🌐 **www.cornwall.gov.uk/transport-and-streets/public-transport/**

They advise that although every effort is made to keep this information as up to date as possible, it is advisable to also check with:

Traveline:
📞 **0871 200 2233**
🌐 **www.travelinesw.com**

Also local bus operator First:
📞 **0345 646 0707**
🌐 **www.firstgroup.com**

Stagecoach run service 6 from Exeter to Bude, if you are coming to the South West by train this may be useful.
🌐 **www.stagecoachbus.com**

South Devon

The coastline between Plymouth and Exeter is accessible by bus from many inland towns. As for North Devon, the Devon County Council web site has a variety of options. There is an interactive bus map to look at and also Area Bus Timetable Booklets to download:
🌐 **www.traveldevon.info/bus/timetables**

Also as for North Devon, when you are at a bus stop, use the 8 letter reference number on the bus stop and text it to 84268. You will receive a reply with the times of the next three buses to come past that stop.

For more timetable enquiries:

Traveline:
📞 **0871 200 2233**
🌐 **www.travelinesw.com**

The main operators are:
Stagecoach: **www.stagecoachbus.com**
First Group: **www.firstgroup.com**
Tally Ho: **01548 853081**
🌐 **www.tallyhoholidays.co.uk/Service-details**

For Plymouth Citybus map and services go to
🌐 **www.plymouth.gov.uk** and follow links for the transport section.

East Devon

The East Devon coastline is accessible by bus from Exeter, Ottery St. Mary, Honiton and Axminster. Trains are also available from London Waterloo stop at Axminster, Honiton and Exeter or the quicker train from London Paddington stops at Exeter as do trains coming from Bristol. Please note, as previously, that the summer and winter timetables do vary a lot.

Dorset

The Dorset Coast is accessible by bus from various inland points with train connections for the distant traveller. For more information:

Traveline:
📞 **0871 200 2233**
🌐 **www.travelinesw.com**

Rock to Padstow ferry

Ferries & River Crossings

The nature of the Coast Path means that many ferries must be used to cross estuaries along the length of the Path.

The ferry crossings below are in Path order.

Ferries can be subject to change due to weather conditions, tides and times of day. Ferry pick up and drop off location can also vary. We advise that you check with the relevant ferry or water taxi before travelling, rather than relying solely on the information below. All information correct at time of going to print.

Instow to Appledore (River Torridge)

Appledore Instow Ferry
- 07710 836317 (daytime only)
- www.appledoreinstowferry.com
- contact@appledoreinstowferry.com

Ferry service runs: 1st April to 31st October.

Padstow to Rock (River Camel)

- 01841 532239 / 07773081574
- www.padstow-harbour.co.uk
- padstowharbour@btconnect.com

		From Padstow	From Rock
First Ferry:		08:00	
Last Ferry:	1 Nov - 31 Mar	16:50	16:30
	1 Apr - 31 May	17:50	17:30
	1 June - mid July	18:50	18:30
	mid July - 31 Aug	19:50	19:30
	1 Sept - mid Sept	18:50	18:30
	mid Sept - 31 Oct	17:50	17:30

See ferry website for departure points as these can vary.

Water taxi:
- 01208 862815 (9am to 5pm)/07778 105297
- www.rock-watertaxi.co.uk
- info@rock-watertaxi.co.uk

Water Taxi service runs: 19.00 until midnight, through to the end of October.

Newquay to Crantock (River Gannel)

Fern Pit Ferry
- 01637 873181
- www.fernpit.co.uk
- info@fernpit.co.uk

Ferry service runs:
Daily from May - mid September
09:30 - 18:00 (weather dependent)

Gillan Creek

Sailaway St. Anthony Ltd
- 01326 231357
- www.sailawaystanthony.co.uk
- info@stanthony.co.uk

Ferry service runs: 1st April to 31st October
The stepping stones of the South West Coast Path across Gillan Creek are submerged roughly 3 hours either side of high water. Sailaway provides a ferry service on demand across the Creek.

Taxi:
For an alternative way around the river, please use one of the following:
Telstar Taxis Tel: 01326 221007
Meneage Taxis Tel: 01326 560530 / 07773 817156

Helford River

Helford River Boats
- 01326 250770
- www.helford-river-boats.co.uk
- info@helford-river-boats.co.uk

Ferry service runs: 1st April to 31st October:
09:30 to 17:00 on demand. July & August ferry may run into the evening.

Taxi:
For an alternative way around the river.
Telstar Taxis Tel: 01326 221007
Meneage Taxis Tel: 01326 560530 / 07773 817156

Falmouth

Cornwall Fal River Ferries - St Mawes Ferry
- 01326 741194
- www.falriver.co.uk
- info@falriver.co.uk

Ferry service runs: 7 Days a week all year round.

Falmouth Water Taxi
- 07522 446659
- www.falmouthwatertaxi.co.uk
- skipper@falmouthwatertaxi.co.uk

Water Taxi runs: 9am - 9pm

St Mawes - Place Creek

Cornwall Fal River Ferries - Place Ferry
- 01326 741194
- www.falriver.co.uk
- info@falriver.co.uk

Ferry service runs: 7 Days a week - April to October.

St Mawes Kayaks Water Taxi
- 07971 846786
- www.stmaweskayaks.co.uk

Fowey to Polruan (River Fowey)

Polruan Ferry Co Ltd
- 📞 **01726 870232**
- 🌐 **www.ctomsandson.co.uk/polruan-ferry**
- ✉ **enquiries@ctomsandson.co.uk**

Ferry service runs:
1st May – 30th September
Monday to Thursday: 07:15- 21:00
Friday: 07:15 – 23:00
Saturday: 07:30 – 23:00
Sunday: 09:00 – 21:00
1st October – 30th April
Monday to Thursday: 07:15 – 19:00
Friday to Saturday: 07:30 – 21:00
Sunday: 09:00 to 19:00

Cremyll (Mount Edgcumbe) to Plymouth (River Tamar)

Plymouth Boat Trips
- 📞 **01752 253153**
- 🌐 **www.plymouthboattrips.co.uk/ferries/cremyll-ferry**
- ✉ **info@plymouthboattrips.co.uk**

Ferry service runs:
Summer Service: 1st April to 30th September
From Cremyll:
Weekdays Monday – Thursday: 06:45 to 21:00
Friday: 06:45 to 22:00
Saturdays: 07:30 to 22:00
Sundays: 08:30 to 21:30

From Plymouth:
Monday to Thursday: 07:15 to 21:15
Friday: 07:15 to 22:15
Saturdays: 07:45 to 22:00
Sundays: 08:45 to 21:45

Winter Service from 1st October - 31st March
From Cremyll:
Monday to Friday: 06:45 to 18:30
Saturdays: 07:30 to 19:00
Sundays: 08:30 to 18:00

From Plymouth:
Monday to Friday: 07:15 to 18:45
Saturdays: 07:45 to 19:15
Sundays: 08:45 to 18:15

Sutton Harbour to Mount Batten (River Plym)

Mount Batten Ferry
- 📞 **07930 838614**
- 🌐 **www.mountbattenferry.co.uk**
- ✉ **mountbattenferry@gmail.com**

Summer ferry service runs:
From April to October:
Monday to Friday: 07:30 to 23:00
Saturday: 09:00 to 23:00
Sunday: 09:00 to 22:00

Winter ferry service runs:
October to March:
Monday to Thursday: 07:45 to 18:15
Friday: 07:45 to 23:00
Saturday 08:45 to 23:00
Sunday   08:45 to 18:15

Wembury (Warren Point) to Noss Mayo (River Yealm)

River Yealm Ferry & Water Taxi
- 📞 **Bill Gregor: 07817 132757**
- 🌐 **www.nationaltrust.org.uk/noss-mayo/features/noss-mayo-ferry**

Ferry service runs: 1st April to 30th September: 10:00 to 16:00.

Mothecombe to Wonwell (River Erme)

There is no ferry at the River Erme. Please refer to the tide times on page 25

Bigbury (Cockleridge) to Bantham Slipway (River Avon)

Ferry operations were not finalised when this Guide went to print, see our website for more up to date information **www.southwestcoastpath.org.uk**

Salcombe to East Portlemouth (Salcombe Estuary)

The Salcombe Ferry
- 📞 **01548 842061/07769 319375**
- 🌐 **www.salcombeinformation.co.uk/advertiser/salcombe-ferry**
- ✉ **simonshortman1@gmail.com**

Ferry service runs: All year, contact Simon Shortman ferry operator for further details.

Dartmouth to Kingswear (River Dart)

Lower Dartmouth Ferry
- 📞 **01803 752342**
- 🌐 **www.southhams.gov.uk/dartmouthlowerferry**
- ✉ **dlf@swdevon.gov.uk**

Ferry operates all year:
From Dartmouth TQ6 9AP:
Monday to Saturday: 07:10 to 22:55
Sunday: 08:10 to 22:45

From Kingswear TQ6 0AA:
Monday to Saturday: 07:00 to 22:45
Sunday: 08:00 to 22:45

Dartmouth (River Dart)

Dartmouth Steam Railway & River Boat Co
Dartmouth to Kingswear passenger ferry
- ☎ **01803 555872**
- ⊕ **www.dartmouthrailriver.co.uk/tours/ dartmouth-to-kingswear-passenger- ferry**

Ferry service runs:
Monday to Saturday: 07:30 to 23:10
Sundays: 09:00 to 23:15

Shaldon to Teignmouth (River Teign)

Teignmouth - Shaldon Ferry
- ☎ **Greg Allen: 07896 711822/07940503314**
- ⊕ **www.teignmouthshaldonferry.co.uk**

Ferry service runs:

April – End July	08:00 to 18:00
End July – End Aug	08:00 to dusk
September – October	08:00 to 18:00
November – January	08:00 to 16:30
February – March	08:00 to 17:00
Winter Weekends	start at 10:00
Summer Weekends	start at 09:00

Starcross to Exmouth (River Exe)

Starcross to Exmouth Ferry
- ☎ **Mark Rackley: 01626 774770/ 07974 022536**
- ⊕ **www.facebook.com/StarcrossExmouthFerry**

Ferry service runs: May to end October.
From Starcross every hour from 10:10 to 16:10,
(and 17:10 mid-May to mid-September)
From Exmouth every hour from 10:40 to 16:40
(and 17:40 (mid-May to mid-September)

Turf to Topsham (River Exe)

- ☎ **Steve Garrett:07778 370582**
- ⊕ **www.topshamtoturfferry.co.uk**
- ✉ **seadreamferry@gmail.com**

Ferry service runs:
Weekends and Bank holiday only:
Easter until Late May Bank Holiday and then
mid – 30th September
From Topsham: 11:30, 12:15, 13:00, 14:15
From Turf: 11:45, 12:30, 14:00, 15:00
Every day:
From Late May Bank Holiday to mid-September,
times as above
July and August weekends only:
From Topsham: 13:40, 15:15
From Turf: 13:15, 16:00

Dawlish Warren to Exmouth (River Exe)

Exeplorer Water Taxi
- ☎ **07970 918418**
- ⊕ **www.watertaxi.squarespace.com**
- ✉ **exeplorerwatertaxis@gmail.com**

Ferry service runs: Daily between 1st April to
31st October. Times vary between 07:20 and 20:00
throughout the year.

Topsham (River Exe)

**Exeter City Council, Canals and Rivers
Department**
- ☎ **07801 203338**
- ⊕ **www.exeter.gov.uk/leisure-and-culture/ sport-and-leisure/waterways/**

Ferry service runs:
Easter to September: 09:30 to 17:30
(daily except Tuesdays)
October to Easter - Weekends and bank holidays:
10:00 to 17:00

Weymouth Harbour

- ☎ **01305 838423**
- ⊕ **www.weymouth-harbour.co.uk**
- ✉ **weymouthharbour@dorset.gov.uk**

Ferry service runs:
Since 16th Century, rowing ferries have
taken passengers across Weymouth Harbour.
Alternatively, contact West Dorset Taxis:
07876 798770

South Haven Point to Sandbanks, Poole

Swanage Motor Road & Ferry Co
- ☎ **01929 450203**
- ⊕ **www.sandbanksferry.co.uk**

Ferry service runs:
Sandbanks: 07:00 to 23:00
Shell Bay: 07:10 to 23:10
Alternatively, contact A1 Taxis: **07758 130281**

If you are relying on a ferry service
we urge you to contact the ferry
operator direct before travelling.

Tide times included in this edition refer to the times of low water at Devonport. These tables act as a guide only for those wishing to paddle across the Gannel (Newquay) or the Erme. Please be sure to read the warnings given under the relevant section in the Guide. Walkers of the Coast Path are advised not to wade across any of the other estuaries around the route. Walkers should consult the local tide times. Those crossing the Gannel or Erme should note that there can be considerable differences in height between spring and neap tides; and the information below should be used for general timing guidance only. Again, details are available in tide tables locally.

- **Newquay (The Gannel) deduct 30 minutes**
- **River Erme tides are the same as Newquay**

The tidal information is reproduced by permission of the Controller of Her Majesty's Stationery Office and the UK Hydrographic Office (www.ukho.gov.uk) ©British Crown copyright. All rights reserved.

* Add 1 hour for Daylight Saving Time from 29th March 2020 to 25th October 2020.
Add 1 hour for Daylight Saving Time from 28th March 2021 to 31st October 2021.

TIDE TIMES FOR 2020

JANUARY		Low Tide Morning		Low Tide Afternoon	
		Time	Height	Time	Height
1	Wednesday	0309	1.8	1537	1.8
2	Thursday	0344	2.0	1616	2.0
3	Friday	0427	2.2	1705	2.2
4	Saturday	0525	2.4	1808	2.3
5	Sunday	0637	2.4	1915	2.2
6	Monday	0747	2.3	2019	2.0
7	Tuesday	0850	2.0	2117	1.8
8	Wednesday	0946	1.7	2210	1.5
9	Thursday	1038	1.4	2300	1.3
10	Friday	1128	1.2	2347	1.1
11	Saturday			1215	1.0
12	Sunday	0033	1.0	1302	0.9
13	Monday	0119	0.9	1347	0.8
14	Tuesday	0203	0.9	1431	0.8
15	Wednesday	0246	1.0	1515	1.0
16	Thursday	0331	1.2	1601	1.2
17	Friday	0418	1.4	1650	1.5
18	Saturday	0511	1.7	1749	1.7
19	Sunday	0617	1.9	1901	1.9
20	Monday	0738	2.0	2021	1.9
21	Tuesday	0856	1.9	2130	1.7
22	Wednesday	1001	1.6	2227	1.5
23	Thursday	1055	1.3	2317	1.3
24	Friday	1142	1.1		
25	Saturday	0001	1.1	1225	1.0
26	Sunday	0041	1.0	1304	1.0
27	Monday	0117	1.1	1339	1.0
28	Tuesday	0149	1.1	1410	1.1
29	Wednesday	0217	1.3	1438	1.3
30	Thursday	0243	1.5	1504	1.5
31	Friday	0307	1.6	1530	1.7

FEBRUARY		Low Tide Morning		Low Tide Afternoon	
		Time	Height	Time	Height
1	Saturday	0336	1.8	1602	1.9
2	Sunday	0415	2.1	1648	2.1
3	Monday	0513	2.3	1802	2.2
4	Tuesday	0644	2.3	1927	2.2
5	Wednesday	0807	2.2	2040	2.0
6	Thursday	0916	1.8	2144	1.7
7	Friday	1017	1.5	2242	1.3
8	Saturday	1113	1.1	2335	1.0
9	Sunday			1204	0.8
10	Monday	0024	0.7	1252	0.5
11	Tuesday	0110	0.5	1337	0.4
12	Wednesday	0154	0.5	1420	0.4
13	Thursday	0235	0.6	1501	0.6
14	Friday	0315	0.8	1541	0.9
15	Saturday	0356	1.1	1622	1.3
16	Sunday	0441	1.5	1710	1.7
17	Monday	0537	1.9	1813	2.0
18	Tuesday	0654	2.1	1944	2.2
19	Wednesday	0836	2.1	2115	2.0
20	Thursday	0950	1.8	2216	1.7
21	Friday	1044	1.4	2305	1.4
22	Saturday	1130	1.1	2347	1.1
23	Sunday			1210	0.9
24	Monday	0026	0.9	1247	0.8
25	Tuesday	0100	0.9	1320	0.8
26	Wednesday	0129	0.9	1347	0.9
27	Thursday	0153	1.1	1410	1.1
28	Friday	0215	1.2	1431	1.3
29	Saturday	0236	1.4	1453	1.4

MARCH		Low Tide Morning		Low Tide Afternoon	
		Time	Height	Time	Height
1	Sunday	0300	1.5	1520	1.6
2	Monday	0334	1.8	1558	1.9
3	Tuesday	0421	2.0	1655	2.2
4	Wednesday	0540	2.3	1837	2.3
5	Thursday	0730	2.2	2009	2.1
6	Friday	0851	1.8	2122	1.7
7	Saturday	0959	1.4	2225	1.3
8	Sunday	1056	0.9	2319	0.8
9	Monday	1148	0.5		
10	Tuesday	0008	0.5	1236	0.2
11	Wednesday	0054	0.3	1320	0.1
12	Thursday	0137	0.2	1401	0.1
13	Friday	0217	0.3	1440	0.4
14	Saturday	0255	0.5	1517	0.8
15	Sunday	0333	0.9	1555	1.2
16	Monday	0414	1.4	1638	1.7
17	Tuesday	0506	1.9	1736	2.2
18	Wednesday	0618	2.2	1904	2.4
19	Thursday	0819	2.2	2058	2.2
20	Friday	0935	1.8	2158	1.8
21	Saturday	1025	1.4	2244	1.4
22	Sunday	1108	1.1	2325	1.1
23	Monday	1146	0.9		
24	Tuesday	0002	0.9	1222	0.8
25	Wednesday	0035	0.8	1252	0.8
26	Thursday	0103	0.9	1318	0.9
27	Friday	0126	1.0	1340	1.0
28	Saturday	0147	1.1	1401	1.1
29	Sunday	0209	1.2	1424	1.3
30	Monday	0234	1.4	1452	1.5
31	Tuesday	0307	1.6	1529	1.8

APRIL		Low Tide Morning		Low Tide Afternoon	
		Time	Height	Time	Height
1	Wednesday	0353	1.9	1623	2.1
2	Thursday	0507	2.2	1800	2.3
3	Friday	0702	2.1	1944	2.1
4	Saturday	0829	1.8	2101	1.7
5	Sunday	0938	1.3	2204	1.2
6	Monday	1035	0.8	2258	0.7
7	Tuesday	1126	0.4	2347	0.4
8	Wednesday			1213	0.1
9	Thursday	0032	0.2	1257	0.1
10	Friday	0115	0.1	1338	0.2
11	Saturday	0155	0.3	1417	0.4
12	Sunday	0233	0.6	1454	0.8
13	Monday	0311	1.0	1531	1.3
14	Tuesday	0353	1.5	1614	1.8
15	Wednesday	0444	1.9	1709	2.2
16	Thursday	0552	2.2	1827	2.4
17	Friday	0738	2.2	2019	2.3
18	Saturday	0902	1.9	2124	1.9
19	Sunday	0953	1.5	2211	1.5
20	Monday	1035	1.2	2252	1.2
21	Tuesday	1113	1.0	2329	1.0
22	Wednesday	1147	0.9		
23	Thursday	0002	1.0	1218	0.9
24	Friday	0031	0.9	1246	0.9
25	Saturday	0057	1.0	1311	1.0
26	Sunday	0122	1.1	1336	1.1
27	Monday	0148	1.2	1403	1.3
28	Tuesday	0218	1.3	1434	1.5
29	Wednesday	0254	1.5	1515	1.8
30	Thursday	0343	1.8	1612	2.0

MAY		Low Tide Morning		Low Tide Afternoon	
		Time	Height	Time	Height
1	Friday	0459	2.0	1742	2.2
2	Saturday	0640	2.0	1918	2.0
3	Sunday	0803	1.7	2034	1.7
4	Monday	0911	1.2	2138	1.2
5	Tuesday	1009	0.8	2233	0.8
6	Wednesday	1101	0.5	2323	0.5
7	Thursday	1148	0.3		
8	Friday	0009	0.3	1233	0.3
9	Saturday	0053	0.3	1315	0.4
10	Sunday	0134	0.4	1355	0.6
11	Monday	0214	0.7	1433	1.0
12	Tuesday	0253	1.1	1511	1.4
13	Wednesday	0336	1.5	1554	1.8
14	Thursday	0424	1.8	1646	2.1
15	Friday	0524	2.1	1750	2.3
16	Saturday	0637	2.2	1909	2.3
17	Sunday	0759	2.0	2026	2.1
18	Monday	0901	1.7	2122	1.8
19	Tuesday	0948	1.5	2207	1.5
20	Wednesday	1029	1.3	2247	1.3
21	Thursday	1106	1.1	2324	1.2
22	Friday	1141	1.1	2358	1.1
23	Saturday			1214	1.1
24	Sunday	0031	1.1	1247	1.1
25	Monday	0103	1.1	1319	1.2
26	Tuesday	0136	1.2	1352	1.3
27	Wednesday	0212	1.3	1430	1.5
28	Thursday	0254	1.4	1515	1.6
29	Friday	0346	1.6	1612	1.8
30	Saturday	0454	1.8	1726	1.9
31	Sunday	0614	1.7	1847	1.9

JUNE		Low Tide Morning		Low Tide Afternoon	
		Time	Height	Time	Height
1	Monday	0732	1.6	2002	1.6
2	Tuesday	0841	1.3	2108	1.3
3	Wednesday	0941	1.0	2206	1.0
4	Thursday	1035	0.8	2259	0.8
5	Friday	1125	0.7	2347	0.6
6	Saturday			1211	0.6
7	Sunday	0033	0.6	1255	0.7
8	Monday	0117	0.7	1337	0.9
9	Tuesday	0158	0.9	1416	1.1
10	Wednesday	0238	1.1	1455	1.4
11	Thursday	0319	1.4	1535	1.7
12	Friday	0402	1.7	1619	2.0
13	Saturday	0450	1.9	1710	2.1
14	Sunday	0546	2.0	1810	2.2
15	Monday	0647	2.0	1914	2.2
16	Tuesday	0750	1.9	2017	2.0
17	Wednesday	0847	1.8	2113	1.8
18	Thursday	0938	1.6	2202	1.6
19	Friday	1024	1.4	2247	1.4
20	Saturday	1106	1.3	2329	1.2
21	Sunday	1148	1.2		
22	Monday	0010	1.1	1228	1.1
23	Tuesday	0051	1.1	1308	1.1
24	Wednesday	0131	1.0	1349	1.2
25	Thursday	0213	1.1	1431	1.3
26	Friday	0257	1.2	1516	1.4
27	Saturday	0346	1.3	1607	1.5
28	Sunday	0441	1.5	1705	1.7
29	Monday	0544	1.6	1813	1.7
30	Tuesday	0655	1.6	1927	1.7

JULY		Low Tide Morning		Low Tide Afternoon	
		Time	Height	Time	Height
1	Wednesday	0808	1.5	2038	1.6
2	Thursday	0914	1.4	2142	1.4
3	Friday	1013	1.2	2240	1.1
4	Saturday	1107	1.0	2331	1.0
5	Sunday	1155	0.9		
6	Monday	0019	0.9	1241	0.9
7	Tuesday	0104	0.8	1323	1.0
8	Wednesday	0145	0.9	1401	1.1
9	Thursday	0223	1.1	1437	1.3
10	Friday	0259	1.3	1511	1.5
11	Saturday	0334	1.5	1545	1.7
12	Sunday	0410	1.7	1623	1.9
13	Monday	0452	1.9	1710	2.1
14	Tuesday	0545	2.1	1811	2.2
15	Wednesday	0647	2.1	1918	2.2
16	Thursday	0751	2.0	2023	2.0
17	Friday	0851	1.8	2122	1.8
18	Saturday	0947	1.6	2216	1.5
19	Sunday	1039	1.4	2306	1.3
20	Monday	1127	1.2	2354	1.1
21	Tuesday			1214	1.0
22	Wednesday	0040	0.9	1300	0.9
23	Thursday	0125	0.8	1344	0.9
24	Friday	0209	0.8	1426	0.9
25	Saturday	0251	0.8	1508	1.0
26	Sunday	0334	1.0	1552	1.2
27	Monday	0420	1.2	1640	1.5
28	Tuesday	0512	1.5	1738	1.7
29	Wednesday	0617	1.7	1851	1.9
30	Thursday	0735	1.9	2013	1.9
31	Friday	0854	1.8	2128	1.7

AUGUST		Low Tide Morning		Low Tide Afternoon	
		Time	Height	Time	Height
1	Saturday	1000	1.5	2229	1.4
2	Sunday	1056	1.3	2322	1.1
3	Monday	1144	1.1		
4	Tuesday	0008	0.9	1228	1.0
5	Wednesday	0051	0.8	1308	0.9
6	Thursday	0129	0.9	1343	1.0
7	Friday	0203	1.0	1414	1.1
8	Saturday	0232	1.1	1441	1.3
9	Sunday	0259	1.3	1506	1.5
10	Monday	0323	1.6	1531	1.8
11	Tuesday	0350	1.8	1602	2.0
12	Wednesday	0427	2.0	1651	2.2
13	Thursday	0532	2.2	1817	2.4
14	Friday	0701	2.3	1941	2.3
15	Saturday	0815	2.1	2050	2.0
16	Sunday	0919	1.8	2152	1.6
17	Monday	1017	1.5	2248	1.2
18	Tuesday	1111	1.2	2339	0.9
19	Wednesday			1200	0.9
20	Thursday	0027	0.7	1247	0.7
21	Friday	0112	0.5	1331	0.6
22	Saturday	0155	0.5	1412	0.6
23	Sunday	0235	0.6	1452	0.7
24	Monday	0315	0.8	1531	1.0
25	Tuesday	0355	1.2	1615	1.4
26	Wednesday	0440	1.6	1707	1.8
27	Thursday	0540	2.0	1819	2.1
28	Friday	0707	2.2	1959	2.2
29	Saturday	0846	2.1	2123	1.9
30	Sunday	0953	1.8	2221	1.5
31	Monday	1045	1.4	2309	1.2

SEPTEMBER		Low Tide Morning		Low Tide Afternoon	
		Time	Height	Time	Height
1	Tuesday	1129	1.1	2352	0.9
2	Wednesday			1210	0.9
3	Thursday	0030	0.8	1247	0.9
4	Friday	0105	0.8	1319	0.9
5	Saturday	0135	0.9	1346	1.1
6	Sunday	0200	1.1	1408	1.2
7	Monday	0220	1.3	1427	1.4
8	Tuesday	0239	1.5	1447	1.6
9	Wednesday	0301	1.7	1514	1.9
10	Thursday	0333	2.0	1555	2.2
11	Friday	0422	2.3	1704	2.4
12	Saturday	0605	2.5	1907	2.4
13	Sunday	0745	2.3	2026	2.1
14	Monday	0857	1.9	2132	1.6
15	Tuesday	0958	1.5	2229	1.1
16	Wednesday	1052	1.1	2320	0.7
17	Thursday	1142	0.7		
18	Friday	0007	0.5	1228	0.5
19	Saturday	0052	0.3	1311	0.4
20	Sunday	0134	0.3	1352	0.4
21	Monday	0213	0.5	1431	0.6
22	Tuesday	0251	0.8	1509	1.0
23	Wednesday	0329	1.3	1551	1.5
24	Thursday	0413	1.8	1642	1.9
25	Friday	0510	2.2	1755	2.3
26	Saturday	0643	2.5	1953	2.3
27	Sunday	0836	2.3	2112	2.0
28	Monday	0937	1.9	2204	1.5
29	Tuesday	1024	1.5	2247	1.2
30	Wednesday	1106	1.2	2327	1.0

OCTOBER		Low Tide Morning		Low Tide Afternoon	
		Time	Height	Time	Height
1	Thursday	1144	1.0		
2	Friday	0003	0.9	1219	0.9
3	Saturday	0035	0.9	1249	1.0
4	Sunday	0102	1.0	1314	1.1
5	Monday	0125	1.1	1335	1.2
6	Tuesday	0145	1.3	1354	1.4
7	Wednesday	0204	1.5	1416	1.6
8	Thursday	0228	1.7	1444	1.8
9	Friday	0301	2.0	1524	2.1
10	Saturday	0347	2.3	1628	2.4
11	Sunday	0514	2.5	1835	2.4
12	Monday	0717	2.4	2002	2.1
13	Tuesday	0834	2.0	2109	1.6
14	Wednesday	0935	1.5	2205	1.1
15	Thursday	1029	1.0	2256	0.7
16	Friday	1118	0.7	2343	0.4
17	Saturday			1205	0.4
18	Sunday	0028	0.3	1248	0.4
19	Monday	0110	0.4	1330	0.5
20	Tuesday	0150	0.6	1410	0.7
21	Wednesday	0228	1.0	1449	1.1
22	Thursday	0307	1.4	1532	1.6
23	Friday	0351	1.9	1623	2.0
24	Saturday	0447	2.3	1734	2.4
25	Sunday	0612	2.6	1923	2.4
26	Monday	0804	2.4	2042	2.0
27	Tuesday	0906	2.0	2133	1.7
28	Wednesday	0953	1.7	2216	1.4
29	Thursday	1034	1.4	2254	1.1
30	Friday	1112	1.2	2329	1.0
31	Saturday	1146	1.1		

TIDE TIMES 2020/2021

NOVEMBER		Low Tide Morning		Low Tide Afternoon	
		Time	Height	Time	Height
1	Sunday	000	1.0	1216	1.1
2	Monday	0028	1.1	1243	1.2
3	Tuesday	0053	1.2	1307	1.3
4	Wednesday	0117	1.3	1331	1.4
5	Thursday	0141	1.5	1357	1.6
6	Friday	0209	1.7	1429	1.8
7	Saturday	0245	1.9	1513	2.0
8	Sunday	0334	2.2	1617	2.3
9	Monday	0454	2.4	1802	2.3
10	Tuesday	0642	2.4	1931	2.0
11	Wednesday	0803	2.0	2040	1.6
12	Thursday	0907	1.6	2138	1.2
13	Friday	1003	1.1	2230	0.8
14	Saturday	1054	0.8	2319	0.6
15	Sunday	1141	0.6		
16	Monday	0004	0.5	1227	0.5
17	Tuesday	0048	0.6	1310	0.6
18	Wednesday	0130	0.8	1352	0.8
19	Thursday	0210	1.1	1434	1.2
20	Friday	0250	1.5	1518	1.6
21	Saturday	0334	1.9	1607	1.9
22	Sunday	0426	2.2	1707	2.2
23	Monday	0532	2.5	1822	2.3
24	Tuesday	0655	2.5	1944	2.2
25	Wednesday	0813	2.2	2045	1.9
26	Thursday	0908	2.0	2132	1.7
27	Friday	0954	1.7	2214	1.5
28	Saturday	1034	1.5	2251	1.3
29	Sunday	1110	1.4	2325	1.3
30	Monday	1144	1.3	2357	1.2

DECEMBER		Low Tide Morning		Low Tide Afternoon	
		Time	Height	Time	Height
1	Tuesday	1216	1.3		
2	Wednesday	0028	1.3	1248	1.3
3	Thursday	0059	1.4	1319	1.4
4	Friday	0130	1.5	1352	1.5
5	Saturday	0204	1.6	1429	1.6
6	Sunday	0244	1.8	1515	1.8
7	Monday	0334	2.0	1613	2.0
8	Tuesday	0439	2.1	1728	2.0
9	Wednesday	0601	2.2	1851	1.9
10	Thursday	0723	2.0	2004	1.7
11	Friday	0834	1.7	2108	1.4
12	Saturday	0935	1.4	2204	1.1
13	Sunday	1030	1.1	2256	0.9
14	Monday	1122	0.9	2345	0.8
15	Tuesday			1210	0.8
16	Wednesday	0031	0.8	1256	0.8
17	Thursday	0115	0.9	1340	0.9
18	Friday	0157	1.1	1423	1.1
19	Saturday	0238	1.4	1505	1.4
20	Sunday	0318	1.7	1548	1.7
21	Monday	0401	1.9	1633	1.9
22	Tuesday	0449	2.2	1725	2.1
23	Wednesday	0546	2.3	1825	2.2
24	Thursday	0652	2.4	1930	2.2
25	Friday	0801	2.2	2031	2.0
26	Saturday	0900	2.0	2124	1.8
27	Sunday	0951	1.8	2210	1.6
28	Monday	1035	1.6	2252	1.5
29	Tuesday	1117	1.4	2332	1.4
30	Wednesday	1156	1.3		
31	Thursday	0010	1.3	1235	1.3

TIDE TIMES FOR 2021

JANUARY		Low Tide Morning		Low Tide Afternoon	
		Time	Height	Time	Height
1	Friday	0049	1.3	1314	1.2
2	Saturday	0127	1.3	1352	1.2
3	Sunday	0205	1.3	1432	1.3
4	Monday	0246	1.4	1515	1.4
5	Tuesday	0330	1.6	1602	1.5
6	Wednesday	0420	1.7	1657	1.7
7	Thursday	0521	1.9	1804	1.8
8	Friday	0636	2.0	1922	1.8
9	Saturday	0757	1.9	2037	1.7
10	Sunday	0911	1.7	2143	1.5
11	Monday	1014	1.4	2241	1.3
12	Tuesday	1109	1.1	2333	1.1
13	Wednesday			1200	0.9
14	Thursday	0021	0.9	1247	0.8
15	Friday	0105	0.9	1330	0.8
16	Saturday	0146	1.0	1410	0.9
17	Sunday	0223	1.1	1447	1.1
18	Monday	0258	1.3	1522	1.4
19	Tuesday	0330	1.6	1556	1.6
20	Wednesday	0404	1.8	1632	1.9
21	Thursday	0444	2.1	1717	2.1
22	Friday	0539	2.3	1816	2.3
23	Saturday	0649	2.4	1925	2.3
24	Sunday	0801	2.3	2031	2.1
25	Monday	0907	2.1	2131	1.9
26	Tuesday	1003	1.8	2224	1.6
27	Wednesday	1054	1.5	2312	1.4
28	Thursday	1140	1.2	2357	1.2
29	Friday			1224	1.0
30	Saturday	0040	1.0	1307	0.9
31	Sunday	0121	0.9	1347	0.8

FEBRUARY		Low Tide Morning		Low Tide Afternoon	
		Time	Height	Time	Height
1	Monday	0201	0.9	1426	0.8
2	Tuesday	0239	1.0	1505	1.0
3	Wednesday	0318	1.1	1544	1.2
4	Thursday	0400	1.3	1629	1.5
5	Friday	0450	1.6	1724	1.8
6	Saturday	0555	1.9	1837	2.0
7	Sunday	0722	2.1	2011	2.0
8	Monday	0856	1.9	2133	1.8
9	Tuesday	1007	1.6	2235	1.5
10	Wednesday	1103	1.2	2326	1.1
11	Thursday	1152	0.9		
12	Friday	0011	0.9	1236	0.7
13	Saturday	0053	0.8	1316	0.6
14	Sunday	0130	0.8	1352	0.7
15	Monday	0203	0.9	1423	0.9
16	Tuesday	0232	1.1	1451	1.1
17	Wednesday	0257	1.3	1516	1.4
18	Thursday	0320	1.6	1539	1.7
19	Friday	0345	1.8	1607	2.0
20	Saturday	0421	2.1	1652	2.2
21	Sunday	0530	2.4	1821	2.4
22	Monday	0709	2.4	1946	2.3
23	Tuesday	0828	2.2	2057	2.1
24	Wednesday	0935	1.8	2159	1.7
25	Thursday	1032	1.4	2253	1.3
26	Friday	1123	1.1	2342	1.0
27	Saturday			1209	0.8
28	Sunday	0026	0.7	1252	0.5

MARCH		Low Tide Morning		Low Tide Afternoon	
		Time	Height	Time	Height
1	Monday	0108	0.6	1333	0.4
2	Tuesday	0147	0.5	1411	0.5
3	Wednesday	0225	0.6	1448	0.6
4	Thursday	0302	0.8	1525	1.0
5	Friday	0341	1.1	1605	1.4
6	Saturday	0426	1.5	1654	1.8
7	Sunday	0527	2.0	1805	2.2
8	Monday	0659	2.2	1958	2.3
9	Tuesday	0853	2.0	2127	1.9
10	Wednesday	1001	1.6	2225	1.5
11	Thursday	1052	1.1	2312	1.1
12	Friday	1136	0.8	2354	0.8
13	Saturday			1217	0.6
14	Sunday	0032	0.7	1254	0.5
15	Monday	0107	0.6	1326	0.6
16	Tuesday	0137	0.8	1354	0.8
17	Wednesday	0202	0.9	1417	1.0
18	Thursday	0223	1.2	1436	1.3
19	Friday	0241	1.4	1454	1.5
20	Saturday	0302	1.7	1518	1.8
21	Sunday	0334	1.9	1556	2.1
22	Monday	0425	2.3	1705	2.4
23	Tuesday	0622	2.4	1907	2.4
24	Wednesday	0754	2.2	2026	2.1
25	Thursday	0906	1.8	2133	1.7
26	Friday	1006	1.3	2229	1.2
27	Saturday	1059	0.9	2319	0.8
28	Sunday	1146	0.5		
29	Monday	0005	0.5	1230	0.3
30	Tuesday	0048	0.3	1312	0.2
31	Wednesday	0128	0.3	1351	0.3

APRIL		Low Tide Morning		Low Tide Afternoon	
		Time	Height	Time	Height
1	Thursday	0207	0.4	1428	0.6
2	Friday	0245	0.7	1506	0.9
3	Saturday	0325	1.1	1546	1.4
4	Sunday	0411	1.5	1636	1.9
5	Monday	0513	2.0	1747	2.3
6	Tuesday	0648	2.2	1945	2.3
7	Wednesday	0839	1.9	2108	1.9
8	Thursday	0941	1.5	2202	1.5
9	Friday	1028	1.1	2247	1.1
10	Saturday	1111	0.8	2328	0.9
11	Sunday	1149	0.7		
12	Monday	0005	0.7	1225	0.6
13	Tuesday	0039	0.7	1255	0.7
14	Wednesday	0107	0.8	1321	0.9
15	Thursday	0131	1.0	1343	1.1
16	Friday	0152	1.2	1403	1.3
17	Saturday	0211	1.4	1423	1.5
18	Sunday	0235	1.6	1450	1.8
19	Monday	0309	1.8	1529	2.0
20	Tuesday	0400	2.1	1633	2.3
21	Wednesday	0542	2.3	1829	2.4
22	Thursday	0720	2.1	1953	2.1
23	Friday	0833	1.7	2101	1.7
24	Saturday	0935	1.2	2159	1.2
25	Sunday	1029	0.8	2251	0.8
26	Monday	1118	0.5	2339	0.5
27	Tuesday			1204	0.3
28	Wednesday	0024	0.3	1248	0.3
29	Thursday	0108	0.3	1330	0.4
30	Friday	0149	0.4	1410	0.7

MAY		Low Tide Morning		Low Tide Afternoon	
		Time	Height	Time	Height
1	Saturday	0230	0.7	1451	1.0
2	Sunday	0313	1.1	1534	1.5
3	Monday	0402	1.5	1626	1.9
4	Tuesday	0504	1.9	1733	2.2
5	Wednesday	0627	2.1	1908	2.2
6	Thursday	0802	1.9	2030	2.0
7	Friday	0905	1.6	2126	1.6
8	Saturday	0953	1.3	2213	1.3
9	Sunday	1036	1.1	2254	1.1
10	Monday	1115	1.0	2332	1.0
11	Tuesday	1150	0.9		
12	Wednesday	0005	1.0	1222	1.0
13	Thursday	0036	1.0	1249	1.1
14	Friday	0102	1.1	1314	1.2
15	Saturday	0127	1.2	1338	1.4
16	Sunday	0152	1.4	1404	1.5
17	Monday	0221	1.6	1436	1.7
18	Tuesday	0259	1.7	1519	1.9
19	Wednesday	0353	1.9	1622	2.1
20	Thursday	0514	2.0	1751	2.2
21	Friday	0642	1.9	1915	2.0
22	Saturday	0755	1.6	2024	1.7
23	Sunday	0900	1.3	2126	1.3
24	Monday	0957	1.0	2222	0.9
25	Tuesday	1050	0.7	2313	0.7
26	Wednesday	1139	0.5		
27	Thursday	0002	0.5	1227	0.5
28	Friday	0049	0.5	1312	0.6
29	Saturday	0135	0.6	1356	0.8
30	Sunday	0219	0.8	1440	1.1
31	Monday	0305	1.1	1525	1.4

JUNE		Low Tide Morning		Low Tide Afternoon	
		Time	Height	Time	Height
1	Tuesday	0354	1.4	1614	1.7
2	Wednesday	0448	1.7	1711	2.0
3	Thursday	0551	1.9	1817	2.1
4	Friday	0702	1.9	1929	2.1
5	Saturday	0810	1.8	2034	1.9
6	Sunday	0905	1.6	2128	1.7
7	Monday	0953	1.5	2214	1.5
8	Tuesday	1035	1.3	2255	1.3
9	Wednesday	1113	1.2	2332	1.3
10	Thursday	1148	1.2		
11	Friday	0006	1.2	1221	1.2
12	Saturday	0039	1.2	1253	1.3
13	Sunday	0111	1.3	1324	1.4
14	Monday	0143	1.4	1358	1.5
15	Tuesday	0219	1.4	1434	1.6
16	Wednesday	0259	1.5	1518	1.7
17	Thursday	0348	1.6	1611	1.8
18	Friday	0449	1.7	1716	1.9
19	Saturday	0600	1.7	1831	1.9
20	Sunday	0714	1.6	1945	1.7
21	Monday	0824	1.4	2053	1.5
22	Tuesday	0927	1.2	2155	1.2
23	Wednesday	1026	1.0	2252	0.9
24	Thursday	1120	0.9	2346	0.8
25	Friday			1211	0.8
26	Saturday	0036	0.7	1259	0.8
27	Sunday	0124	0.7	1345	0.9
28	Monday	0210	0.8	1429	1.0
29	Tuesday	0255	1.0	1512	1.2
30	Wednesday	0338	1.2	1554	1.5

JULY		Low Tide Morning		Low Tide Afternoon	
		Time	Height	Time	Height
1	Thursday	0422	1.5	1638	1.8
2	Friday	0508	1.7	1727	2.0
3	Saturday	0600	1.9	1824	2.1
4	Sunday	0659	2.0	1927	2.1
5	Monday	0801	2.0	2030	2.0
6	Tuesday	0859	1.8	2127	1.8
7	Wednesday	0951	1.7	2217	1.7
8	Thursday	1037	1.5	2302	1.5
9	Friday	1119	1.4	2343	1.3
10	Saturday	1159	1.3		
11	Sunday	0022	1.2	1238	1.3
12	Monday	0100	1.2	1315	1.2
13	Tuesday	0138	1.2	1353	1.3
14	Wednesday	0215	1.2	1430	1.3
15	Thursday	0254	1.2	1510	1.4
16	Friday	0335	1.3	1554	1.5
17	Saturday	0423	1.5	1645	1.7
18	Sunday	0520	1.6	1749	1.8
19	Monday	0630	1.7	1907	1.9
20	Tuesday	0750	1.7	2026	1.7
21	Wednesday	0905	1.6	2138	1.5
22	Thursday	1011	1.4	2241	1.2
23	Friday	1109	1.1	2336	0.9
24	Saturday			1201	0.9
25	Sunday	0027	0.7	1249	0.8
26	Monday	0114	0.6	1333	0.8
27	Tuesday	0157	0.7	1414	0.9
28	Wednesday	0236	0.8	1451	1.0
29	Thursday	0313	1.0	1525	1.3
30	Friday	0347	1.3	1559	1.6
31	Saturday	0421	1.6	1635	1.9

AUGUST		Low Tide Morning		Low Tide Afternoon	
		Time	Height	Time	Height
1	Sunday	0501	1.9	1722	2.1
2	Monday	0553	2.2	1825	2.3
3	Tuesday	0659	2.2	1935	2.3
4	Wednesday	0807	2.2	2044	2.1
5	Thursday	0911	2.0	2144	1.9
6	Friday	1007	1.7	2236	1.6
7	Saturday	1056	1.5	2323	1.3
8	Sunday	1141	1.3		
9	Monday	0006	1.1	1224	1.1
10	Tuesday	0047	1.0	1304	1.0
11	Wednesday	0126	0.9	1341	1.0
12	Thursday	0203	0.9	1418	1.0
13	Friday	0240	0.9	1454	1.1
14	Saturday	0316	1.1	1533	1.3
15	Sunday	0357	1.4	1618	1.6
16	Monday	0446	1.7	1716	1.9
17	Tuesday	0552	2.0	1836	2.1
18	Wednesday	0725	2.1	2013	2.0
19	Thursday	0857	1.9	2134	1.7
20	Friday	1006	1.6	2237	1.3
21	Saturday	1102	1.2	2329	0.9
22	Sunday	1150	0.9		
23	Monday	0015	0.7	1235	0.7
24	Tuesday	0057	0.5	1315	0.7
25	Wednesday	0136	0.6	1351	0.7
26	Thursday	0210	0.7	1422	0.9
27	Friday	0240	1.0	1450	1.2
28	Saturday	0306	1.3	1515	1.5
29	Sunday	0330	1.6	1539	1.8
30	Monday	0354	2.0	1609	2.2
31	Tuesday	0432	2.3	1712	2.5

SEPTEMBER		Low Tide Morning		Low Tide Afternoon	
		Time	Height	Time	Height
1	Wednesday	0558	2.5	1850	2.5
2	Thursday	0726	2.5	2009	2.3
3	Friday	0839	2.2	2117	2.0
4	Saturday	0941	1.8	2213	1.6
5	Sunday	1034	1.5	2301	1.2
6	Monday	1121	1.2	2346	0.9
7	Tuesday			1204	0.9
8	Wednesday	0027	0.7	1245	0.8
9	Thursday	0107	0.6	1323	0.7
10	Friday	0144	0.6	1400	0.7
11	Saturday	0220	0.8	1436	0.9
12	Sunday	0255	1.0	1513	1.2
13	Monday	0333	1.4	1556	1.6
14	Tuesday	0420	1.8	1653	2.0
15	Wednesday	0527	2.2	1821	2.3
16	Thursday	0719	2.4	2017	2.1
17	Friday	0858	2.1	2132	1.7
18	Saturday	0959	1.6	2226	1.2
19	Sunday	1048	1.2	2312	0.9
20	Monday	1132	0.9	2354	0.6
21	Tuesday			1212	0.7
22	Wednesday	0033	0.6	1249	0.7
23	Thursday	0108	0.6	1322	0.8
24	Friday	0138	0.8	1350	1.0
25	Saturday	0203	1.1	1413	1.2
26	Sunday	0223	1.4	1432	1.5
27	Monday	0240	1.7	1450	1.8
28	Tuesday	0259	1.9	1515	2.1
29	Wednesday	0330	2.3	1559	2.4
30	Thursday	0429	2.6	1803	2.7

OCTOBER		Low Tide Morning		Low Tide Afternoon	
		Time	Height	Time	Height
1	Friday	0647	2.6	1936	2.4
2	Saturday	0808	2.3	2047	2.0
3	Sunday	0913	1.9	2144	1.6
4	Monday	1006	1.5	2233	1.1
5	Tuesday	1054	1.1	2319	0.8
6	Wednesday	1139	0.8		
7	Thursday	0002	0.6	1221	0.6
8	Friday	0043	0.5	1301	0.6
9	Saturday	0122	0.6	1340	0.6
10	Sunday	0159	0.8	1418	0.9
11	Monday	0236	1.1	1457	1.2
12	Tuesday	0316	1.5	1543	1.7
13	Wednesday	0405	2.0	1644	2.1
14	Thursday	0516	2.4	1819	2.3
15	Friday	0716	2.5	2009	2.1
16	Saturday	0842	2.1	2114	1.7
17	Sunday	0938	1.6	2203	1.3
18	Monday	1024	1.3	2247	1.0
19	Tuesday	1106	1.0	2326	0.8
20	Wednesday	1144	0.8		
21	Thursday	0003	0.8	1220	0.8
22	Friday	0036	0.8	1251	0.9
23	Saturday	0104	1.0	1317	1.1
24	Sunday	0127	1.2	1340	1.3
25	Monday	0147	1.5	1359	1.6
26	Tuesday	0205	1.7	1419	1.8
27	Wednesday	0228	1.9	1448	2.1
28	Thursday	0302	2.2	1533	2.4
29	Friday	0356	2.5	1710	2.6
30	Saturday	0601	2.7	1857	2.4
31	Sunday	0730	2.4	2009	2.0

NOVEMBER		Low Tide Morning		Low Tide Afternoon	
		Time	Height	Time	Height
1	Monday	0837	2.0	2109	1.6
2	Tuesday	0933	1.5	2201	1.2
3	Wednesday	1024	1.2	2249	0.9
4	Thursday	1111	0.8	2335	0.7
5	Friday	1156	0.7		
6	Saturday	0018	0.6	1240	0.6
7	Sunday	0101	0.7	1322	0.7
8	Monday	0141	0.9	1404	0.9
9	Tuesday	0223	1.2	1449	1.3
10	Wednesday	0307	1.6	1538	1.7
11	Thursday	0359	2.0	1639	2.0
12	Friday	0507	2.3	1801	2.2
13	Saturday	0642	2.4	1933	2.1
14	Sunday	0805	2.2	2039	1.8
15	Monday	0903	1.8	2130	1.5
16	Tuesday	0951	1.5	2214	1.3
17	Wednesday	1034	1.3	2254	1.1
18	Thursday	1113	1.1	2330	1.1
19	Friday	1148	1.1		
20	Saturday	0003	1.1	1221	1.2
21	Sunday	0032	1.2	1249	1.3
22	Monday	0058	1.3	1315	1.4
23	Tuesday	0122	1.5	1340	1.6
24	Wednesday	0147	1.7	1407	1.8
25	Thursday	0215	1.9	1440	2.0
26	Friday	0253	2.1	1526	2.1
27	Saturday	0345	2.3	1635	2.3
28	Sunday			1806	2.3
29	Monday	0507	2.4	1924	2.0
30	Tuesday	0753	2.0	2029	1.7

DECEMBER		Low Tide Morning		Low Tide Afternoon	
		Time	Height	Time	Height
1	Wednesday	0856	1.7	2127	1.3
2	Thursday	0953	1.3	2220	1.1
3	Friday	1045	1.0	2310	0.9
4	Saturday	1135	0.8	2358	0.8
5	Sunday			1223	0.7
6	Monday	0044	0.8	1310	0.8
7	Tuesday	0130	0.9	1357	0.9
8	Wednesday	0215	1.2	1444	1.1
9	Thursday	0302	1.4	1533	1.4
10	Friday	0351	1.8	1626	1.7
11	Saturday	0446	2.0	1726	1.9
12	Sunday	0550	2.2	1834	2.0
13	Monday	0703	2.2	1943	2.0
14	Tuesday	0812	2.1	2043	1.9
15	Wednesday	0909	1.9	2134	1.7
16	Thursday	0957	1.7	2218	1.5
17	Friday	1040	1.5	2257	1.4
18	Saturday	1120	1.4	2333	1.4
19	Sunday	1155	1.4		
20	Monday	0007	1.4	1229	1.4
21	Tuesday	0039	1.4	1300	1.4
22	Wednesday	0109	1.5	1332	1.5
23	Thursday	0141	1.6	1404	1.6
24	Friday	0214	1.7	1440	1.7
25	Saturday	0251	1.8	1521	1.8
26	Sunday	0336	1.9	1610	1.9
27	Monday	0431	2.1	1712	2.0
28	Tuesday	0541	2.1	1828	2.0
29	Wednesday	0701	2.1	1944	1.8
30	Thursday	0817	1.9	2053	1.6
31	Friday	0924	1.6	2155	1.4

The Environment of the South West Coast Path

The South West Coast Path is one of the country's National Trails. Indeed, it is the longest of them at 630 miles/1,105 km. In common with all National Trails, the Coast Path passes through an outstanding environment, and Coast Path walkers will experience the finest coastal landscapes in the country. This range of coastal landscapes includes high cliffs, extensive beaches, wide bays, tiny coves, wooded estuaries and prominent headlands.

This range of outstanding landscapes has been recognised officially by the large number of formal designations, both international and national, around the length of the Coast Path.

International Designations

UNESCO has designated certain world-class environments as Biosphere Reserves. These are areas with a special blend of landscapes and wildlife, a rich cultural heritage and a community that cares about it and wishes to sustain it for the future. The Coast Path passes through the North Devon Biosphere Reserve, which has as its core the dunes of Braunton Burrows – See Section 7, but includes as its outer areas, the whole Coast Path between Lynton and Marsland Mouth – See Section 3-13.

World Heritage Sites

(WHSs) are also designated by UNESCO, in this case for their "Outstanding Universal Value". The South West Coast Path passes through two World Heritage Sites. The Cornwall and West Devon Mining Landscape WHS is defined by the mining landscape which was formed by the cultural tradition of non-ferrous hard-rock mining. It contributed to developing the Industrial Revolution in Britain and pioneered its transfer overseas. The designation covers ten distinct areas and includes iconic relic mining landscapes, with their old engine houses, as well as old harbours. Five of these areas relate to the Coast Path – the St Agnes area – See Section 24, the Port of Hayle – See Sections 25 and 26, the St Just area – See Sections 27-28, the area around Rinsey and Trewavas – See Section 32 and Charlestown See Section 41.

The Coast Path's second WHS is the Jurassic Coast, England's first such site to be designated for its natural properties. It is designated as it clearly depicts a geological "walk through time" of 185 million years of Earth's history in 95 miles/152 km. Geological history, and resulting landscapes, of the Triassic, Jurassic and Cretaceous periods are successively exposed over the length of the WHS, which stretches between Exmouth and Swanage – See Section 58-70.

National Designations

The country's finest landscapes are designated nationally as National Parks or Areas of Outstanding Natural Beauty. In landscape terms these designations are regarded as of equal value. Most of the South West Coast Path is covered by such designations.

Exmoor – See Sections 1-3 with its cliffs and deep wooded valleys, has National Park status. Most of the remainder of the Coast Path is covered by Area of Outstanding Natural Beauty (AONB) status.

The North Devon AONB extends along much of the coast between Exmoor and the Devon/Cornwall border - See Sections 4 -7 and 11-13 excluding only Ilfracombe and the area around the Taw-Torridge estuary. The Cornwall AONB covers the vast majority of the Cornish coast – See Sections 13-25 and 27-46 excluding only a few mainly urban lengths. The whole length of coast between Plymouth and Brixham – See Sections 47-54 falls within the South Devon AONB. East of the River Exe, most of the coast, excluding only the urban areas, as far as the Devon/Dorset border, is covered by the East Devon AONB. And finally, all of the Dorset coast, except the largely urban Weymouth and Portland, is within the Dorset AONB.

The wealth of landscape and environmental designations outlined above gives some idea of the quality of the landscape through which the South West Coast Path passes. However, this hides the fact that there is a wide range of landscape types to be experienced. For an idea of the more detailed landscape types, a description will be found at the start of each of the seven lengths we have divided the Coast Path into – Exmoor, North Devon, North Cornwall, West Cornwall, South Cornwall, South Devon and the Jurassic Coast.

Heritage of the Coast Path

Along the Coast Path you will discover evidence left behind from millennia of people living, working and fighting along our coastline.

The Coast Path has a long history. Right up until 1913 the whole length of the Path was regularly patrolled by the coastguards and excise officers in the constant struggle to apprehend lawbreakers. They needed to be able to look down into every bay and cove, on the lookout for smugglers, and, as a result the Path closely hugs the coast, providing excellent views but rarely the most direct path between two points.

A number of sites along the South West Coast Path have Bronze or Iron Age burial features known as barrows or tumuli. Coastal cliffs must have provided a very dramatic setting for prehistoric burials and other rituals, as they still do for the churches and chapels from later periods, found along the Coast Path.

The coast has always been the front line for repelling invaders. Forts and castles dating from the Iron Age, right through to the Second World War, provide some of the most dramatic and obvious man-made structures along the entire length of the South West Coast Path.

Headlands provide excellent vantage points and are comparatively easy to defend. Iron Age forts with earth ramparts and ditches are common on headlands along the Coast Path.

In several later periods the need to control the English Channel led to construction of major defences along the south coast of Cornwall, Devon and Dorset. Some of these were reoccupied during the nineteenth century, and a further ring of forts ('Palmerston follies') were created around Plymouth at that time.

The Coast Path also links together numerous traces of Second World War defences. These range from individual pillboxes to an entire deserted village at Tyneham in Dorset. Tyneham was one of two sites depopulated to allow military training to take place, but its inhabitants were never allowed to return.

There is a rich industrial heritage relating to quarrying, mining, lime burning, fishing and boat building along the Coast Path. Trade with other coastal settlements near and far has also taken place over many centuries.

The rocks that have been exploited around the coast of the South West vary from the limestones of Dorset (Purbeck marble and Portland Limestone) and Devon to slates in North Cornwall and the multicoloured serpentine of the Lizard.

Beam engine houses on rugged cliffs are an icon of the Cornish landscape and often feature on postcards and in advertisements. They are important relics of a distinctive industrial landscape created by hard-rock mining for metals during the eighteenth and nineteenth centuries. Six areas adjacent to the Coast Path are now part of the Cornish Mining World Heritage Site – the St Agnes Mining District, Portreath Harbour, the ports of Hayle and Charlestown, the St Just Mining District and Trewavas.

Along the whole length of the Coast Path you'll find the lime kilns that were used to supply burnt lime, in order to sweeten the naturally acid soils to make crops and grass grow better.

Wheal Owles, Botallack

Below we've split the path into 52 day lengths. Each of these allows time for breaks and covers what we think is a comfortable day's walking, whilst finishing at places where you can find accommodation. If you think you'd like to go slower or faster than this, you can find alternative itinerary suggestions on our website.

Week 1 (Seven days)

Day	Distance (Rounded)		From - to
1	9mi	14km	Minehead – Porlock Weir *Take National Rail main line to Taunton; bus Taunton - Minehead; or National Express coach to Minehead*
2	12mi	20km	Porlock Weir – Lynton
3	13mi	21km	Lynton – Combe Martin
4	13mi	20km	Combe Martin – Woolacombe
5	16mi	27km	Woolacombe – Braunton
6	12mi	20km	Braunton – Instow
7	11mi	18km	Instow – Westward Ho!
Total	**86mi**	**140km**	*Take bus Westward Ho! - Barnstaple; train Barnstaple - Exeter; National Rail main line from Exeter; or National Express coach from Westward Ho!*

Week 2 (Seven days)

Day	Distance (Rounded)		From - to
1	11mi	18km	Westward Ho! – Clovelly *National Rail main line to Exeter; train Exeter - Barnstaple; bus Barnstaple - Westward Ho!; or National Express coach to Westward Ho!*
2	10mi	16km	Clovelly – Hartland Quay
3	15mi	25km	Hartland Quay – Bude
4	10mi	16km	Bude – Crackington Haven
5	11mi	18km	Crackington Haven – Tintagel
6	9mi	15km	Tintagel – Port Isaac
7	12mi	19km	Port Isaac - Padstow
Total	**78mi**	**127km**	*Bus to Bodmin Parkway; National Rail main line from Bodmin Parkway*

Week 3 (Six days)

Day	Distance (Rounded)		From - to
1	14mi	22km	Padstow – Porthcothan *National Rail main line to Bodmin Parkway; bus Bodmin Parkway - Padstow*
2	11mi	18km	Porthcothan – Newquay
3	11mi	18km	Newquay – Perranporth
4	12mi	20km	Perranporth – Portreath
5	12mi	20km	Portreath – Hayle
6	6mi	9km	Hayle – St Ives
Total	66mi	107km	*Train St Ives-St Erth; National Rail main line from St Erth; or National Express coach from St Ives*

Week 4 (Six days)

Day	Distance (Rounded)		From - to
1	14mi	22km	St Ives – Pendeen Watch *National Rail main line to St Erth; train St Erth - St Ives; or National Express coach to St Ives*
2	9mi	15km	Pendeen Watch – Sennen Cove
3	12mi	19km	Sennen Cove – Lamorna Cove
4	9mi	15km	Lamorna Cove – Marazion
5	11mi	17km	Marazion – Porthleven
6	13mi	22km	Porthleven – Lizard
Total	**68mi**	**110km**	*Bus Lizard Town - Redruth; National Rail main line from Redruth*

Week 5 (Six days)

Day	Distance (Rounded)		From - to
1	11mi	17km	Lizard – Coverack *National Rail main line to Redruth; Bus Lizard Town - Redruth*
2	13mi	21km	Coverack – Helford
3	10mi	16km	Helford – Falmouth
4	14mi	22km	Falmouth – Portloe
5	12mi	20km	Portloe – Mevagissey
6	12mi	19km	Mevagissey – Par
Total	**72mi**	**115km**	*National Rail main line from Par*

Week 6 (Seven days)

Day	Distance (Rounded)		From - to
1	13mi	21km	Par – Polperro *National Rail main line to Par*
2	12mi	20km	Polperro – Portwrinkle
3	13mi	21km	Portwrinkle – Plymouth
4	15mi	24km	Plymouth – Wembury (ferry crossing)
5	14mi	22km	Wembury (ferry crossing) – Bigbury on Sea
6	14mi	22km	Bigbury on Sea – Salcombe
7	13mi	21km	Salcombe – Torcross
Total	94mi	151km	*Bus Torcross - Plymouth; National Rail main line or National Express coach from Plymouth*

Week 7 (Six days)

Day	Distance (Rounded)		From - to
1	10mi	16km	Torcross – Dartmouth *National rail main line or National Express coach to Plymouth; bus Plymouth - Torcross*
2	11mi	17km	Dartmouth – Brixham
3	11mi	17km	Brixham – Babbacombe
4	16mi	27km	Babbacombe – Exmouth
5	13mi	21km	Exmouth – Sidmouth
6	11mi	17km	Sidmouth – Seaton (Devon)
Total	**72mi**	**115km**	*Bus Seaton - Exeter; National Rail main line or National Express Coach from Exeter*

Week 8 (Seven days)

Day	Distance (Rounded)		From - to
1	14mi	23km	Seaton (Devon) – Seatown (Dorset) *National Rail main line or National Express coach to Exeter; bus Exeter - Seaton*
2	12mi	19km	Seatown (Dorset) – Abbotsbury
3	11mi	17km	Abbotsbury – Ferry Bridge (Wyke Regis)
4	13mi	21km	Isle of Portland
5	14mi	23km	Ferry Bridge (Wyke Regis) – Lulworth Cove
6	14mi	23km	Lulworth Cove – Worth Matravers
7	14mi	22km	Worth Matravers – South Haven Point (Poole Harbour)
Total	**92mi**	**148km**	*Ferry South Haven Point-Sandbanks; bus Sandbanks-Poole or Bournemouth; National Rail main line or National Express coach from Poole or Bournemouth*

Walking Guides

The Association has published a series of Walking Guide booklets which break down the whole of the Coast Path into easy to follow sections of between 5 and 17 miles per booklet. Each walking guide gives detailed walking directions as well as pointing out items of interest along the route, These Walking Guides provide detailed instructions for short sections of the Path, laid out in both directions. They include maps and photos as well as offering interesting facts, history, wildlife and geological information. These are available to buy at **www.southwestcoastpath.org.uk** or by telephoning the office on **01752 896237**. They are an excellent addition to this Guide.

Walk No.	Section Name	Distance (miles)	Distance (km)
1	Minehead to Porlock Weir	8.9	14.3
2	Porlock Weir to Lynton	12.1	19.5
3	Lynton to Combe Martin	13.7	22.0
4	Combe Martin to Ilfracombe	5.4	8.7
5	Ilfracombe to Woolacombe	8.5	13.7
6	Woolacombe to Croyde Bay	5.2	8.4
7	Croyde Bay to Braunton	9.8	15.8
8	Braunton to Barnstaple	5.4	8.7
9	Barnstaple to Bideford	10.7	17.2
10	Bideford to Westward Ho!	8	12.9
11	Westward Ho! to Clovelly	11.1	17.9
12	Clovelly to Hartland Quay	10.3	16.6
13	Hartland Quay to Bude	15.2	24.5
14	Bude to Crackington Haven	9.8	15.8
15	Crackington Haven to Boscastle	6.7	10.8
16	Boscastle to Tintagel	4.7	7.6
17	Tintagel to Port Isaac	9.1	14.6
18	Port Isaac to Padstow	11.7	18.8
19	Padstow to Harlyn Bay	6.5	10.5
20	Harlyn Bay to Porthcothan	6.7	10.8
21	Porthcothan to Newquay	10.3	16.6
22	Newquay to Holywell Bay	8.1	13.0
23	Holywell Bay to Perranporth	4.5	7.2
24	Perranporth to Portreath	12.4	20.0
25	Portreath to Hayle	11.7	18.8
26	Hayle to St Ives	6.1	9.8
27	St Ives to Pendeen	13.7	22.0
28	Pendeen to Sennen Cove	9.1	14.6
29	Sennen Cove to Porthcurno	6.3	10.1
30	Porthcurno to Lamorna	5.4	8.7
31	Lamorna to Marazion	9.2	14.8
32	Marazion to Porthleven	10.8	17.4
33	Porthleven to Poldhu Cove	5.2	8.4
34	Poldhu Cove to The Lizard	8.2	13.2
35	The Lizard to Coverack	10.4	16.7
36	Coverack to Helford	12.9	20.8
37	Helford to Falmouth	10.3	16.6
38	Falmouth to Portscatho	6.2	10.0
39	Porthscatho to Portloe	7.4	11.9
40	Portloe to Mevagissey	12.2	19.6
41	Mevagissey to Par	10.7	17.2
42	Par to Fowey	6.8	10.9
43	Fowey to Polperro	7.1	11.4
44	Polperro to Looe	5	8.0
45	Looe to Portwrinkle	7.7	12.4
46	Portwrinkle to Plymouth	13.2	21.2
47	Plymouth (Admiral's Hard) to Mount Batten	7.5	12.1
48	Mount Batten to Wembury (ferry)	7.5	12.1
49	Wembury to River Erme	10.3	16.6
50	River Erme to Hope Cove	9.3	15.0
51	Hope Cove to Salcombe	8.1	13.0
52	Salcombe to Torcross	12.6	20.3
53	Torcross to Dartmouth	10.3	16.6
54	Dartmouth to Brixham	10.9	17.5
55	Brixham to Babbacombe	13.2	21.2
56	Babbacombe to Teignmouth	6.4	10.3
57	Teignmouth to Exmouth	8	12.9
58	Exmouth to Budleigh Salterton	5.4	8.7
59	Budleigh Salterton to Sidmouth	7.1	11.4
60	Sidmouth to Seaton	10.3	16.6
61	Seaton (Devon) to Lyme Regis	7.1	11.4
62	Lyme Regis to West Bay	10	16.1
63	West Bay to Abbotsbury	9.3	15.0
64	Abbotsbury to Ferry Bridge (Weymouth)	10.9	17.5
65	Ferrybridge around Isle of Portland	13	20.9
66	Ferrybridge (Weymouth) to Lulworth Cove	14.4	23.2
67	Lulworth Cove to Kimmeridge Bay	7.1	11.4
68	Kimmeridge Bay to Worth Matravers (Winspit)	7.1	11.4
69	Worth Matravers (Winspit) to Swanage	6.5	10.5
70	Swanage to South Haven Point	7.5	12.1
71	Alternative route between West Bexington and Osmington Mills along the South Dorset Ridgeway	17.1	

Coast Path Walk Sections

Based on the 630 miles in 8 weeks itinerary on pages 34-35, the South West Coast Path has been divided into 70 Sections. Each Section represents a day's or half-day's walk of the Itinerary. However, it must be emphasised that these Sections should not be confined to use by those walking long stretches of the Coast Path. Each Section is designed to be used on its own as a one-off if so wished, as well as by those planning long walks of several days. The Sections are arranged in anti-clockwise order, from Minehead to Poole, with an additional Section 71 for the alternative inland South Dorset Ridgeway. In a number of coastal locations it is now necessary to pay for the toilet facilities. Also be aware that in winter a number of toilets close, or are only opened at weekends.

Key to Walk Sections - Pages 38-197

Each walk section starts with an overview as well as a map illustration of the walk Section, covering the landscape, it's general character and some of it's highlights.

Next, there is a short description of how the Section can be undertaken as a day or part-day walk with public transport or a local circular walk.

Finally, the main body of the Section description contains simplified instructions for walking in a Minehead – Poole direction, generally only highlighting those locations where it is possible to go astray.

At the end of each of the 7 Coast Path areas are places to **Sleep**, places to **Eat & Drink** and **Activities/Transport options** in that area.

Please note that this guide is produced annually and changes occur to the landscape of the Coast Path, so using out-of date literature can be misleading. If in doubt, follow the signs and waymarks on the ground.

Walk section table format:

 Distance – length of the Section in miles and kilometres;

 Cumulative distance – total length of the Coast Path from Minehead to the end of the Section in miles and kilometres;

 Ascent – height climbed during the Section in feet and metres;

 Cumulative ascent – total height climbed on the Coast Path from Minehead to the end of the Section in feet and metres;

 Grading – each Section is graded as Easy, Moderate, Strenuous or Severe. Inevitably, such grading is subjective to an extent, and not all of any Section will be identical throughout, but the grading will give an idea of the effort required;

 Timing – this is an estimated fair average for completing the Section. Times will vary depending on weather, number in party, gear carried, number of refreshment or photograph stops. The estimate should be an aide in planning;

 OS Maps – the reference numbers of the OS Maps needed to walk the Section are given. Both Landranger (1:50,000) and Explorer (1:25,000) maps are given;

 Area – for those not geographically acquainted with the South West, the Coast Path has been sub-divided into 7 areas for ease of identification, Exmoor, North Devon, North Cornwall, West Cornwall, South Cornwall, South Devon and Jurassic coast. These can be seen on the map on the inside cover of the Guide.

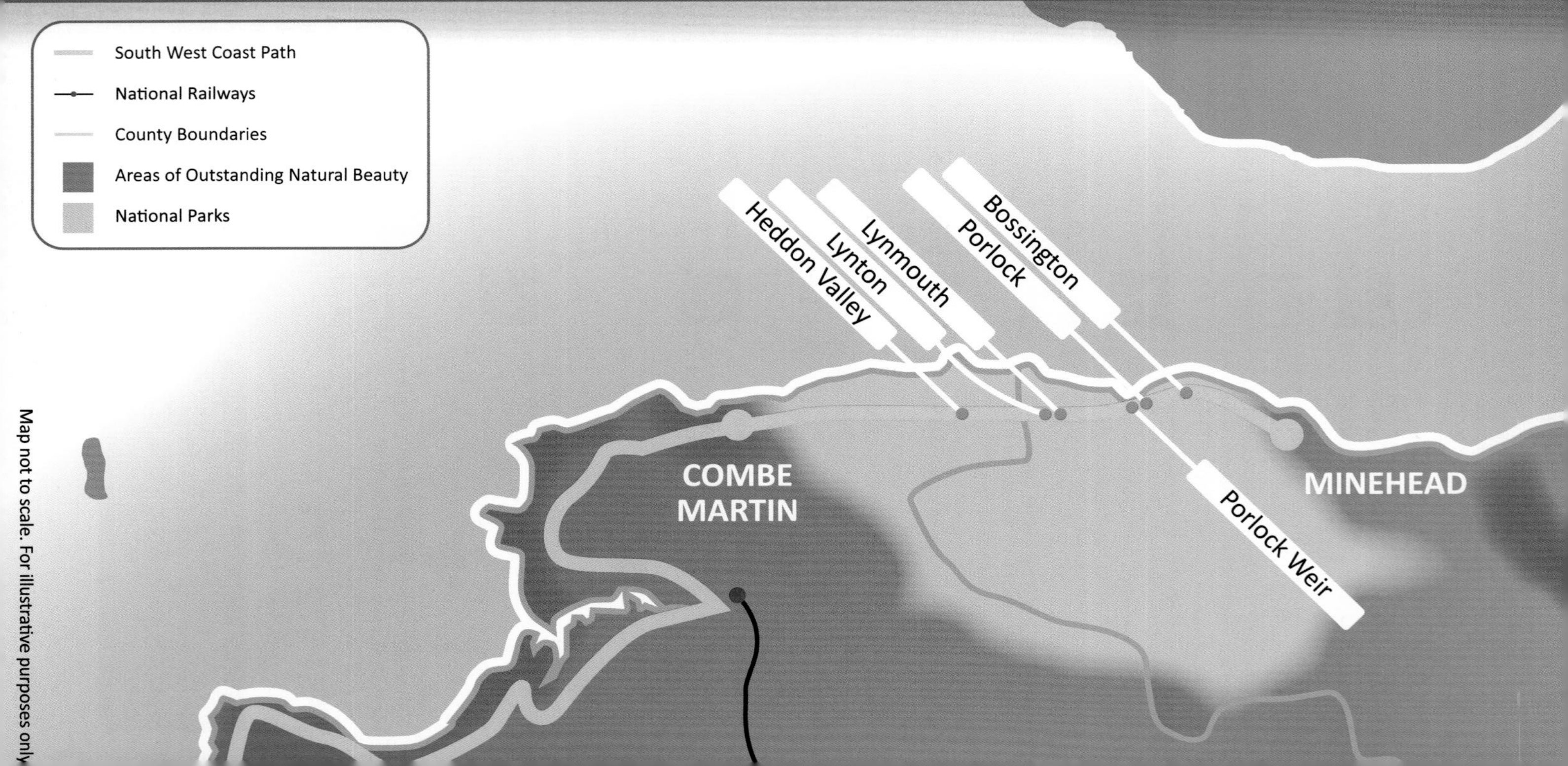

MINEHEAD

Porlock Weir

Bossington

Porlock

Lynmouth

Lynton

Heddon Valley

COMBE MARTIN

South West Coast Path

National Railways

County Boundaries

Areas of Outstanding Natural Beauty

National Parks

Map not to scale. For illustrative purposes only

Exmoor
Minehead to Combe Martin

(Sections 1-3)

The Exmoor coast is characterised by two main landscape types. The first is the meeting of the rolling expanse of high moorland and the sea. The coastline itself is one of high cliffs, some of them among the highest sea cliffs in England, but this height is sometimes disguised by the cliffs' convex shape, usually referred to as "hog's back". Views are often extensive inland, over the undulating moorland, while seaward in good visibility the coast of Wales may be seen across the Bristol Channel. The second main landscape type comprises steep and deep valleys which cut across the moorland cliffs. These valleys, known as "combes", are typically ancient oak woodland. Often this woodland spreads along the adjacent cliff faces, also convex in shape. Views from the Coast Path here are inevitably less extensive, and sometimes quite limited by the woodland, but the nature of the ancient woodland makes for an environment of considerable ecological interest. The combes and the height of the cliffs in the Exmoor length result in some notable gradients for walkers in places. Contrasting with these main landscape types is the Vale of Porlock, a flat-floored break in the cliffs crossed by the South West Coast Path over marshland at its mouth.

All of the locations on the map illustration to the left, have at least one facility including toilets, a cafe/restaurant, shop or pub.

Great Hangman

OS Maps: Landranger 181; Explorer OL9

	This Walk	Cumulative	This Walk	Cumulative	Grading	Timing
Ascent	1,824ft	1,824ft	556m	556m	Official: Moderate Alternative: Strenuous	4.5 hours
Distance	8.9mi	8.9mi	14.3km	14.3km		

For detailed directions see our Walking Guide no. 1, Minehead to Porlock Weir.

This is a classic example of where moorland meets the sea. Inland, the high expanse of Exmoor rolls away, broken by deep wooded valleys; where it meets the Bristol Channel there are high, convex cliffs, cut by deep and narrow "combes". This is a lonely, remote length, away from main roads and settlements, with often the only evidence of modern life being development far away on the opposite shore of the Bristol Channel on the South Wales coast. At the western end is the contrasting landscape of Porlock Vale, a flat-floored area of farmland and marshland behind its shingle ridge, quite different in character from the rest of this Section.

Directions

Regular buses run between Minehead and Porlock Weir.

The South West Coast Path starts from the celebratory marker on the sea front. The current route, which may not be shown on older maps, proceeds along the sea front, past the quay. Just before Greenaleigh Farm it turns left on ascending zigzags to North Hill.

At the summit of North Hill follow the acorn symbol towards Selworthy and Bossington. At the next Coast Path sign there is a fork, the route to the right being marked "Rugged Cliff Top Path", and either option can be taken. Do not be put off by the description of the seaward path as "rugged" , it is a splendid alternative and although a little longer, it is not too strenuous and gives much better sea views than the inland "official" path. It is well waymarked, and dogs are permitted but must be under very close control. There is likely to be cattle grazing.

On the "rugged" Path, at the stile, take the left fork towards a bench, then continue downhill to take the lower Path by a "Rugged Path" signpost. From Grexy Combe (GR 937 481) take the well-defined diagonal path up the hill to a wall, which is then followed first towards the sea then parallel to it to Western Brockholes. Here it turns inland to re-join the inland "official" path behind Hurlstone Point. (This seaward Path will add about an hour to the estimated time.)

The inland route, meanwhile, follows good tracks parallel to the sea. Joining the "rugged" path on Bossington Hill, the now-combined route descends the steep Hurlstone Combe. There is an optional diversion out to Hurlstone Point which gives a superb view. From Hurlstone, take care not to follow the obvious path to the left which contours round Bossington Hill.

The Path descends and goes inland to Bossington village and then just past the car park out towards the sea again. The route now crosses the marsh to Porlock Weir, easy to follow the whole way. At high spring tides it can become impassable, and signs to Porlock village should be followed. For tidal information contact Minehead Tourist Information Centre (TIC) - see page 200.

If the diversion via Porlock village is taken, leave the village on the Toll Road then bear right on a footpath that goes behind West Porlock to Porlock Weir.

OS Maps: Landranger 181 (eastern half); Landranger 180 (western half); Explorer OL9

	This Walk	Cumulative	This Walk	Cumulative	Grading	Timing
Ascent	3,156ft	4,980ft	962m	1,518m	Moderate, strenuous in parts	5.5 hours
Distance	12.1mi	21.0mi	19.5km	33.8km		

For detailed directions see our Walking Guide no. 2, Porlock Weir to Lynmouth.

This is a Section of two halves. In the east, approximately between Porlock Weir and the Devon/Somerset border, Exmoor meets the sea at a run of high, convex but well-wooded cliffs. The Coast Path here is a woodland walk with frequent glimpses of the sea, quiet and remote in character. To the west the cliffs become more open and steeper and the area around The Foreland and Countisbury is a spectacular viewpoint with panoramas over the double-decker towns of Lynton and Lynmouth. The section is lonely and remote, with no facilities, except a pub at Countisbury.

Directions

The bus service which linked Porlock Weir and Lynton ended in September 2014 after the bus company which operated it ceased trading. The route is covered by a vintage bus, which makes two trips daily in the high summer season only. For up to date details, it is recommended you visit www.travelinesw.com, or telephone 0871 200 2233.

The official route is signposted left of the hotel at Porlock Weir but it is possible to go in front of the hotel, past the shops then left signposted to Culbone.

Reaching Culbone turn right to visit the charming tiny church, which is recommended. From the church, retrace steps and turn right uphill on the Coast Path. After about 300 yards/275m bear right into Culbone, Embelle and Yenworthy Woods. This route may not be shown on some older maps. Unfortunately, recent land slippages towards the end of Yenworthy Wood have forced an inland diversion via Yenworthy Combe.

Continue to Sister's Fountain, where the access path to the bus route at County Gate on the A39 leaves the Coast Path. Go uphill through a pair of wild boar head gateposts, then take care not to miss the narrow signposted path 300 yards/275 metres past the cottage as the drive bears left. An alternative waymarked route may be taken between Culbone and Yenworthy Wood. Although slightly more inland, it offers better views than the mainly woodland more coastal route.

At Coddow Combe, the route is signposted left off the lighthouse track "Countisbury 1.5 miles". From Countisbury the now spectacular Path continues down the seaward side of the A39 road. Lower down it joins the road for a short way before descending on zigzags to the foreshore. Walk into Lynmouth, crossing the footbridge, then turn right to the sea front. Lynton is vertically above Lynmouth and is reached by turning left up the steps before the cliff railway (which can be taken as an interesting alternative). A new route is also available past the Esplanade car park at the end of the sea front, where a pleasant path, signposted to Lynton, goes left up the steep wooded hillside to emerge on the Coast Path west of Lynton. Both Lynmouth and Lynton have all facilities.

It is interesting to know that from Lynmouth it is possible to walk Devon's Coast to Coast route using the Two Moors Way and its southern extension to the south coast at Wembury. Guide books are available from Lynton Tourist Information Centre (TIC).

OS Maps: Landranger 180; Explorer OL9

	This Walk	Cumulative	This Walk	Cumulative	Grading	Timing
Ascent	3,766ft	8,746ft	1,148m	2,666m	Strenuous	7 hours
Distance	13.7mi	34.7mi	22.0km	55.8km		

For detailed directions see our Walking Guide no. 3, Lynton to Hunter's Inn and Hunter's Inn to Combe Martin.

This generally quiet and remote Section passes through a series of spectacular coastal landscapes: the Valley of Rocks with its rocky crags and pinnacles; the steep wooded cliffs at Woody Bay; the breathtaking scenery of the deep and steep crevice carved through the cliffs at Heddon's Mouth; the wide open spaces of Holdstone Down; and the heights of the Great Hangman, the highest point on the entire Coast Path and one of the highest coastal locations in the country.

Directions

Lynton and Combe Martin are connected by a summer bus service (year-round at weekends). Heddon's Mouth (6.5 miles/10.5km from Lynton) makes a good break in this length (though not on the bus route). There is a pub with accommodation at nearby Hunters Inn.

The Coast Path out of Lynton is on North Walk, and this Path leads to Castle Rock in the Valley of Rocks. The next section follows a minor but sometimes busy road, but a diversion to the right from the turning circle at the end of the Valley avoids its first length. Continue past the Toll House and up the hill. A permissive path on the right to Crock Point then avoids another length, and also gives stunning views.

The Coast Path leaves the road just before the hotel opposite the Red House. Arriving at another road turn left uphill. Follow the next Coast Path sign ahead. When this superb stretch reaches the dramatic Heddon's Mouth valley, follow it down to the valley floor. On reaching the stone bridge over the Heddon River, turn right over the river, and at the next Path turn hard left. Continue for 100 yards/91metres to the signpost on the right to Combe Martin. (Inland on either side of the river the Path leads to the pub at Hunter's Inn.)

Climb steeply away from the valley floor, keeping right at the top where the Path levels off. Continue round the headland (take care in windy conditions) then the Path heads inland to reach a stone wall; this is followed parallel to the sea. The wall ends and the signed Path continues across the heathland of Holdstone Down. At Sherrycombe the route follows the grass track along the top of the combe to the inland end and then down. Ascending Great Hangman from Sherrycombe, bear away from the wall on the left and ignore the many paths going to the right, meeting the wall higher up. From Great Hangman the Path is obvious to Little Hangman and beyond to Combe Martin.

If you enjoy sleeping, eating or drinking at any business on the Path please suggest they join us as Business Members so that we can share their brilliance!

The businesses listed here are all supporters and members of the South West Coast Path Association. Please find more details on our website www.southwestcoastpath.org.uk

- **GR** Grid Reference
- **DP** Distance from the Path
- **N** Nearest Town/Village with facilities
- **3** Number Of Rooms
- 🐕 Dogs Welcome
- 🍴 Evening Meal Available
- 📶 Wifi
- 🚗 Parking
- 🛒 Grocery Shop On Site

Bed & Breakfast and Hotels

NAME	OTHER INFO		
Yarn Market Hotel High Street, Dunster, Minehead, TA24 6SF 📞 01643 821425 ✉ enquiries@yarnmarkethotel.co.uk 🌐 www.yarnmarkethotel.co.uk	GR: SS991438	DP: 2 miles	
	N: **MINEHEAD**		
	Offers one night stays		
	28 🐕 🍴 📶 🚗		Other info: Annual Guided Walks along the Path.
Sunfield B&B 83 Summerland Avenue, Minehead, TA24 5BW 📞 01643 703565 ✉ stay@sunfieldminehead.co.uk 🌐 www.sunfieldminehead.co.uk	GR: SS972462	DP: 0.4 miles	
	N: **MINEHEAD**		
	Offers one night stays		
	6 🐕 📶		Other info:
Northfield Hotel Northfield Road, Minehead, TA24 5PU 📞 01643 705155 ✉ res@nfhotel.co.uk 🌐 www.northfield-hotel.co.uk	GR: SS970466	DP: 0 miles	
	N: **MINEHEAD**		
	Offers one night stays		
	30 🐕 🍴 📶 🚗		Other info: Limited dog friendly rooms
The Parks Guest House 26 The Parks, Minehead, TA24 8BT 📞 01643 703547 ✉ info@parksguesthouse.co.uk 🌐 www.parksguesthouse.co.uk	GR: SS964462	DP: 0.8 miles	
	N: **MINEHEAD**		
	Offers one night stays		
	3 🐕 📶 🚗		Other info: Open Mar-Nov
Exmoor Country House Minehead Road, Porlock, TA24 8EY 📞 01643 863599 ✉ info@exmoor-house.co.uk 🌐 www.exmoor-house.co.uk	GR: SS892467	DP: 1 mile	
	N: **PORLOCK**		
	Offers one night stays		
	5 🍴 📶 🚗		Other info:
Glen Lodge Luxury B&B Hawkcombe, Porlock, TA24 8LN 📞 01643 863371 / 07771 558263 ✉ glenlodge@gmail.com 🌐 www.glenlodge.net	GR: SS884459	DP: 1 mile	
	N: **PORLOCK**		
	Offers one night stays		
	5 🐕 📶 🚗		Other info: Hot Tub available after long walk!
The Cottage B&B High Street, Porlock, TA24 8PU 📞 01643 862996 ✉ cottageporlock@gmail.com 🌐 www.cottageporlock.co.uk	GR: SS885467	DP: 0.5 miles	
	N: **PORLOCK**		
	Offers one night stays		
	4 📶 🚗		Other info: Guest lounge
Myrtle Cottage High Street, Porlock, TA24 8PU 📞 01643 862978 ✉ enquiries@myrtleporlock.co.uk 🌐 www.myrtleporlock.co.uk	GR: SS884467	DP: 0.25 miles	
	N: **PORLOCK**		
	Offers one night stays		
	4 🐕 📶 🚗		Other info:
Sea View B&B West End, Porlock, TA24 8NP 📞 01643 853456 ✉ seaview.porlock@btconnect.com 🌐 www.seaviewporlock.co.uk	GR: SS884467	DP: 0.25 miles	
	N: **PORLOCK**		
	4 📶		Other info: Packed lunch/homemade pies.

EXMOOR - MINEHEAD TO COMBE MARTIN

NAME	OTHER INFO	
Ash Farm B&B Ash Farm, Porlock Weir, TA24 8JN ☎ 01643 862414 ✉ jenniferwren@jenniferwren.plus.com 🌐 www.southwestcoastpath.org.uk/ash-farm-porlock-hill	GR: SS842478	DP: 2 miles
	N: **PORLOCK WEIR**	
	Offers one night stays	
	3 📶 🚗	Other info: Open Apr-Oct
The Old Sea Captains House 1 Tors Road, Lynmouth, EX35 6ET ☎ 01598 753369 ✉ thecaptainshouse@btinternet.com 🌐 www.thecaptainshouseinlynmouth.co.uk	GR: SS727493	DP: 0.7 miles
	N: **LYNMOUTH**	
	Offers one night stays	
	9 🐕 📶 🚗	Other info: Centre of Lynmouth with full view of the Coast Path.
Orchard House Hotel 12 Watersmeet Road, Lynmouth, EX35 6EP ☎ 01598 753247 ✉ info@orchardhousehotel.co.uk 🌐 www.orchardhousehotel.co.uk	GR: SS726493	DP: 0.4 miles
	N: **LYNMOUTH**	
	Offers one night stays	
	6 🐕 🍴 📶	Other info:
Sinai House Lynway, Lynton, EX35 6AX ☎ 01598 753227 ✉ enquiries@sinaihouse.co.uk 🌐 www.sinaihouse.co.uk	GR: SS721491	DP: 0.5 miles
	N: **LYNTON**	
	Offers one night stays	
	8 📶 🚗	Other info:
St Vincent Guest House Market Street, Lynton, EX35 6AF ☎ 0781 131 3850 ✉ emma.anderson@zen.co.uk 🌐 www.stvincentlynton.co.uk	GR: SS720493	DP: 0.25 miles
	N: **LYNTON**	
	Offers one night stays	
	7 📶	Other info: Gluten-free specialists! Happy to make a packed lunch. Book direct.
The Crown Hotel Market Street, Lynton, EX35 6AG ☎ 01598 752253 ✉ thecrownhotellynton@outlook.com 🌐 www.thecrownlynton.co.uk	GR: SS720493	DP: 0.25 miles
	N: **LYNTON**	
	Offers one night stays	
	10 🐕 🍴 📶 🚗	Other info: Request packed lunches, extra charge.
South View Guest House 23 Lee Road, Lynton, EX35 6BP ☎ 01598 753728 ✉ jubrey@hotmail.co.uk 🌐 www.southviewguesthouselynton.co.uk	GR: SS718494	DP: 0.5 miles
	N: **LYNTON**	
	Offers one night stays	
	5 📶 🚗	Other info:
Gable Lodge Guest House 35 Lee Road, Lynton, EX35 6BS ☎ 01598 752367 ✉ gablelodge@btconnect.com 🌐 www.gablelodgelynton.com	GR: SS717494	DP: 0.25 miles
	N: **LYNTON**	
	Offers one night stays	
	6 🍴 📶 🚗	Other info:
Longmead House 9 Longmead, Lynton, EX35 6DQ ☎ 01598 752523 ✉ info@longmeadhouse.co.uk 🌐 www.longmeadhouse.co.uk	GR: SS714493	DP: 0.1 miles
	N: **LYNTON**	
	Offers one night stays	
	8 📶 🚗	Other info:
Blair Lodge Moory Meadow, Combe Martin, EX34 0DG ☎ 01271 882294 ✉ info@blairlodge.co.uk 🌐 www.blairlodge.co.uk	GR: SS578472	DP: 0.3 miles
	N: **COMBE MARTIN**	
	Offers one night stays	
	8 🍴 📶 🚗	Other info: Open Feb-Oct
Newberry Beach Lodge Newberry Road, Combe Martin, EX34 0AP ☎ 01271 883709 /07922571331 ✉ cjg0040@msn.com 🌐 www.newberrybeachlodge.co.uk	GR: SS574471	DP: 0 miles
	N: **COMBE MARTIN**	
	Offers one night stays	
	4 🐕 🍴 📶 🚗	Other info: Open all year

NAME	OTHER INFO	
Mellstock House B&B Woodlands, Combe Martin, EX34 0AR ☎ 01271 882592 ✉ enquiries@mellstockhouse.co.uk 🌐 www.mellstockhouse.co.uk	GR: SS574471	DP: 0 miles
	N: **COMBE MARTIN**	
	Offers one night stays	
	[5] 📶 🚗	Other info: Discounts available for all SWCP walkers and members.
Channel Vista Guest House Woodlands, Combe Martin, EX34 0AT ☎ 01271883514 ✉ info@channelvista.co.uk 🌐 www.channelvista.co.uk	GR: SS574470	DP: 0.1 miles
	N: **COMBE MARTIN**	
	Offers one night stays	
	[7] 📶 🚗	Other info:
Marlyn B&B Home Barton Farmhouse, Barton Lane, Berrynarbour, EX34 9SU ☎ 07952 244874 ✉ info@marlynbb.co.uk 🌐 www.marlynbb.co.uk	GR: SS567470	DP: 0.3 miles
	N: **COMBE MARTIN**	
	Offers one night stays	
	[3] 📶 🚗 🛒	Other info: Open Feb-Oct

Self Catering

NAME	OTHER INFO	
Keepers House Dunster, TA24 6SQ ☎ 0344 800 2070 ✉ cottages@nationaltrust.org.uk 🌐 www.nationaltrust.org.uk/holidays/keepers-house-dunster	GR: SS991436	DP: 3 miles
	N: **DUNSTER**	
	[3] 🚗	Other info:
Anchor Cottage 1 Quay Street, Minehead, TA24 5UL ☎ 0770 2985261 ✉ enquiries@anchorcottageminehead.co.uk 🌐 www.anchorcottageminehead.co.uk	GR: SS971469	DP: 0 miles
	N: **MINEHEAD**	
	[2] 🐕 📶 🚗	Other info: At the very start of the Coast Path.
Ivy's Cottage Selworth, TA24 8TP ☎ 0344 800 2070 ✉ cottages@nationaltrust.org.uk 🌐 www.nationaltrust.org.uk/holidays/ivys-cottage-somerset	GR: SS919468	DP: 1 mile
	N: **PORLOCK**	
	[1] 🚗	Other info: Parking is 180 metres up hill from the cottage.
Lower House Bossington, Minehead, TA24 8HQ ☎ 0344 800 2070 ✉ cottages@nationaltrust.org.uk 🌐 www.nationaltrust.org.uk/holidays/lower-house-somerset	GR: SS898479	DP: 1 mile
	N: **PORLOCK**	
	[5] 🐕 🚗	Other info:
Butter Hill Barn Lynmouth, EX35 6NE ☎ 0344 335 1296 ✉ bunkhouses@nationaltrust.org.uk 🌐 www.nationaltrust.org.uk/holidays/butter-hill-barn-devon	GR: SS898483	DP: 0 miles
	N: **LYNMOUTH**	
	[1] 🐕 🚗	Other info:
Kipscombe Cottage Countisbury, Lynmouth, EX35 6NE ☎ 0345 800 2070 ✉ cottages@nationaltrust.org.uk 🌐 www.nationaltrust.org.uk/holidays/kipscombe-cottage-devon	GR: SS898482	DP: 0 miles
	N: **LYNMOUTH**	
	[2] 🐕 📶 🚗	Other info:
Berry Lawn Linhay Bothy Lymouth, EX35 6NE ☎ 0344 335 1296 ✉ bunkhouses@nationaltrust.org.uk 🌐 www.nationaltrust.org.uk/holidays/berry-lawn-linhay-bothy	GR: SS898485	DP: 0 miles
	N: **LYNMOUTH**	
	Offers one night stays	
	[1] 🐕 📶	Other info:

NAME	OTHER INFO	
Exmoor Bunkhouse Lymouth, EX35 6NE 0344 335 1296 bunkhouses@nationaltrust.org.uk www.nationaltrust.org.uk/holidays/exmoor-bunkhouse	GR: SS898486	DP: 0 miles
	N: **LYNMOUTH**	
	3 🚗	Other info: Sleeps 18
Countisbury Hill Cottage Lynton, EX35 6NE 0344 800 2070 cottages@nationaltrust.org.uk www.nationaltrust.org.uk/holidays/countisbury-hill-cottage-devon	GR: SS898484	DP: 0 miles
	N: **LYNTON**	
	2 🐕 📶 🚗	Other info:
Foreland Bothy Countisbury, Lynton, EX35 6NE 0344 335 1296 bunkhouses@nationaltrust.org.uk www.nationaltrust.org.uk/holidays/foreland-bothy-devon	GR: SS898480	DP: 0 miles
	N: **LYNTON**	
	Offers one night stays	
	1 🐕 🚗	Other info:
The Lighthouse Keepers Cottage Lynton, EX35 6NE 0345 800 2070 cottages@nationaltrust.org.uk www.nationaltrust.org.uk/holidays/the-lighthouse-keepers-cottage-devon	GR: SS898479	DP: 0 miles
	N: **LYNTON**	
	6 📶 🚗	Other info:
Coombe Park Lodge Lynton, EX35 6LE 0344 800 2070 cottages@nationaltrust.org.uk www.nationaltrust.org.uk/holidays/combe-park-lodge-devon	GR: SS736475	DP: 1 mile
	N: **LYNTON**	
	2 🐕 📶 🚗	Other info:
Martinhoe Cleave Cottages Martinhoe, Parracombe, EX31 4PZ 01598 753987 info@exmoorhideaway.co.uk www.exmoorhideaway.co.uk	GR: SS656483	DP: 0.75 miles
	N: **LYNTON**	
	4 🐕 📶 🚗	Other info:
Heddon Lodge Heddon Valley, EX31 4PY 01598 763230 info@huntersinnhotel.com www.nationaltrust.org.uk/holidays/heddon-lodge-devon	GR: SS654482	DP: 1 mile
	N: **HEDDON VALLEY**	
	2 🐕 🍴 📶 🚗	**Other info:** The Hunters Inn is adjacent to the cottage.
Heddon's Gate Hotel Heddon Valley, EX31 4PZ 01598 763481 stay@heddonsgatehotel.co.uk www.heddonsgatehotel.co.uk	GR: SS656483	DP: 0.5 miles
	N: **HEDDON VALLEY**	
	Offers one night stays	
	11 🐕 📶 🚗	**Other info:** Bar, sun terrace, free lift from Hunter's Inn after evening meal. Packed lunch.
Heddon Orchard Bothy Parracombe, Barnstaple, EX31 4PY 0344 335 1296 bunkhouses@nationaltrust.org.uk www.nationaltrust.org.uk/holidays/heddon-orchard-bothy-devon	GR: SS654481	DP: 1 mile
	N: **HEDDON VALLEY**	
	Offers one night stays	
	1 🐕	Other info:
The Hunters Inn Hotel Parracombe, Barnstaple, EX31 4PY 01599 763230 info@huntersinnhotel.com www.nationaltrust.org.uk/holidays/the-hunters-inn-exmoor	GR: SS654481	DP: 10 miles
	N: **HEDDON VALLEY**	
	Offers one night stays	
	1 🐕 🍴 📶 🚗	Other info:

NAME	OTHER INFO	
West Challacombe Cottage Coombe Martin, EX34 0DS 📞 0345 800 2070 ✉ cottages@nationaltrust.org.uk 🌐 www.nationaltrust.org.uk/holidays/west-challacombe-cottage-devon	GR: SS589478	DP: 0 miles
	N: **COMBE MARTIN**	
	2 🛜 🚗	Other info:
West Challacombe Manor Coombe Martin, EX34 0DS 📞 0345 800 2070 ✉ cottages@nationaltrust.org.uk 🌐 www.nationaltrust.org.uk/holidays/west-challacombe-manor-devon	GR: SS589477	DP: 0.5 miles
	N: **COMBE MARTIN**	
	3 🛜 🚗	Other info:

Campsites and Holiday Parks

NAME	OTHER INFO	
Sparkhayes Farm Campsite Sparkhayes Lane, Porlock, TA24 8NE 📞 07721 05123 / 01643 862470 ✉ sparkhayes@hotmail.com 🌐 www.sparkhayes.co.uk	GR: SS886468	DP: 0.1 miles
	N: **MINEHEAD**	
	Offers one night stays	
	🐕 🍴 🛒 🚗	Other info: Meals, Groceries and Wifi all within 100m all year.
Kipscombe Farm Campsite Countisbury, Lynmouth, EX35 6NE 📞 01598 763556 ✉ northdevoncamping@nationaltrust.org.uk 🌐 www.nationaltrust.org.uk/holidays/kipscombe-farm-campsite	GR: SS898481	DP: 0 miles
	N: **LYNMOUTH**	
	Offers one night stays	
	🐕 🚗	Other info: This campsite is only open for a few weeks during August.
Combe Martin Beach Holiday Park Woodlands, Combe Martin, EX34 0AS 📞 01271 882 563 🌐 www.johnfowlerholidays.com/devon-holiday-park/ combe-martin-beach-holiday-park	GR: SS575470	DP: 0.7miles
	N: **COMBE MARTIN**	
	111 🐕 🍴 🛜 🚗	Other info: Caravans, chalets, manor house & apartments set in the valley.
Sandaway Beach Holiday Park Berrynarbor, Combe Martin, EX34 9ST 📞 01271 883 155 🌐 www.johnfowlerholidays.com/devon-holiday-park/ sandaway-beach-holiday-park	GR: SS571472	DP: 0.8 miles
	N: **COMBE MARTIN**	
	120 🐕 🍴 🛒 🛜 🚗	Other info: Range of self catering & camping options.

Information

NAME	OTHER INFO	
Minehead Information Centre The Beach Hotel, The Avenue, Minehead, TA24 5AP 📞 01643 702624 ✉ minehead.visitor@hotmail.com 🌐 www.mineheadbay.co.uk	GR: SS974464	DP: 0.5 miles
	N: **MINEHEAD**	
	🐕	Other info: We carry a great selection of maps & books to help make the most of your trip.
Lynton and Lynmouth TIC Town Hall Lee Road, Lynton, EX35 6BT 📞 01598 752225 ✉ info@lyntourism.co.uk 🌐 www.visitlyntonandlynmouth.com	GR: SS718804	DP: 0.2 miles
	N: **LYNTON**	
		Other info:

Activities

NAME	OTHER INFO	
Exmoor Rambler High Street, Porlock, Minehead, TA24 8PY 📞 01643 862429 ✉ exmoorrambler@btinternet.com 🌐 www.exmoorrambler.uk	GR: SS885467	DP: 0.25 miles
	N: **MINEHEAD**	
	🐕	Other info: Post office services available in store.

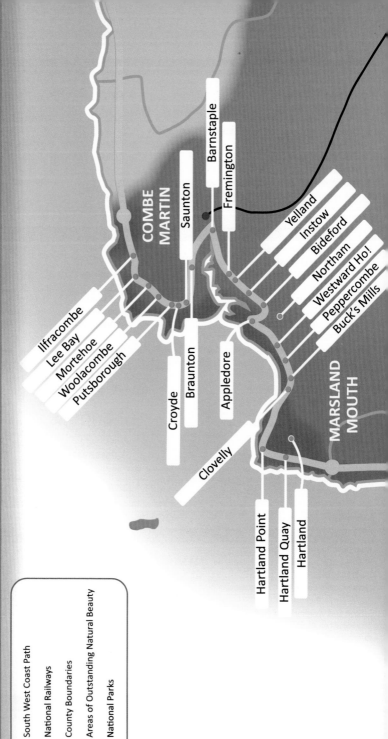

COMBE MARTIN

MARSLAND MOUTH

Barnstaple
Saunton
Fremington
Yelland
Instow
Bideford
Northam
Westward Ho!
Peppercombe
Buck's Mills

Ilfracombe
Lee Bay
Mortehoe
Woolacombe
Putsborough

Croyde
Braunton
Appledore
Clovelly

Hartland Point
Hartland Quay
Hartland

South West Coast Path

National Railways

County Boundaries

Areas of Outstanding Natural Beauty

National Parks

Map not to scale. For illustrative purposes only

North Devon
Combe Martin to Marsland Mouth

(Sections 4-13)

Most of the North Devon coast faces north over the Bristol Channel. Much of this length comprises cliffs of moderate height with, in the east, some prominent headlands like Morte Point and Baggy Point which offer fine coastal vistas. In the centre of the North Devon length is the large joint estuary of the Taw and Torridge Rivers, flanked by areas of sand dunes and marshland. The South West Coast Path partly uses old railway lines around the estuary, crossing the rivers at the towns of Barnstaple and Bideford. Adjacent to the estuary are extensive sandy beaches, popular with surfers and families. The north facing cliffs continue to Hartland Point, one of the Coast Path's major headlands (referred to as the 'Promontory of Hercules' by the Romans). Seascapes typically have the coast of Wales beyond the Bristol Channel as the backdrop; in the west the offshore island of Lundy, at the "mouth" of the Bristol Channel, is the focal point. Hartland Point marks an abrupt change in direction from the east-west of most of North Devon to the north-south beyond. This north-south length is very dramatic, with high cliffs fronted by jagged fingers of rock stretching into the Atlantic. Deep and steep valleys cut the coastline, making for some considerable gradients for walkers, but there are no bays or harbours other than the tiny harbour at Hartland Quay.

All of the locations on the map illustration to the left, have at least 1 facility including toilets, a cafe/restaurant, shop or pub.

Combe Martin

OS Maps: Landranger 180; Explorer 139 or OL9

	This Walk	Cumulative	This Walk	Cumulative	Grading	Timing
Ascent	1,280ft	10,026ft	390m	3,056m	Moderate, strenuous in parts	2.5 hours
Distance	5.4mi	40.1mi	8.7km	64.5km		

For detailed directions see our Walking Guide no. 4, Combe Martin to Ilfracombe.

This is a Section of rocky inlets, one of which, Watermouth, is spacious enough for boats to be moored. These bays are divided by rugged headlands. The cliffs here are grey and slatey, making for a forbidding looking coastline, notwithstanding the little bays. At the western end, the site of a prehistoric hill fort gives a panoramic view over Ilfracombe. This Section is never far from the A399 coast road and various tourist facilities, so despite the impressive cliffs it is not a lonely length.

Directions

Combe Martin and Ilfracombe are linked by a regular bus service, allowing a bus-walk to be easily undertaken on this Section.

The Coast Path leaves the Lime Kiln car park in Combe Martin, passing the Tourist Information Centre (TIC), then forks right. Turn right (Seaside Hill Road) above the beach. Turn right onto a narrow tarmac lane and follow the acorn signs as the path winds below the houses, and uphill to finally join the A399 at Sandaway holiday park. Walk on the slightly raised Path along the roadside through two gates. Go along a Path beside a field to a flight of steps, then turn left up the slip road back to the main road and on to the brow, passing the bus shelter. Turn right to follow the road down to the old main road, with a bus shelter, now used as an Information Point, over to the right. Here turn left beside the entrance to the hotel, to follow a track towards Watermouth Cove.

At Watermouth it is possible to cross the foreshore from the harbour office, keeping to the left of the bay for some 110 yards/100 metres to a flight of steps at most states of the tide; take care, as the rocks can be slippery. However, if the tide is high, use the route running parallel to the main road. (Check the Watermouth tide timings by contacting Ilfracombe or Combe Martin Tourist Information Centres (TICs) - see page 200).

This roadside Path is a great improvement as it avoids the need to walk in the road carriageway. It was completed in late 2013 following the Association's offer of £50,000 from our reserves towards its cost, because of our safety concerns. The offer enabled the remainder of the funding to be secured from the Rural Development Fund for England and Devon County Council, a successful conclusion to a decade of pressure.

The next pleasant section of Path passes the western side of Watermouth Cove and on around Widmouth Head and then Rillage Point. There is then a roadside section into Hele. Turn right here, then climb some steps on the far left of the beach. The Path zigzags up past Beacon Point to the top of Hillsborough. Follow the waymarks down the hill to Ilfracombe Harbour.

OS Maps: Landranger 180; Explorer 139

	This Walk	Cumulative	This Walk	Cumulative	Grading	Timing
Ascent	2,037ft	12,063ft	621m	3,677m	Easy to moderate; strenuous west of Lee Bay	3.5 hours
Distance	8.5mi	48.6mi	13.7km	78.2km		

For detailed directions see our Walking Guide no. 5, Ilfracombe to Woolacombe.

Most of this Section is characterised by grass-topped cliffs, fronting numerous small coves and a foreshore of rock ledges. Half-way along is the focal point of Bull Point lighthouse. At Morte Point the character of the coastline changes abruptly, as the enormous beach of Woolacombe Sands in its vast bay comes into view, often dotted with surfers. The dark jagged rocks of Morte Point give this headland a superb brooding atmosphere.

Directions

Ilfracombe and Woolacombe are linked by a regular bus service, allowing a bus-walk to be easily undertaken on this Section.

From Ilfracombe Harbour walk along Capstone Road. After some 170 yards/150 metres turn right to pass around Capstone Point. At the far end take a flight of steps that goes up behind the back of the Landmark Theatre. Follow this path to the top of the gardens and through a gate by a shelter. Bear right along Granville Road, then right again onto an unmetalled road which leads to the Torrs Walk on the right; the Torrs Walk is well waymarked.

At the top of the Torrs Walk, bear right and follow the Path down the field to the stile in the corner. Continue ahead around the hill to another stile, then cross the field to meet the old coach road ahead. Bear right on this track, which later becomes a minor road into Lee Bay.

The next length from Lee Bay is quite strenuous. Proceed up the road from Lee, turning right at the top of the hill through a brick-pillared gate. Two steep valleys are crossed before Bull Point and its lighthouse are reached. The Path continues on and out around Morte Point, a spectacular jagged, slate ridge like a dinosaur's back emerging from the sea. The Path leaves Morte Point, and crosses the road and heads slightly inland before turning back to arrive at the edge of Woolacombe.

Bull Point towards Morte Point

OS Maps: Landranger 180; Explorer 139

	This Walk	Cumulative	This Walk	Cumulative	Grading	Timing
Ascent	725ft	12,788ft	221m	3,898m	Moderate	3 hours
Distance	5.2mi	53.8mi	8.4km	86.6km		

For detailed directions see our Walking Guide no. 6, Woolacombe to Croyde Bay.

The main feature of this Section is the vast sandy beach of Woolacombe Sands, backed by a substantial line of dunes. Busy with families and surfers close to the town, it becomes surprisingly empty away from the facilities. Beyond the beach is the superb headland of Baggy Point, a contrast to the beach with its steep cliffs and broad, grassy top. Rounding the headland, another smaller sandy bay comes into view, Croyde Bay, with the wider vista of Bideford Bay beyond.

Directions

Croyde Bay is an excellent centre for a circular walk using the Coast Path, around Baggy Point to Putsborough, giving views over Woolacombe Sands while experiencing the superb character of the headland.

At Woolacombe the Coast Path runs parallel to the Esplanade road, then turns up Challacombe Road. It leaves this road on the right at approximately the National Trust sign – at a waymark. The Path continues through the enormous dunes of Woolacombe Warren – the waymarking means that going astray is unlikely. An alternative is to follow Marine Drive and the track beyond, which gives better views. If the tide is low many walk the length of Woolacombe Sands but this should not be attempted on a high or rising tide.

The official Path leaves the Warren by a set of steep steps, joining the extension to Marine Drive and the alternative route. It continues along the track then a road, leaving it to the right after the entrance to the beach and caravan site. As an alternative, take the earlier Path on the right to the car park at Putsborough, where there are seasonal refreshments and toilets (the beach route joins here). Go left of the caravan site to a stile and up the cliff slope to re-join the official Path.

The excellent high level Path continues to the end of Baggy Point, giving superb views. At the end of the headland, bear right to join the lower Path towards Croyde. Follow the road, partly on a parallel Path. Do not leave the road at the first slipway. The official Path leaves the road a little further on to cross the beach, but many will continue on to visit Croyde and its facilities.

The Esplanade, Woolacombe

OS Maps: Landranger 181 (eastern half); Landranger 180 (western half); Explorer OL9

	This Walk	Cumulative	This Walk	Cumulative	Grading	Timing
Ascent	506ft	13,294ft	154m	4,052m	Easy	3.25 hours
Distance	9.8mi	63.6mi	15.8km	102.4km		

For detailed directions see our Walking Guide no. 7, Croyde Bay to Braunton.

The length immediately adjacent to Croyde Bay follows a low cliff, and gives stunning views over the truly enormous length of Saunton Sands, with the dune complex of Braunton Burrows behind. Beyond is the sweep of Bideford Bay, with the possibility of seeing as far as Hartland Point lighthouse, many miles away. Offshore on the horizon is the Isle of Lundy. The remainder of this Section is low and level, through a huge range of dunes (the official route) or along the seemingly endless Saunton Sands. Then comes the twin estuary of the Rivers Taw and Torridge, with mudbanks and reclaimed marshes making for a birdwatcher's delight. This is a length displaying a relatively rare aspect of the South West coast.

Directions

Croyde Bay and Braunton are linked by a regular year-round bus service, making this a good bus-walk possibility.

The Coast Path leaves Croyde Bay via the beach (no dogs May-September), and on to the low cliffs at Down End. After climbing up some steep steps, turn left at the old coastguard lookout onto the B3231 road, and walk back in the direction of Croyde for a few yards before crossing the road with care, turn right at the waymark then climb some stone steps. The Path now contours round Saunton Down, parallel to and above the road. This ends opposite the large white building of the hotel.

From here there are optional routes. The first option is to cross the road and pass around the hotel to the Saunton Sands car park, where there are toilets and seasonal refreshments. Leave the car park by the entrance road, and after 55 yards/50 metres bear right along a stony lane to the B3231. Continue carefully along the road for some 400 yards/365 metres, past the Golf Club driveway, turning right at a red brick partially rendered house.

If there is no need for the toilets or refreshments, a better option is to turn left uphill opposite the hotel, away from the road. Follow the Path as it bears round to the right, until it arrives at the B3231 opposite the red brick house described above. Cross the road to continue on the same route as above.

This route now enters the Braunton Burrows nature reserve, designated a UNESCO Biosphere Reserve for its nature conservation importance. The route through the Burrows is well waymarked; first follow a clear track through patchy woodland along the edge of the golf course with the military training area on the right. After the Sandy Lane car park, follow the signing for nearly two miles along a rough, traffic-free, military dirt road known as the American Road, to arrive at Crow Point by the estuary of the Taw and Torridge rivers. Follow another dirt road, approximately eastwards, to arrive at the White House, a well-known local landmark.

Many walkers prefer to miss the Burrows and walk from Saunton Sands car park the length of the beach, for some 3.5 miles/5.5 kilometres. Near the end of the beach, just after a wooden groyne, look out for a slatted wooden boardwalk entering the dunes to the left. Follow this to arrive at the Broad Sands car park. This beach route keeps the sea in sight, not the case with the Burrows route.

From the White House following the Path diversion signs, walk on top of the inner sea defence bank. This is followed, between estuary and reclaimed marshes, to the old quay at Velator on the edge of Braunton. To visit Braunton and its facilities, turn left at Velator along the footpath and cycleway, following the former railway track.

Male stonechat taken at Baggy Point, Croyde

OS Maps: Landranger 180; Explorer 139

	This Walk	Cumulative	This Walk	Cumulative	Grading	Timing
Ascent	16ft	13,310ft	5m	4,057m	Easy	2 hours
Distance	5.4mi	69.0mi	8.7km	111.0km		

For detailed directions see our Walking Guide no. 8, Braunton to Barnstaple.

This is a flat, low-level Section, following the line of the former railway track once used by the Atlantic Coast Express. As well as the Coast Path, it is also used by Devon's Coast to Coast Cycle Route. At the Braunton end, the main item of interest is the Royal Marines air base at Chivenor, next to the Path, but further on, the Path runs alongside the estuary of the River Taw, with its interplay of water and sand and mud banks. This makes for a pleasant environment; in character, however, this length is semi-urban.

Directions

There is a regular and year-round bus service between Braunton and Barnstaple, which can also be accessed at Chivenor, approximately mid-way along the route, giving various short walk options.

From Braunton's main car park the signed route to Barnstaple leads to the Coast Path at Velator, and from here the Path follows the former railway past Chivenor Royal Marines base, and then alongside the Taw Estuary all the way to Barnstaple.

The new high level bridge across the River Taw can be used as an alternative to the Coast Path and offers a superb view down the river. However, most will prefer to continue on the riverside Path into Barnstaple, an attractive town with many facilities for walkers.

Approaching Barnstaple on the former railway (signed as Tarka Trail), the Path crosses a bridge over the tributary River Yeo and then passes the old railway station to a riverside embankment. Leave this at steps climbing to Barnstaple's historic Long Bridge. Barnstaple, North Devon's major centre, is a pleasant and interesting historic town well worth exploring, as well as offering a range of facilities, including a branch line railway to the main line at Exeter.

Barnstaple Bridge

9 BARNSTAPLE TO BIDEFORD

OS Maps: Landranger 180; Explorer 139

	This Walk	Cumulative	This Walk	Cumulative	Grading	Timing
Ascent	40ft	13,350ft	12m	4,069m	Easy	4 hours
Distance	10.7mi	79.7mi	17.2km	128.3km		

For detailed directions see our Walking Guide no. 9, Barnstaple to Bideford.

This is a flat, low-level Section, much of it following a former railway line on the south side of the Taw Estuary. It passes through a landscape of marshland and pastures, with the tidal expanses and sand banks of the river never far away. This is an area of great value for birdlife. Approaching Instow the estuary opens out as the Taw's sister river, the Torridge, joins and there are wide areas of sand bars and dunes. This Section, despite its proximity to "civilisation" and the use of the former railway as part of the Devon Coast to Coast Cycle Route, is nevertheless one of much interest and character.

Directions

There is a regular and frequent all-year bus service between Barnstaple and Bideford, which can also be accessed at Fremington and Instow along the route. A variety of short walk options is therefore available.

Cross Barnstaple's historic Long Bridge then keep to the right of the large roundabout, following Tarka Trail signing, then cross a mini-roundabout to a Path which curves around to a subway under the approach road for the high-level bridge. A link path to the railway station goes off to the left here. The main Path, signed Coast Path and Tarka Trail, then links to the former railway line. The direct Coast Path route across the high-level bridge joins here.

The former railway continues past the delightfully restored Fremington Quay, with its all-year cafe and Information Point. At Yelland look out for the Path leaving the railway to the right, which takes the Coast Path behind the site of an old power station. After passing inland of the cricket ground, the route then crosses an area of dunes to arrive at the estuary-side road through Instow, which has all facilities. Go through the old railway station and follow the former railway to the restored Bideford station. Leave the station to cross Bideford Long Bridge, then turn right along the bustling quay. Bideford has all facilities.

Bideford Bridge

OS Maps: Landranger 180; Explorer 139

	This Walk	Cumulative	This Walk	Cumulative	Grading	Timing
Ascent	524ft	13,871ft	159m	4,228m	Easy	3 hours
Distance	8.0mi	87.7mi	12.9km	141.1km		

For detailed directions see our Walking Guide no. 10, Bideford to Westward Ho!

Much of this Section follows the estuary of the River Torridge, first on its east bank then turning back on its west. The estuary is largely enclosed by green hills, but houses and roads are ever-present and a high-level road bridge over the estuary is a major feature. The Coast Path crosses the river at the charming old port of Bideford. Passing beyond the estuary and through the characterful old fishing town of Appledore, the Path crosses the open spaces of Northam Burrows and its surrounding marshlands, and then alongside an enormous pebble ridge as it arrives again at the open sea. As an alternative option, missing out Bideford, a ferry service is now operating between Instow and Appledore, for details see page 22.

Directions

A regular bus service links Bideford and Westward Ho! and another connects Bideford to Appledore. These services allow for a range of Coast Path-based walk options.

From Bideford Quay keep alongside the river past the car park, then next to the rugby club to a lane which passes under the high-level bridge. Follow the waymarked tracks to a riverside lane, then after the old tank traps, fork right to a small woodland area.

Descend to a boardwalk, then continue on the old sea wall. Follow the waymarked route round Appledore shipyard, and at the road turn right into Appledore via Myrtle Street. Continue along the quay and on into the charming old part of the town, along Irsha Street and past the lifeboat station. Here the route follows a Path along the edge of low cliffs and across a field to a slipway. When the tide is low continue along The Skern around another wooden slipway following the high water mark, then cross a stile to enter Northam Burrows. When the tide is high follow the slipway where the route joins a road. Follow the road for approximately 0.3 miles/0.5 metres to a crossroads and here turn right.

Follow the track ahead alongside the marshes, then on the seaward side of the dunes to the pebble ridge. Continue ahead on the landward side of the ridge. On the approach to Westward Ho! leave Northam Burrows by the pedestrian gate to the right of the cattle grid by the toll booth. Proceed up Pebble Ridge Road using the right side pavement to the crossroads. Turn right into Golf Links Road, then after the Tesco Express store, turn right into Westbourne Terrace. Just before the slipway turn left onto the promenade to Westward Ho!

OS Maps: Landranger 180 (eastern half) ; Explorer 139 (eastern half); Landranger 190 (western half); Explorer 126 (western half)

	This Walk	Cumulative	This Walk	Cumulative	Grading	Timing
Ascent	2,995ft	16,866ft	913m	5,141m	Strenuous	6 hours
Distance	11.1mi	98.8mi	17.9km	159.0km		

For detailed directions see our Walking Guide no. 11, Westward Ho! to Clovelly

This Section is one of cliffs and woods. The eastern half is an area of undulating cliffs, cut in places by substantial valleys, though in the length closest to Westward Ho!, where the line of an old railway is used, the Path is generally level. The western half passes through lengthy wooded stretches, much of it along the old carriage road known as the Hobby Drive. At the western end, Clovelly is probably one of the most picturesque villages in England.

Directions

There is no direct bus route between Westward Ho! and Clovelly. However, there is one between Bideford and Clovelly, as well as a frequent link to Bideford from Westward Ho! Peppercombe and Buck's Mills, about two thirds of the way along this length towards Clovelly, are on the Bideford-Clovelly bus route, giving possible bus-walks at this end.

At Westward Ho! walk along the Path above the beach. After passing the last of the holiday chalets, the Path follows the track of the long-disused Bideford to Westward Ho! railway. This makes a fine easy scenic walk. Where the railway turns inland, the Path continues along the cliffs, rising and falling to cross a short pebble beach before climbing again. At Peppercombe turn inland to cross the stream and then continue through woodland. Note that some old maps may not show the correct route at Worthygate Wood. The Path drops to Buck's Mills, a picturesque little spot, then climbs again into more woods. On leaving Barton Wood, keep to the bottom edge of the field until crossing a bridge to the Hobby Drive at the end of a second field. The Hobby Drive section is nearly 3 miles/5 kilometres long, and although very pleasant, offers sea glimpses rather than sea views. The Path arrives at Clovelly at the top of the steep village street. Clovelly is very picturesque and has most facilities, though perhaps limited in range.

Pebble Ridge at Westward Ho!

OS Maps: Landranger 190; Explorer 126

	This Walk	Cumulative	This Walk	Cumulative	Grading	Timing
Ascent	2,382ft	19,248ft	726m	5,867m	Moderate to strenuous	5 hours
Distance	10.3mi	109.1mi	16.6km	175.6km		

For detailed directions see our Walking Guide no. 12, Clovelly to Hartland Quay.

There is a great contrast in this Section between east and west. In the east the landscape is one of parkland, the domesticated and partly ornamental landscape of the grounds of Clovelly Court. After leaving the parkland a run of high cliffs culminates at Hartland Point, one of the great defining headlands of the Coast Path. Here the coast turns from east-west to north-south and its character changes into one of the Coast Path's most breathtaking stretches, with dark brooding cliffs behind jagged fingers of rock stretching into the Atlantic Ocean. Experiencing its magnificent scenery is well worth the effort of crossing the spectacular deep valleys which cut the coast. The Section ends at the pub and hotel at Hartland Quay, which has a wonderful remote atmosphere.

Bucks Mills

Directions

Hartland Quay has no public transport. However, there are numerous walking links from the Coast Path to Hartland village, 2.5 miles/4km inland, which is on the bus route to Clovelly.

If using Clovelly as a base, it is requested that visitors use the main car park. If you're walking on your own, it might be worth paying for a village visit at £7 which includes car parking.

From the main car park, walk out of the entrance and turn right down the road for some 220 yards/200 metres to a black gate on the left. Go through and follow the track first right and through a gap in the wall, then leave the track and follow the marked path down to the right. After a while go through a kissing-gate then follow the fence on the right to another gate into shrubbery. Continue through the shrubbery through more gates. Turn right at a T-junction and right again at the next fork. Soon the Path arrives at an unusual seat known as the "Angel's Wings". At the track, turn hard right – not along the track. After passing a superb viewpoint the Path descends steeply into a valley to another track. Go right here. The signed detour to the viewpoint is well worth the effort.

The Coast Path goes down the valley to Mouth Mill. Turn left before reaching the shore on to a substantial track. Turn right to cross the new steel and timber bridge.

Turn right after the bridge, then left to climb the valley side. Half-way up, follow the steps to the right. On reaching the top, pass through fields to a stile on the right leading to some descending zigzags. Cross the bridge at the bottom, turn left then take the first right.

After the prehistoric earthwork of Windbury Castle, the Path continues on the cliff-top to Shipload Bay and then on to Hartland Point, where there are seasonal refreshments. The Coast Path turns sharp left off the lighthouse track, towards the coastguard lookout before the lighthouse gate. A short diversion gives a good view of a wreck on the rocks below.

From Hartland Point the Path descends into an unusual valley, almost parallel to the coast, at Smoothlands, before climbing again. Descending then to the valley at the Abbey River, the Path goes inland to cross at a stone bridge. At the next cliff top, past an old folly tower, the Path arrives at a road by the old Rocket House. Bear right to follow the Path downhill to Hartland Quay, a lonely outpost with car park, toilets and refreshments, as well as a hotel.

Looking towards Hartland Quay

OS Maps: Landranger 190; Explorer 126 (most of length); Explorer 111 (Bude)

	This Walk	Cumulative	This Walk	Cumulative	Grading	Timing
Ascent	4,170ft	23,418ft	1,271m	7,138m	Severe	8.5 hours
Distance	15.2mi	124.3mi	24.5km	200.0km		

For detailed directions see our Walking Guide no. 13, Hartland Quay to Morwenstow and Morwenstow to Bude.

This is an awe-inspiring and dramatic coastline. Great jagged ridges of rock stretch out into the Atlantic Ocean, backed by high, surf-fringed cliffs. The coast is punctuated by jutting headlands and tiny, often inaccessible beaches. In the south, towards Bude, the coast softens a little, and at low tide, long sandy beaches appear. This is a spectacular Section.

(Note that although for convenience this Section is included in the North Devon length, the southern half of the Section is within Cornwall.)

Directions

Hartland Quay has no public transport connections. There is, however, an infrequent bus service between Bude and Morwenstow, half-way along, which could be used for a bus-walk on the southern half of this Section.

Note that this is probably the most arduous of all the days in the suggested itinerary. It is necessary to cross ten river valleys to complete the length, all of them steep and deep. Because of this, many may prefer to split the length at Morwenstow, where there is a tea room and the pub also offers some accommodation.

From Hartland Quay a track then a grassy path passes behind St Catherine's Tor. There is a climb, then the cliff Path reaches the dramatic waterfall at Speke's Mill Mouth. Keep to the eastern side of the stream here for some 150 yards/135 metres then cross by the wooden footbridge. Follow the signs up the valley inland of Swansford Hill. Take care at Sandhole Cliff, after joining the metalled road, to look out for the signpost after about 0.3 mile/0.5 kilometres indicating the turn right back to the coast. (It is hoped this length of road may be eliminated in the near future.) After Welcombe Mouth, Marsland Mouth marks the Cornish border, indicated by a wooden sign. The ascents and descents continue, and a diversion to Morwenstow might be worth considering. The church is picturesque and interesting and there are seasonal refreshments nearby. At the radio dishes do not miss the sign directing right towards the cliff edge. Descending to Duckpool, cross the stream by a footbridge. There are toilets here. Continue on to Sandy Mouth where there are more toilets and seasonal refreshments. The going now eases at last, and after passing over the open cliffs at Maer Down the Path arrives at Crooklets Beach at Bude. Follow the Path along the low cliffs behind the beaches into the town, which has all facilities.

If you enjoy sleeping, eating or drinking at any business on the Path please suggest they join us as Business Members so that we can share their brilliance!

The businesses listed here are all supporters and members of the South West Coast Path Association. Please find more details on our website www.southwestcoastpath.org.uk

GR Grid Reference
DP Distance from the Path
N   Nearest Town/Village with facilities

[3] Number Of Rooms
[Dog] Dogs Welcome
[Meal] Evening Meal Available

[Wifi] Wifi
[Car] Parking
[Cart] Grocery Shop On Site

Bed & Breakfast and Hotels

NAME	OTHER INFO	
Collingdale Guest House 13 Larkstone Terrace, Ilfracombe, EX34 9NU ☎ 01271 863770 ✉ thecollingdale@gmail.com ⊕ www.thecollingdale.co.uk	GR: SS526475	DP: 0.3 miles
	N: **ILFRACOMBE**	
	Offers one night stays	
	[9] [Wifi]	**Other info:** Award winning Guest House metres from SWCP Harbour views.
Harcourt Hotel 49 Fore Street, Ilfracombe, EX34 9DJ ☎ 01271 862931 ✉ enquiries@harcourthotel.co.uk ⊕ www.harcourthotel.co.uk	GR: SS520477	DP: 0 miles
	N: **ILFRACOMBE**	
	Offers one night stays	
	[8] [Dog] [Wifi]	**Other info:**
Brookdales B&B 23 Brookdale Avenue, Ilfracombe, EX34 8DB ☎ 01271 269388 ✉ christine_goodenough@sky.com ⊕ www.brookdales.co.uk	GR: SS513474	DP: 0 miles
	N: **ILFRACOMBE**	
	Offers one night stays	
	[3] [Wifi]	**Other info:** Open all year
Marine House B&B South Street, Woolacombe, EX34 7BB ☎ 01271 870972 ✉ marinehousedevon@gmail.com ⊕ www.marinehouse.co.uk	GR: SS459436	DP: 0.25 miles
	N: **WOOLACOMBE**	
	Offers one night stays	
	[2] [Wifi]	**Other info:** Parking permit available on first come first served basis.
Combas Farm Meadow lane, Croyde, EX33 1PH ☎ 01271 890398 ✉ info@combasfarm.co.uk ⊕ www.combasfarm.co.uk	GR: SS449396	DP: 0.5 miles
	N: **CROYDE**	
	Offers one night stays	
	[4] [Wifi] [Car]	**Other info:**
The Whiteleaf The Whiteleaf At Croyde, Croyde, EX33 1PN ☎ 01271 890266 ✉ bookings@thewhiteleaf.co.uk ⊕ www.thewhiteleaf.co.uk	GR: SS441 389	DP: 1 mile
	N: **BRAUNTON**	
	Offers one night stays	
	[5] [Wifi] [Car]	**Other info:** Dinner must be booked in advance
Breakers B&B Breakers, Downend, Croyde, EX33 1QE ☎ 01271 890101 ✉ croydebreaksbookings@gmail.com ⊕ www.croydebreaksindevon.co.uk	GR: SS436386	DP: 0.1 miles
	N: **CROYDE**	
	Offers one night stays	
	[4] [Wifi] [Car]	**Other info:** Open Easter - End October.
Saunton Sands Hotel Saunton Sands, Braunton, EX33 1LQ ☎ 01271 890212 ✉ reservations@sauntonsands.com ⊕ www.sauntonsands.com	GR: SS446378	DP: 0 miles
	N: **SAUNTON**	
	Offers one night stays	
	[82] [Meal] [Wifi] [Car]	**Other info:**

NAME	OTHER INFO
North Cottage 14 North Street, Braunton, EX33 1AJ ☎ 01271 812703 ✉ north_cottage@hotmail.com 🌐 www.northcottagebraunton.co.uk	GR: SS485366 DP: 0.5 miles N: **BRAUNTON** Offers one night stays [4] 🐕 🛜 🚗 Other info:
Silver Cottage B&B 14 Silver Street, Braunton, EX33 2EN ☎ 07974017663 / 01271 814165 ✉ silvercottage.braunton@gmail.com 🌐 www.bedandbreakfast-braunton.co.uk	GR: SS489372 DP: 1.5 miles N: **BRAUNTON** Offers one night stays [2] 🛜 Other info:
The Laurels B&B 26 Church Street, Braunton, EX33 2EL ☎ 01271 812872 ✉ info@thelaurelsbraunton.co.uk 🌐 www.thelaurelsbraunton.co.uk	GR: SS489370 DP: 1 mile N: **BRAUNTON** Offers one night stays [3] 🐕 🛜 🚗 Other info:
Marsdens Devon Cottages 2, The Square, Braunton, EX33 2JB ☎ 01271 813777 ✉ devon@marsdens.co.uk 🌐 www.marsdens.co.uk	GR: SS488366 DP: 0 miles N: **BRAUNTON** 🐕 🛜 🚗 Other info: Open all year
Trojen Bed & Breakfast Franklyn Avenue, Braunton, EX33 2JY ☎ 01271 814019 / 07890885825 ✉ jennyjcocker@yahoo.co.uk 🌐 www.staybandbnorthdevon.com	GR: SS490365 DP: 0.5 miles N: **BRAUNTON** Offers one night stays [2] 🛜 🚗 Other info: Can sleep 4. Homemade cakes on arrival.
Bennings B&B The Firs, Higher Park Road, Braunton, EX33 2LG ☎ 01271 814358 ✉ info@bennings.co.uk 🌐 www.bennings.co.uk	GR: SS499364 DP: 1 mile N: **BRAUNTON** Offers one night stays [3] 🐕 🛜 🚗 Other info: Open all year.
The Old Vicarage B&B Barbican Terrace, Barnstaple, EX32 9HQ ☎ 01271 328504 ✉ contact@oldvicaragebarnstaple.co.uk 🌐 www.oldvicaragebarnstaple.co.uk	GR: SS562328 DP: 0.25 miles N: **BARNSTAPLE** Offers one night stays [2] 🛜 🚗 Other info: Daily homemade cakes.
Herton Guest House Herton, Lake Hill, Barnstaple, EX31 3HS ☎ 01271 323302 ✉ janmanning.herton@gmail.com 🌐 www.herton-guesthouse.co.uk	GR: SS555073 DP: 0.25 miles N: **BARNSTAPLE** Offers one night stays [2] 🚗 Other info: Open all year except Christmas.
The Poplars B&B Rumsam Road, Barnstaple, EX32 9EW ☎ 01271 378773 ✉ thepoplarsbarnstaple@gmail.com 🌐 www.barnstaplebedandbreakfast.co.uk	GR: SS567319 DP: 0.75 miles N: **BARNSTAPLE** Offers one night stays [3] 🛜 🚗 Other info: Storage for bicycles if needed
Honeysuckle Cottage B&B Bideford, EX39 4NL ☎ 01271 861067 ✉ bedandbreakfast@honeysucklecottagewestleigh.com 🌐 www.honeysucklecottagewestleigh.com	GR: SS472287 DP: 0.25 miles N: **INSTOW** Offers one night stays [2] 🛜 🚗 Other info:

NAME	OTHER INFO	
Culloden House Fosketh Hill, Westward Ho!, EX39 1UL ☎ 01237 479421 ✉ cullodenhouse@gmail.com 🌐 www.culloden-house.co.uk	GR: SS430289 DP: 0.15 miles N: **WESTWARD HO!** Offers one night stays	[8] 🛜 **Other info:** 5 minutes walk to SWCP, restaurants, shops.
Tors Top Bed and Breakfast Cornborough Road, Westward Ho, EX39 1AA ☎ 07894 065324 ✉ bedandbreakfastwestwardho@gmail.com 🌐 www.torstopbedandbreakfast.co.uk	GR: SS427286 DP: 0.44 miles N: **WESTWARD HO!** Offers one night stays	[2] 🛜 🚗 **Other info:** Packed Lunches available
Corner House B&B 14 The Strand, Bideford, EX39 2ND ☎ 01237 473722 ✉ cornerhousestrand@gmail.com 🌐 www.facebook.com/pages/Corner-House/151170201580574	GR: SS452268 DP: 0.1 miles N: **BIDEFORD** Offers one night stays	🐕 🛜 **Other info:** Close to the Path and ideally located to Bideford's Town centre.
SeaLily 7 Clifton Street, Bideford, EX39 4ET ☎ 07795 480353 ✉ hello.sealily@hotmail.com 🌐 www.tiny.cc/AirBnB-Nicola	GR: SS458261 DP: 0.2 miles N: **BIDEFORD** Offers one night stays	[1] 🛜 **Other info:** On-street parking.
Old Keepers Cottage Bed and Breakfast Tennacott Lane, Bideford, EX39 4QD ☎ 01237 479113 ✉ lucygiddy@btinternet.com 🌐 www.oldkeeperscottage.net	GR: SS475247 DP: 3 miles N: **BIDEFORD** Offers one night stays	[4] 🛜 🚗 **Other info:** Situated 1 mile down a single track country lane.
Pillowery Park Burscott, Higher Clovelly, Bideford, EX39 5RR ☎ 01237 431668 ✉ info@clovellyrooms.co.uk 🌐 www.clovellyrooms.co.uk	GR: SS313241 DP: 0.75 miles N: **HIGHER CLOVELLY** Offers one night stays	[3] 🛜 🚗 **Other info:** Lifts by arrangement.
The Old Smithy B&B 147 Slerra Hill, Clovelly, EX39 5ST ☎ 01237 431202 ✉ oldsmithybandb@gmail.com 🌐 www.oldsmithybandbclovelly.co.uk	GR: SS311242 DP: 0.5 miles N: **CLOVELLY** Offers one night stays	[2] 🛜 🚗 **Other info:**
Harbour View Cottage 77 High Street, Clovelly, EX39 5TQ ☎ 01237 432215 ✉ harbourview77@yahoo.com 🌐 www.clovellycottage.co.uk	GR: SS317248 DP: 0 miles N: **CLOVELLY** Offers one night stays	[4] 🐕 🛜 **Other info:** Small fee for luggage transfers from Clovelly Visitor Centre to cottage.
Southdown B&B 1 Southdown Cottages, Higher Clovelly, EX39 5SA ☎ 01237 431504 ✉ southdownhartland@gmail.com 🌐 www.southdownhartland.co.uk	GR: SS298235 DP: 2 miles N: **CLOVELLY** Offers one night stays	[2] 🐕 🍴 🛜 🚗 **Other info:**
West Titchberry Farm West Titchberry, Hartland Point, EX39 6AU ☎ 01237 441287 🌐 www.westtitchberryfarm.weebly.com	GR: SS241271 DP: 0.25 miles N: **HARTLAND POINT** Offers one night stays	[3] 🍴 🛜 🚗 **Other info:** Open all year

NAME	OTHER INFO	
Hartland Quay Hotel Hartland, Bideford, EX39 6DU ☏ 01237 441218 ✉ info@hartlandquayhotel.co.uk 🌐 www.hartlandquayhotel.co.uk	GR: SS222247	DP: 0 miles
	N: **HARTLAND**	
	Offers one night stays	
	14 🐕 🛏 🍽 📶 🚗	Other info:
Clouds Bed & Breakfast Stoke, Hartland, Bideford, EX39 6DU ☏ 01237 440236 / 07479 592729 ✉ paul-summers1@hotmail.co.uk 🌐 www.cloudsatstoke.com	GR: SS237246	DP: 0.75 miles
	N: **HARTLAND**	
	Offers one night stays	
	2 📶 🚗	Other info: Packed lunches available.
Elmscott Farm B&B Elmscott, Hartland, EX39 6ES ☏ 01237 441276 ✉ john.goa@virgin.net 🌐 www.elmscott.org.uk	GR: SS231217	DP: 1 mile
	N: **HARTLAND**	
	Offers one night stays	
	3 🛒 🚗	Other info: Open Easter-End Oct.
Gawlish Farm B&B Hartland, Bideford, EX39 6AT ☏ 01237 441320 ✉ jillygeorge@icloud.com 🌐 www.southwestcoastpath.org.uk/gawlish-farm-near-hartland	GR: SS260267	DP: 0.25 miles
	N: **HARTLAND**	
	Offers one night stays	
	4 🍽 📶 🚗	Other info: Ensuite rooms. Happy to take to local pub for meals.

Campsites and Holiday Parks

NAME	OTHER INFO	
Stowford Farm Meadows Berry Down, Combe Martin, EX34 0PW ☏ 01271 882476 ✉ enquiries@stowford.co.uk 🌐 www.stowford.co.uk	GR: SS559426	DP: 3 miles
	N: **ILFRACOMBE**	
	Offers one night stays	
	🐕 🍽 🛏 🛒 📶 🚗	Other info: Family Friendly. Swimming Pool.
Hele Valley Holiday Park Hele Bay, Ilfracombe, EX34 9RD ☏ 01271 862460 ✉ holidays@helevalley.co.uk 🌐 www.helevalley.co.uk	GR: SS533472	DP: 0.5 miles
	N: **ILFRACOMBE**	
	Offers one night stays	
	3 🐕 📶 🚗	Other info: Open 31 Mar - 31 Dec
Sunnymead Farm Camping & Touring Site Mortehoe Road, Ilfracombe, EX34 8NZ ☏ 01271 879845 ✉ info@sunnymead-farm.co.uk 🌐 www.sunnymead-farm.co.uk	GR: SS500442	DP: 1 mile
	N: **WOOLACOMBE**	
	Offers one night stays	
	🐕 🛒 📶 🚗	Other info: Shop open in high season, bus stops on demand at our entrance, dogs FOC.
Lee Meadow Farm Camping Shaftsborough Lane, Lee, Woolacombe, EX34 8FF ☏ 01271 879825 ✉ info@leemeadowcamping.co.uk 🌐 www.leemeadowcamping.co.uk	GR: SS488448	DP: 0.3 miles
	N: **WOOLACOMBE**	
	Offers one night stays	
	🐕 🍽 🛒 🚗	Other info: Open - 21/05/2020 to 6/09/2020.
Little Roadway Farm Camping Park Georgeham Road, Woolacombe, EX34 7HL ☏ 01271 870313 ✉ enquiries@littleroadway.co.uk 🌐 www.littleroadway.co.uk	GR: SS467422	DP: 0.5 miles
	N: **WOOLACOMBE**	
	Offers one night stays	
	🐕 🍽 🛒 🚗	Other info: Glamping Pods, Bell Tents, Caravan & Holiday Cottage. Take-away in high season.
Greencliff Farm Campsite Abbotsham, Bideford, EX39 5BL ☏ 01237 424674 ✉ greencliff.farm@gmail.com 🌐 www.greencliff-farm.co.uk	GR: SS410268	DP: 0.25 miles
	N: **BIDEFORD**	
	Offers one night stays	
	🐕 🚗	Other info:

NAME	OTHER INFO	
Westacott Farm Camping	GR: SS410261	DP: 0.5 miles
Abbotsham, Bideford, EX39 5BN	N: **BIDEFORD**	
📞 01237 472351		
✉ enquiries@westacottfarm.co.uk		Other info:
🌐 www.westacottfarm.co.uk	🚗	
Stoke Barton Farm Campsite	GR: SS235246	DP: 0.5 miles
Stoke, Hartland, EX39 6DU	N: **HARTLAND**	
📞 01237 441238	Offers one night stays	
✉ stokebartoncampsite@gmail.com	🐕 🛒 🚗	Other info: 2 Pixie Huts available to hire with sprung king sized beds and electric point.
🌐 www.westcountry-camping.co.uk		
Cheristow Lavender Campsite	GR: SS250254	DP: 1.25 miles
Higher Cheristow, Hartland, EX39 6DA	N: **HARTLAND**	
📞 01237 440101	Offers one night stays	
✉ cheristow77@yahoo.com	🐕 🚗	Other info:
🌐 www.cheristow.co.uk		

Self Catering

NAME	OTHER INFO	
Fisherman's Cottage	GR: SS535477	DP:
29 Beach Road, Hele, Ilfracombe, EX34 9QZ	N: **ILFRACOMBE**	
📞 07809 096036	2 🐕 🛒 📶	Other info: 50 metres from Coast Path, sleeps up to 4 in two bedrooms, 2 mins to pub & shop.
✉ ruth@inspire.uk.com	🚗	
🌐 www.facebook.com/HeleDevon		
Ocean Backpackers	GR: SS522478	DP: 0.3 miles
29 St James Place, Ilfracombe, EX34 9BJ	N: **ILFRACOMBE**	
📞 01271 867835	Offers one night stays	
✉ info@oceanbackpackers.co.uk	12 🐕 📶 🚗	Other info: Self catering. Drying room available.
🌐 www.oceanbackpackers.co.uk		
Gordons Cabin	GR: SS457452	DP: 1 mile
Mortehoe, Woolacombe, EX34 7DR	N: **WOOLACOMBE**	
📞 0350 800 1895		
✉ cottages@nationaltrust.org.uk	1 🐕 🚗	Other info:
🌐 www.nationaltrust.org.uk/holidays/gordons-cabin-devon		
The Beach House Hostel	GR: SS458 437	DP: 0 miles
3 Granville Terrace, 3 West Road, Woolacombe, EX34 7BW	N: **WOOLACOMBE**	
📞 07500 701982 / 01271 871727	Offers one night stays	
✉ hello@thebeachhousedevon.co.uk	6 🍴 📶 🚗	Other info:
🌐 www.thebeachhousedevon.co.uk		
Pickwell Barton	GR: SS456410	DP: 0.5 miles
Georgeham, Braunton, EX33 1LA	N: **BRAUNTON**	
📞 01271 890994		
✉ holidays@pickwellbarton.co.uk	6 📶 🚗	Other info: Open all year
🌐 www.pickwellbarton.co.uk		
The Slipway	GR: SS430398	DP: 1 mile
Croyde, EX33 1PA	N: **CROYDE**	
📞 0344 800 2070		
✉ cottages@nationaltrust.org.uk	2 🚗	Other info:
🌐 www.nationaltrust.org.uk/holidays/the-slipway-north-devon		
Mulberry	GR: SS458301	DP: 1 mile
Churchill Way Appledore, Bideford, EX39 1PA	N: **APPLEDORE**	
📞 01237 426710		
✉ info@stayin.co.uk	5 🐕	Other info:
🌐 www.stayindevon.co.uk/cottages		

NAME	OTHER INFO	
Peppercombe Bothy Horns Cross, Bideford, EX39 5EA 📞 0344 335 1296 ✉ bunkhouses@nationaltrust.org.uk 🌐 www.nationaltrust.org.uk/holidays/peppercombe-bothy-devon	GR: SS380234 N: **BUCKS MILLS** Offers one night stays 1 🐕🚗	DP: 0.5 mile **Other info:** Parking nearby.
Coastguard Cottage 1 Peppercombe, Clovelly, EX39 5QD 📞 0345 800 2070 ✉ cottages@nationaltrust.org.uk 🌐 www.nationaltrust.org.uk/holidays/coastguard-cottage-1-devon	GR: SS38313 N: **CLOVELLY** 2 🚗	DP: 0.5 mile **Other info:**
Coastguard Cottage 2 Peppercombe, Clovelly, EX39 5QD 📞 0345 800 2070 ✉ cottages@nationaltrust.org.uk 🌐 www.nationaltrust.org.uk/holidays/coastguard-cottage-2-devon	GR: SS38313 N: **CLOVELLY** 2 🚗	DP: 0.5 mile **Other info:**
Coastguard Cottage 3 Peppercombe, Clovelly, EX39 5QD 📞 0345 800 2070 ✉ cottages@nationaltrust.org.uk 🌐 www.nationaltrust.org.uk/holidays/coastguard-cottage-3-devon	GR: SS38313 N: **CLOVELLY** 1 🚗	DP: 0.5 mile **Other info:**
Combe Cottage Peppercombe, Clovelly, EX39 5QD 📞 0345 800 2070 ✉ cottages@nationaltrust.org.uk 🌐 www.nationaltrust.org.uk/holidays/combe-cottage-devon	GR: SS38313 N: **CLOVELLY** 3 🐕🚗	DP: 0.5 mile **Other info:**
Cheristow Farm Cottages Cheristow, Bideford, EX38 6DA 📞 01237 441522 ✉ stay@cheristow-cottages.co.uk 🌐 www.cheristow-cottages.co.uk	GR: SS250252 N: **HARTLAND** 9 🐕📶🚗	DP: 1.5 mile **Other info:** 20 mins walk from Hartland pubs. Hot tub & sauna.
Hartland Caravan Holidays South Lane, Hartland, EX39 6DG 📞 01237 441664 ✉ info@hartlandcaravanholidays.co.uk 🌐 www.hartlandcaravanholidays.co.uk	GR: SS263242 N: **HARTLAND** Offers one night stays 🐕🚗	DP: 3 miles **Other info:** Open all year
Little Barton Hartland, Bideford, EX39 6DY 📞 01237 441259 ✉ enquiries@littlebartonhartland.co.uk 🌐 www.littlebartonhartland.co.uk/work	GR: SS241237 N: **HARTLAND** Offers one night stays 3 🐕📶🚗	DP: 3 miles **Other info:** Out of season the Cottage can be booked for a couple at a reduced rate.
Elmscott Youth Hostel Elmscott, Hartland, EX39 6ES 📞 01237 441367 ✉ john.goa@virgin.net 🌐 www.elmscott.org.uk	GR: SS231217 N: **BIDEFORD** Offers one night stays 7 🛒🚗	DP: 1 mile **Other info:** Open all year

Eat and Drink

NAME	OTHER INFO	
Lee Meadow Farm Shop Shaftsborough Lane, Lee, Woolacombe, EX34 8FF 📞 01271 879825 ✉ info@leemeadowcamping.co.uk 🌐 www.leemeadowcamping.co.uk	GR: SS490448 N: **WOOLACOMBE** 🍴	DP: 1.5 miles **Other info:**
The Quay Cafe Velator, Braunton, EX33 2DX 📞 01271 268180 ✉ office.thequay@gmail.com 🌐 www.thequaycafe.com	GR: SS486357 N: **BRAUNTON** 🐕📶🚗	DP: 0miles **Other info:** Monthly music nights.

Did you know?

The longest flight of wooden steps along the South West Coast Path can be found on Salcombe Hill near Sidmouth and consists of 185 steps.

The coastal cliffs of North Cornwall are likely to experience at least 40 metres of erosion in the next century. That is the same height as the giant statue of Christ that towers over Rio de Janeiro which is 39.6m tall when you include the pedestal.

Around 9 million visitors visit the Path each year, the Path creates around 10,000 jobs and generates over £500 million for the region.

Walking the entire South West Coast Path is the equivalent of scaling Everest, the world's tallest mountain, four times.

The South West Coast Path is the longest section of the England Coast Path, which will be the longest waymarked coastal footpath in the world.

The South West Coast Path Association is a membership charity working with many partners to ensure the Coast Path is looked after and people can continue to use it. However, it costs over £1,400 per mile per year to do so!

The Association is made up of 10 part time and full-time members of staff and nearly 90 volunteers!

Damian Hall, a record breaking ultra-marathon runner, currently holds the record for completing the full 630 miles of South West Coast Path. His record is 10 days, 15 hours, 18 minutes.

Approximately 71% of the Path is in either a National Park or Area of Outstanding Natural Beauty and you'll also pass through 2 World Heritage Sites, a UNESCO Biosphere and a UNESCO Geopark.

In England and Wales, the Exmoor Coast holds titles for; the highest coastline, soaring to a heady 433m (1,421 ft) at Culbone Hill, the highest sea cliff with Great Hangman peaking at 244m (800ft) and the longest stretch of coastal woodland between The Foreland and Porlock. The Exmoor coast is also home to one of the highest tidal ranges in the world, second only to Fundy Bay in Eastern Canada.

At the last count there were over 4,000 way markers guiding you along the whole 630 miles of South West Coast Path.

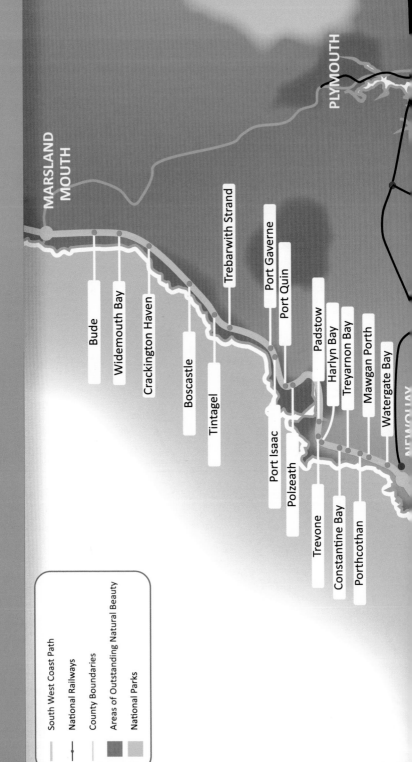

MARSLAND MOUTH

PLYMOUTH

Bude

Widemouth Bay

Crackington Haven

Boscastle

Tintagel

Trebarwith Strand

Port Gaverne

Port Quin

Port Isaac

Polzeath

Trevone

Constantine Bay

Porthcothan

Padstow

Harlyn Bay

Treyarnon Bay

Mawgan Porth

Watergate Bay

NEWQUAY

South West Coast Path

National Railways

County Boundaries

Areas of Outstanding Natural Beauty

National Parks

Map not to scale. For illustrative purposes only

North Cornwall
Marsland Mouth to Newquay

(Sections 14-21)

This length of coast faces the prevailing Atlantic westerlies, making for a sometimes exposed landscape. This is exacerbated by the fact that much of this length comprises of high cliffs, often quite sheer, with prominent headlands giving excellent coastal vistas. In places these cliffs are fronted by sandy beaches, as around Bude and Newquay. In the centre of this length is the mouth of the Camel Estuary, also flanked by sandy beaches. The uncompromising nature of the cliffs also means there are few ports or harbours; those that do exist tend to be sheltered from the Atlantic winds – Padstow within the Camel Estuary, Newquay behind Towan Head, Boscastle sheltered in its narrow inlet while Bude is a relatively recent development which owes much of its existence to the arrival of a canal here in the early 19th century. North of the Camel is a length of coast with an untamed atmosphere and including some sometimes challenging gradients for walkers; to the south the extensive beaches are popular among families and surfers alike and the cliffs are kinder to walkers.

All of the locations on the map illustration to the left, have at least 1 facility including toilets, a cafe/restaurant, shop or pub. There are water refill points at Port Quin, Polzeath and, around 3 miles South of Polzeath at Rock.

North Cornwall cliffs

OS Maps: Landranger 190; Explorer 111

	This Walk	Cumulative	This Walk	Cumulative	Grading	Timing
Ascent	2,494ft	25,912ft	760m	7,898m	Easy then strenuous	4.75 hours
Distance	9.8mi	134.1mi	15.8km	215.8km		

For detailed directions see our Walking Guide no. 14, Bude to Crackington Haven.

Low grassy cliffs and surfing beaches south of Bude give way to an ever higher and more rugged coastline fronted by rough rock ledges and cut by deep and steep valleys. There are some superb viewpoints along this quiet and remote-feeling length which reward the effort. Crackington Haven is a pleasant spot and on the cliffs above, St Gennys Church is a superb spot for contemplation.

Directions

A regular bus service links Bude with Crackington Haven, and also serves Widemouth Bay, about 3 miles/4.8 km from Bude, thus offering a number of bus-walk options.

The Path south from Bude starts at the sea lock on the historic Bude Canal, then climbs to the cliff top at Compass Point and on to Efford Beacon. There are excellent views from here. The Path over Efford Down to Upton and on to Widemouth Bay is easy to follow. Widemouth has toilets and refreshments, the last before Crackington Haven. (There are further refreshment facilities a little inland at Whalesborough, reached by a scenic footpath from Widemouth.)

South of Widemouth the Path follows the low cliff for a short distance then diverts inland slightly at Wanson Mouth to join the coast road in the stream valley. Turn right and follow the road as it climbs steeply to Penhalt Cliff. There are more magnificent views from the cliff-top car park.

From the southern end of the car park the Coast Path crosses a field and descends steeply to Millook Haven. Now follow the steep road uphill for a short distance then turn right onto the cliff top at Raven's Beak. From here the Path climbs steadily past the stunted oak woodland at Dizzard Point and on to Chipman Point. Two further deep and steep valleys are crossed, then a ridge walk leads to Castle Point, which gives tremendous views. Another steep valley crossing leads on to Pencannow Point and views over Crackington Haven. The Path descends easily into the cove, where there are toilets, refreshments, buses and accommodation.

Near Bude

OS Maps: Landranger 190; Explorer 111

	This Walk	Cumulative	This Walk	Cumulative	Grading	Timing
Ascent	2,264ft	28,176ft	690m	8,588m	Strenuous	3.75 hours
Distance	6.7mi	140.8mi	10.8km	226.6km		

For detailed directions see our Walking Guide no. 15, Crackington Haven to Boscastle.

This is a Section of high cliffs, the highest, indeed in Cornwall. Not only are they high, but they also present an appearance of bulk, of being literally massive, and the walker will often feel dwarfed by them, especially on a climb or descent or perhaps on a headland. Much of this Section is also quite lonely, and this combination makes this a coast with an imposing character.

Directions

Crackington Haven and Boscastle are linked by a regular bus service, making this an option for a bus-walk.

There are toilets and seasonal shops, cafes and a pub at Crackington Haven. Leave behind the beach near the toilets and head out for the headland of Cambeak. Rounding the headland, keep away from its high and sheer cliff edges. Beyond Cambeak the Path is relatively level, passing above the landslip zone at Strangles Beach. Ahead looms High Cliff, the appropriately-named highest cliff in Cornwall. There is a steady ascent but the descent on the south side is very steep. The Path then climbs through a landfall at Rusey Cliff, twisting and turning to the top. A cliff top section through fields follows to the sheer black cliff at Buckator. The Path then dips slightly before continuing at high level to Fire Beacon Point. Here the descent is steep, but helped by attractive slate steps. The Path then follows the cliff face into the inlet of Pentargon, with its impressive waterfall. This is best seen from the southern side – do not be tempted to leave the Path for a better view.

The now easy Path continues on to Boscastle. Aim for the white mast on Penally Hill, then follow the Path alongside the beautiful harbour inlet into Boscastle, now happily restored after a huge flood washed through the valley in 2004.

Boscastle Harbour

OS Maps: Landranger 190 (eastern half); Landranger 200 (western half); Explorer 111

	This Walk	Cumulative	This Walk	Cumulative	Grading	Timing
Ascent	1,230ft	29,406ft	375m	8,963m	Moderate	2.25 hours
Distance	4.7mi	145.5mi	7.6km	234.2km		

For detailed directions see our Walking Guide no. 16, Boscastle to Tintagel.

This fairly short Section is a great local favourite, as it combines all the best of the Coast Path – headlands, sandy bays, historic features and, yes, steep valleys, all in a manageable but picturesque length which is not too taxing. In addition, although popular, it never seems crowded and is, indeed, a "real" walk. With all this and its convenient bus links it is a perfect Coast Path taster.

Directions

Boscastle and Tintagel are linked by a regular bus service. It also serves Rocky Valley, half-way between the two, enabling a variety of bus-walks to be undertaken.

Boscastle has been attractively rebuilt after the floods of 2004, and has all facilities.

The Coast Path leaves the south side of the harbour over the new stone bridge and climbs towards the headland of Willapark, with its prominent white watch tower. The Path cuts across the neck of the headland, but a diversion to the end is worthwhile.

After a steep descent and climb at Grower Gut, the Path continues easily, turning seaward of the Manor House at Trevalga. The headland beyond gives views over the rocky offshore islands important for breeding seabirds. The Path continues past Firebeacon Hill – look out for the Ladies Window rock arch in the gully to the right – then passes seaward of a cliff-top caravan and camping site. There is then a descent into the exquisite Rocky Valley. There is a path up the valley to a bus stop on the coast road, passing prehistoric carvings in the cliff wall.

From the footbridge in the valley the Path climbs again, round the edge of the grassy Bossiney Common and above the sandy bay at Bossiney Haven. Another climb then leads to another headland also, confusingly, called Willapark. Again the Coast Path cuts across the neck of the headland and, again, a diversion to the end is worthwhile.

The Path now continues to Barras Nose headland, from where it descends to Tintagel Haven below the castle ruins. Here are toilets, cafe and English Heritage gift shop. A good but steep path leads inland to the village.

In the summer of 2019 a new and quite spectacular cantilever footbridge was opened between the mainland and Tintagel Island at Tintagel Castle, just beyond the Haven.

OS Maps: Landranger 200; Explorer 111 (eastern half); Explorer 106 (western half)

	This Walk	Cumulative	This Walk	Cumulative	Grading	Timing
Ascent	2,589ft	31,995ft	789m	9,752m	Severe	4.75 hours
Distance	9.1mi	154.6mi	14.6km	248.8km		

For detailed directions see our Walking Guide no. 17, Tintagel to Port Isaac.

Both ends of this Section are relatively popular and accessible. At Tintagel the Coast Path passes the remains of the medieval castle perched on its isolated headland. Since the summer of 2019 a new spectacular cantilever footbridge allows easier access to the castle, readily visible from the Coast Path. The Path then passes the atmospherically located cliff-top church and the now picturesque evidence of coastal slate quarrying. At the other end is the beautifully quaint village of Port Isaac in its scenic bay. The long central length, though, comprises high cliffs cut by sometimes precipitously steep valleys. It is remote, lonely and often tough, and will be especially appreciated by those who relish an empty, arduous and dramatic coastline.

Directions

It is possible to take a bus between Tintagel and Port Isaac although it is usually necessary to change at Camelford. A bus-walk is therefore possible, particularly using Camelford as a base.

Tintagel has all necessary facilities. Surprisingly, however, little in the village is very old other than the Old Post Office, once a local manor house.

From the village walk down the Path to Tintagel Haven. From here the Coast Path climbs past the entrance to the Castle and gives excellent views over the headland which forms the castle site. A good path continues seaward of the church and on beyond past the Youth Hostel in its former quarry building and round Penhallic Point with its superb views.

The Path drops steeply to Trebarwith Strand, where there are toilets, refreshments and pub, the last facilities before Port Isaac. The next part is particularly tough as it climbs steeply out of the Trebarwith valley then almost immediately drops down to sea level and up again at Backways Cove. There follows a level stretch of about a mile/1.5 kilometres to the stream valley behind Tregardock Beach. Descend on the inland side of the detached piece of cliff known as The Mountain, then climb again to Tregardock Cliff. Another level length follows, before the deepest and steepest valley yet at Jacket's Point. At the top yet another deep valley almost immediately follows. Then comes a further valley, at Barrett's Zawn. This is an area of massive rock falls. The next valley follows, this one with exceptionally steep and stony sides.

At last the Path levels out again through cliff-top meadows, with just a small valley to cross at St Illickswell Gug. Eventually, the Path reaches the road at Cartway Cove. Take the Path on the right and round the headland to Port Gaverne, a charming spot. Follow the road uphill to the car park at the edge of Port Isaac. Go through this and follow the well-signed path above the attractive harbour inlet into the village.

Port Isaac is a very picturesque village clustered round the little harbour at the head of a sheltered bay. It has all facilities.

OS Maps: Landranger 200; Explorer 106

	This Walk	Cumulative	This Walk	Cumulative	Grading	Timing
Ascent	2,923ft	34,918ft	891m	10,643m	Strenuous then easy	5.5 hours
Distance	11.7mi	166.3mi	18.8km	267.6km		

For detailed directions see our Walking Guide no. 18, Port Isaac to Padstow.

This Section can be divided into three distinct characters. From Port Isaac to Port Quin is a rollercoaster of a Path, closely following the ups and downs and ins and outs of the quiet, scenic but energy-sapping coast. From Port Quin to Polzeath the character becomes rather more open, if still very scenic, including the broad headland of the Rumps and Pentire Point, a wonderful airy lookout. From Polzeath to the Padstow ferry the landscape is tamer, more domesticated, often with housing or tourist development and more estuarine than maritime as it reaches the mouth of the River Camel.

Directions

There is a regular bus service between Port Isaac and Rock, the ferry point for Padstow. This service also passes through Polzeath at the mouth of the Camel estuary, giving several scenic bus-walk options, including an almost level estuary-side one. There is a popular circuit using the Coast Path between Port Isaac and Port Quin and others from Polzeath around Pentire Point.

Port Isaac has all necessary facilities, and is a scenic gem. To leave the village, take the road to the right behind the fish market. Climbing, it bears right and becomes a cliff Path, soon dropping into Pine Haven. From here to Port Quin the Path is magnificent and clear, but tough as it follows the cliff edge next to a fence line. There is an optional diversion to the end of Varley Head.

The Path enters the beautiful Port Quin inlet, descending to what was once a busy pilchard port, though there are no permanent facilities here now. Follow the road westbound up the steep hill and a little way up the Coast Path leaves to the right, towards Doyden Point. The Path follows above the cove, keeping seaward of and below the large house. Head to a prominent stone cairn, then continue ahead on a grassy path and past some old mineshafts. From the cairn a diversion to the right goes to the folly of Doyden Castle and to Doyden Point, where there is a superb view back to Port Quin.

There is a sharp descent to Epphaven Cove then the Path passes through a delightful little wooded valley before climbing past the impressive Lundy Hole. The clear cliff path now heads for the Iron Age fortress on the Rumps headland. A detour to the end is well worthwhile.

From the Rumps the Path climbs through a little former quarry area then continues at high level round Pentire Point, giving spectacular views. An easy descent follows into Polzeath, all well marked. Polzeath has a great surf beach, and so has all the normal facilities such as café, pubs, accommodation, food and surf shops. The Path follows the road past the beach car park where an H_2O water bottle filling facility can be found. The Path then turns right by the cottages, where the road bends sharp left on the steep hill. It now follows a low cliff to Daymer Bay, where there are toilets and a seasonal cafe, then down steps to the beach. At the far end of the beach it leaves through dunes and over a footbridge below Brea Hill. It is possible to detour to visit the little St Enodoc Church from here.

To continue on the Coast Path follow the Path around the side of Brea Hill, following the signs for the realigned path. It is also possible to go over the top or, at low tide, along the beach. On the far south side of Brea Hill the well-signed Path continues through dunes to arrive at Rock car park. Another H_2O water bottle facility can be found at the Rock ferry terminal. A ferry service operates between Rock and Padstow all year but much less frequently in low season. See page 22 for details.

A water taxi service operates between Rock and Padstow, weather and tides permitting. For further details see page 22.

Note that it is possible to walk Coast to Coast across Cornwall between Padstow and Fowey on the south coast, using the Saints' Way. A guidebook is available from Padstow Tourist Information Centre (TIC).

The Rumps

OS Maps: Landranger 200: Explorer 106

	This Walk	Cumulative	This Walk	Cumulative	Grading	Timing
Ascent	810ft	35,728ft	247m	10,890m	Easy	2 hours
Distance	6.5mi	172.8mi	10.5km	278.1km		

For detailed directions see our Walking Guide no. 19, Padstow to Harlyn Bay.

The length from Padstow to Stepper Point, at the mouth of the Camel, is a scenic length of ever-changing estuarine views with sandy stretches, especially at low tide. Beyond, the coast is an easy but picturesque length of cliffs, which include occasional views right across the headland at the mouth of the estuary and up the Camel as well as west to Trevose Head. The two elements of this Section combine to form a popular local walk.

Directions

A regular bus service links Padstow with Harlyn Bay. This allows for a possible bus-walk. There are also a number of possible circular walks from Padstow using the Coast Path which take in the Stepper Point headland.

Padstow is a charming and bustling little harbour town a short way up the Camel Estuary. If arriving from Rock, notice that normally the ferry arrives in Padstow at the harbour, but at low tide it lands a short distance downstream at St Saviour's Point.

The Coast Path leaves the north end of the harbour and proceeds on low cliffs alongside the estuary. After passing a wooded little stream valley at St George's Cove the Path heads inland of a marshy area before going back to the cliffs and on to Hawker's Cove. Refreshments are available at Rest a While Tea Garden at Hawker's Cove. Pass behind the old pilots' houses here then fork right to climb to Stepper Point, with its Daymark tower. From here there are remarkable views, inland to Bodmin Moor as well as along the coast.

The Path is now on the exposed Atlantic coast. Go round the precipitous inlet of Butter Hole Cove, looking out for the small Pepper Hole to the right of the Path just before. An easy length to Gunver Head follows, with excellent sea views. Approaching Trevone the Path skirts the impressive Round Hole collapsed cave – approach this with caution as the sides are sheer. Follow the cliffs round into the bay at Trevone, which has toilets, cafe and pub, as well as a car park. The Path crosses the rear of the beach and leaves behind the little headland on the south-west side of the bay, following the cliff edge to Harlyn Bay, where there are seasonal refreshments and toilets.

OS Maps: Landranger 200; Explorer 106

	This Walk	Cumulative	This Walk	Cumulative	Grading	Timing
Ascent	751ft	36,479ft	229m	11,119m	Easy	3.5 hours
Distance	6.7mi	179.5mi	10.8km	288.9km		

For detailed directions see our Walking Guide no. 20, Harlyn Bay to Porthcothan.

This is a popular Section, never far from a variety of holiday accommodation. It is perhaps most associated with a range of scenic sandy surfing beaches, some of them quite extensive. As a contrast, around the middle of the length is the great landmark of Trevose Head and its lighthouse, visible from great swathes of the North Cornwall coast and an atmospheric location.

Directions

A regular bus service passes Harlyn Bay and links to Porthcothan. The same route serves Constantine Bay, about two-thirds of the way along the coast from Harlyn, giving a potential for a variety of bus-walks.

Harlyn has seasonal refreshments and toilets. From the car park cross the stream on the road bridge then follow the beach below the low cliff. At high spring tides the footpath across the beach is briefly inaccessible. After some 330 yards/300 metres climb the concrete steps on the left onto the cliff and then continue to the headland at Cataclews Point and Mother Ivey's Bay.

The Path passes inland of Padstow's lifeboat station, accessible by a cul-de-sac path, and then goes on to Trevose Head, passing the lighthouse. On a clear day the coastal views are incredibly extensive, ranging from the satellite dishes north of Bude to the granite hills of West Penwith behind St Ives. This is an atmospheric headland.

After an old quarry the Path passes a Round Hole collapsed cave and descends to the partly rocky Booby's Bay. Continue on to the rear of Constantine Bay, a very attractive and extensive beach at low tide. Walk the length of the beach. There are toilets and seasonal refreshments at the far end and a bus stop a little way inland. Beyond the dunes the Path rounds Treyarnon Head to cross another attractive beach at Treyarnon Bay, with seasonal toilets and refreshments.

An unusually indented coastline follows, with sheer-sided headlands and impressive coves. Near Pepper Cove the ramparts of an Iron Age cliff fort may be seen, and the whole coastline is quite spectacular. The Path then turns into another sandy cove, at Porthcothan Bay, which has toilets and refreshments and also has a pub, the Tredrea Inn, about 500 yards/458 metres inland up the road.

OS Maps: Landranger 200; Explorer 106

	This Walk	Cumulative	This Walk	Cumulative	Grading	Timing
Ascent	1,447ft	37,926ft	441m	11,560m	Moderate	5 hours
Distance	10.3mi	189.8mi	16.6km	305.5km		

For detailed directions see our Walking Guide no. 21, Porthcothan to Newquay.

This is a relatively well-walked Section, particularly around Newquay. It shows the interplay of high cliffs and sandy beaches particularly well. Almost the whole length is characterised by high, flat-topped cliffs, sometimes with prominent headlands, which for long stretches form the back of extensive attractive sandy beaches, many of them popular with surfers. While never a lonely Section, its cliffs and bays make it one well worth exploring, helped by the relatively easy terrain.

Directions

Porthcothan and Newquay are linked by a regular bus service. This route follows a road parallel and close to the coast, meaning that there are a number of possible links to the Coast Path from this bus, allowing for quite a range of possible bus-walks.

Porthcothan has all facilities that may be needed. The Coast Path leaves past the shop and keeps in front of the houses and on around the headland. After a short steep descent and climb, an easy level walk leads to Park Head, an excellent viewpoint. There have been numerous landslips here so keep to the Path inland of the white posts. The whole headland is worth wandering over and exploring. Ahead now is the National Trust's Carnewas property, with its spectacular beach. The Trust's cafe and Information Centre are open throughout the summer. On the beach below are the massive stacks forming Bedruthan Steps.

The Bedruthan Steps area can be busy, but the steps to the beach are closed in the winter months. A quieter length follows to Trenance Point and into the sandy bay of Mawgan Porth, where there are toilets, refreshments and a pub as well as a bus stop. Surprisingly, this was once the site of an unfinished canal project.

Cross the stream using the road then leave it to the right on the sharp bend on the hill out of Mawgan Porth. There then follows a long high level length to Watergate Bay on airy flat-topped cliffs, cut by a couple of minor descents. The Path passes Iron Age remains here while inland is the contrast of Newquay Airport. The Path continues on the cliff top behind the magnificent Watergate Beach, much used for surfing and other activities. The Path then descends to the road by the Watergate Bay Hotel, and here there are toilets, refreshments and another bus stop.

Cross the stream at the road then turn right by the car park and climb back to the cliffs, which are now followed to the outskirts of Newquay. The coastal view ahead to the town and its headlands is excellent. The Coast Path leaves the road to pass round the headland of Trevelgue Head, an important prehistoric location. Although the Path bypasses the island at the very end, this can be visited via the footbridge, and is worth the diversion for the views. The Path returns to the road by Porth Beach before leaving it at steps down on the left, to pass underneath the main road and cross the next little headland to emerge above Lusty Glaze beach – look for the information board here relating to the canal previously encountered at Mawgan Porth.

The Path continues into the park at Barrowfields, skirting its seaward side, to reach the main road into Newquay town centre. Follow this just past the railway station then take the old tramway road on the right. Follow the waymarked route along the footpath above Towan Beach.

At the corner go down the steps on the right then from the car park cross Beach Road and follow the tarmac path ahead. At the end follow the steps on the left to pass a bowling green and public toilets to Fore Street. Turn right here as far as the Red Lion and here turn right again to the harbour down North Quay Hill.

As well as all facilities, Newquay has a branch line railway station linking to the main line to Penzance and is the centre of a network of local bus routes.

Looking towards Merope Rocks, Polventon Bay near Harlyn Bay

If you enjoy sleeping, eating or drinking at any business on the Path please suggest they join us as Business Members so that we can share their brilliance!

The businesses listed here are all supporters and members of the South West Coast Path Association. Please find more details on our website www.southwestcoastpath.org.uk

- **GR** Grid Reference
- **DP** Distance from the Path
- **N** Nearest Town/Village with facilities
- **3** Number Of Rooms
- **Dogs Welcome**
- **Evening Meal Available**
- **Wifi**
- **Parking**
- **Grocery Shop On Site**

Bed & Breakfast and Hotels

NAME	OTHER INFO	
Wyvern House B&B 7 Downs View, Bude, EX23 8RF 01288 352205 booking@wyvernhouse.co.uk www.wyvernhouse.co.uk	GR: SS209070	DP: 0.4 miles
	N: **BUDE**	
	Offers one night stays	
	6 🛜 Other info: Single night stays not offered July or August. Open 1/02-30/11.	
Sunrise Guest House 6 Burn View, Bude, EX23 8BY 01288 353214 info@sunrise-bude.co.uk www.sunrise-bude.co.uk	GR: SS209066	DP: 1 mile
	N: **BUDE**	
	🐕 🛜 Other info:	
Tee-side Guest House 2 Burn View, Bude, EX23 8BY 01288 352351 teeside.bude@gmail.com www.tee-side.co.uk	GR: SS209066	DP: 0.5 miles
	N: **BUDE**	
	Offers one night stays	
	5 🛜 Other info:	
Links Side Guest House 7 Burn View, Bude, EX23 8BY 01288 352410 linksidebude@hotmail.com www.linkssidebude.co.uk	GR: SS209066	DP: 0.5 miles
	N: **BUDE**	
	Offers one night stays	
	7 🛜 Other info: Open all year.	
Sea Jade Guest House 15 Burn View, Bude, EX23 8BZ 01288 353404 seajadeguesthouse@yahoo.co.uk www.seajadeguesthouse.co.uk	GR: SS209066	DP: 0.25 miles
	N: **BUDE**	
	Offers one night stays	
	7 🍴 🛜 🚗 Other info: 2 night stay recommended if walking south. Good bus service.	
Beach House B&B Marine Drive, Widemouth Bay, Bude, EX23 0AW 01288 361256 enquiries@beachhousewidemouth.co.uk www.beachhousewidemouth.co.uk	GR: SS199 028	DP: 0 miles
	N: **BUDE**	
	Offers one night stays	
	10 🛜 Other info: Beach Bar/Restaurant/Ice-cream kiosk onsite - Closed Jan.	
Visit The Linhay The Linhay, North Tamerton, EX22 6SF 01409 271235 / 07964 140467 info@visitthelinhay.co.uk www.visitthelinhay.co.uk	GR: SX312992	DP: 9 miles
	N: **BUDE**	
	Offers one night stays	
	🐕 🍴 🛜 🚗 Other info: We offer B&B and self catering, all dog friendly.	
Wild Cyclamen B & B 2 Rosecare St Genny's, Bude, EX23 0BE 07770838472 gmt2858@gmail.com www.wildcyclamen.co.uk	GR: SX169956	DP: 2 miles
	N: **CRACKINGTON HAVEN**	
	Offers one night stays	
	1 🛜 Other info: Packed lunches. Lifts to and from walks. Dogs welcome by prior arrangement.	
The Wellington Hotel The Harbour, Boscastle, PL35 0AQ 01840 250202 info@wellingtonhotelboscastle.com www.wellingtonhotelboscastle.com	GR: SX098912	DP: 0.1 miles
	N: **BOSCASTLE**	
	Offers one night stays	
	17 🐕 🍴 🛜 🚗 Other info:	

NAME	OTHER INFO		
The Slipway Harbour Front, Port Isaac, PL29 3RH ☏ 01208 880264 ✉ slipway@portisaachotel.com 🌐 www.portisaachotel.com	GR: SW996807	DP: 0 miles	
	N: **PORT ISAAC**		
	Offers one night stays		
	7 ⧉ 🍴 📶	Other info: Terraced Cafe and B&B serving all day food.	
Trewetha Cottage B&B Trewetha, Port Isaac, PL29 3RU ☏ 01208 880877 ✉ dijohnsalisbury1@btinternet.com 🌐 www.southwestcoastpath.org.uk/trewetha-cottage-port-isaac	GR: SX004800	DP: 0.4 miles	
	N: **PORT ISAAC**		
	Offers one night stays		
	2 📶 🚗	Other info: Take and pick up from Port Isaac in the evening if required.	
South Quay B&B 4 Riverside, Padstow, PL28 8BY ☏ 01841 532383 ✉ thepadstowcullinans@gmail.com 🌐 www.southquaybedandbreakfastpadstow.co.uk	GR: SW919753	DP: 0.1 miles	
	N: **PADSTOW**		
	Offers one night stays		
	2 🐕 📶	Other info: Open Apr-Feb	
Coswarth House 12 Dennis Road, Padstow, PL28 8DD ☏ 07907 626084 ✉ coswarth@cawlimited.co.uk 🌐 www.coswarthhouse.com	GR: SW919751	DP: 0.5 miles	
	N: **PADSTOW**		
	Offers one night stays		
	4 🐕 📶 🚗	Other info: Single night supplement of £20 waived for SWCP walkers.	
Sunny Corner Main Road, Trevone PL28 8QX ☏ 01841 520476 ✉ mo@wizadora.com 🌐 www.sunnycorner.info	GR: SW892758	DP: 0.2 miles	
	N: **TREVONE**		
	Offers one night stays		
	2 🐕 📶 🚗	Other info: Open all year.	
Penhalonga B&B Constantine Bay, Padstow, PL28 8JG ☏ 01841 521122 / 078158 33158 ✉ lizkennerley@btinternet.com 🌐 www.southwestcoastpath.org.uk/penhalonga-constantine-bay	GR: SW869743	DP: 0.5 miles	
	N: **PADSTOW**		
	Offers one night stays		
	3 🐕 📶 🚗	Other info: Open all year	
Penlan B&B Penlan, Porthcothan Bay, PL28 8LP ☏ 01841 520440 ✉ mary@idenna.com 🌐 www.porthcothanbay.co.uk	GR: SW860718	DP: 0.12 miles	
	N: **PORTHCOTHAN**		
	Offers one night stays		
	2 🐕 📶 🚗	Other info:	

Campsites and Holiday Parks

NAME	OTHER INFO		
Wooda Lakes Holiday Park Pancrasweek, Holsworthy, EX22 7JN ☏ 01409 241934 ✉ info@woodalakes.co.uk 🌐 www.woodalakes.co.uk	GR: SS306088	DP: 7 miles	
	N: **BUDE**		
	11 🐕 📶 🚗	Other info: Open all year.	
Widemouth Bay Caravan Park Poundstock, Bude, EX23 0DF ☏ 01288 361 208 🌐 www.johnfowlerholidays.com/cornwall-holiday-park/ widemouth-bay-caravan-park	GR: SS195009	DP: 0.75 miles	
	N: **BUDE**		
	188 🐕 🍴 🛒 📶 🚗	Other info: Single stays in touring field. Open 01/03-01/11.	
Penhalt Farm Holiday Park Widemouth Bay, Bude, EX23 0DG ☏ 01288 361210 ✉ info@penhaltfarm.co.uk 🌐 www.penhaltfarm.co.uk	GR: SS194002	DP: 0.25 miles	
	N: **WIDEMOUTH BAY**		
	🐕 🛒 📶 🚗	Other info:	

NAME	OTHER INFO	
Dennis Cove Campsite	GR: SW920743	DP: 0.5 miles
Dennis Lane, Padstow, PL28 8DR	N: **PADSTOW**	
📞 01841 532349	Offers one night stays	
📧 hello@denniscovecampsite.co.uk	🐕🚗	**Other info:** Open Easter-End Oct.
🌐 www.denniscovecampsite.co.uk		
Carnevas Holiday Park	GR: SW861726	DP: 0.5 miles
St Merryn, Padstow, PL28 8PN	N: **PORTHCOTHAN**	
📞 01841 520230	Offers one night stays	
📧 carnevascampsite@aol.com	🐕🍴🛒📶🚗	**Other info:** Open Easter-End Oct.
🌐 www.carnevasholidaypark.com		
Old Macdonalds Farm	GR: SW860711	DP: 0.5 miles
Porthcothan Bay, Padstow, PL28 8LT	N: **PORTHCOTHAN**	
📞 01841 540829	Offers one night stays	
📧 info@oldmacdonalds.co.uk	3 📶🚗	**Other info:**
🌐 www.oldmacdonalds.co.uk		
Treago Farm Caravan & Camping Site	GR: SW781600	DP: 0 miles
Treago Farm, Newquay, TR8 5QS	N: **CRANTOCK**	
📞 01637 830277	Offers one night stays	
📧 info@treagofarm.co.uk	🐕🛒📶🚗	**Other info:** 80 pitches. Shop and takeaway. Open Easter - 1st Oct.
🌐 www.treagofarm.co.uk		

Self Catering

NAME	OTHER INFO	
Welcombe Cottage	GR: SS224176	DP: 0.5 miles
Welcombe, EX39 6HH	N: **BUDE**	
📞 07855302242		
📧 info@welcombecottage.holiday	8 📶🚗	**Other info:** Sleeps 18
🌐 www.welcombecottage.holiday		
Valley View Holiday Cottage	GR: SS212136	DP: 0.7 miles
Valley View Woodford, Bude, EX23 9JQ	N: **BUDE**	
📞 07855 302242		
📧 info@valleyview.holiday	3 🐕📶🚗	**Other info:** A short walk from the Coast Path. Open all year.
🌐 www.valleyview.holiday		
Bude Holiday Resort	GR: SS207079	DP: 0 miles
Maer Lane, Bude, EX23 9EE	N: **BUDE**	
📞 01288 355955		
📧 reception.bude@ariaresorts.co.uk	50 🐕🍴📶	**Other info:**
🌐 www.araresorts.co.uk/bude-holiday-resort		
Gwelmor	GR: SS201022	DP: 0.25 miles
Long Park Drive Widemouth Bay, Bude, EX23 0AN	N: **WIDEMOUTH BAY**	
📞 07711 264087		
📧 jaynefreer@hotmail.com	3 🐕📶🚗	**Other info:** Open all year.
🌐 www.facebook.com/GwelmorWidemouthBay		
The Clinker	GR: SX098913	DP: 0 miles
Boscastle, PL35 0HD	N: **BOSCASTLE**	
📞 0345 800 2070		
📧 cottages@nationaltrust.org.uk	1 📶🚗	**Other info:**
🌐 www.nationaltrust.org.uk/holidays/the-clinker-cornwall		
The Gaffer	GR: SX098913	DP: 0 miles
Boscastle, PL35 0HD	N: **BOSCASTLE**	
📞 0345 800 2070		
📧 cottages@nationaltrust.org.uk	1 📶🚗	**Other info:**
🌐 www.nationaltrust.org.uk/holidays/the-gaffer-cornwall		

NAME	OTHER INFO		
The Lugger Boscastle, PL35 0HD 📞 0345 800 2070 ✉ cottages@nationaltrust.org.uk 🌐 www.nationaltrust.org.uk/holidays/the-lugger-cornwall	GR: SX098913	DP: 0 miles	
	N: **BOSCASTLE**		
	⟦2⟧ ⟦📶⟧		Other info:
Harbour View Boscastle, PL35 0AG 📞 0345 800 2070 ✉ cottages@nationaltrust.org.uk 🌐 www.nationaltrust.org.uk/holidays/harbour-view-cornwall	GR: SX097913	DP: 0 miles	
	N: **BOSCASTLE**		
	⟦3⟧ ⟦🐕⟧ ⟦📶⟧ ⟦🚗⟧		Other info:
Beaver Cottages Tregatta, Tintagel, PL34 0DY 📞 01840 770378 ✉ beavercottages@outlook.com 🌐 www.beaver-cottages.co.uk	GR: SX056873	DP: 0.25 miles	
	N: **TINTAGEL**		
	Offers one night stays		
	⟦3⟧ ⟦🐕⟧ ⟦📶⟧ ⟦🚗⟧		Other info: Open all year. 2 cottages sleeping up to 4 and 6.
The White Cottage Port Isaac, PL29 3SQ 📞 0345 800 2070 ✉ cottages@nationaltrust.org.uk 🌐 www.nationaltrust.org.uk/holidays/the-white-cottage-cornwall	GR: SX003807	DP: 0.25 miles	
	N: **PORT ISAAC**		
	⟦3⟧ ⟦🐕⟧ ⟦📶⟧ ⟦🚗⟧		Other info:
Guy's Cottage Port Quin, PL29 3SQ 📞 0345 800 2070 ✉ cottages@nationaltrust.org.uk 🌐 www.nationaltrust.org.uk/holidays/guys-cottage-cornwall	GR: SX003807	DP: 0.25 miles	
	N: **PORT QUIN**		
	⟦3⟧ ⟦🐕⟧ ⟦🚗⟧		Other info:
Moyles Farm Nr Polzeath, Wadebridge, PL27 6RA 📞 01208 862331 ✉ mail@moylesfarm.co.uk 🌐 www.moylesfarm.co.uk	GR: SW956785	DP: 1 mile	
	N: **POLZEATH**		
	Offers one night stays		
	⟦8⟧ ⟦🐕⟧ ⟦🍴⟧ ⟦📶⟧ ⟦🚗⟧		Other info: Pick up & drop off to Path. Luggage Transfer. Open all year.
The Old Farmhouse St Minver, PL27 6QY 📞 0345 800 2070 ✉ cottages@nationaltrust.org.uk 🌐 www.nationaltrust.org.uk/holidays/the-old-farmhouse-cornwall	GR: SW943799	DP: 1 mile	
	N: **POLZEATH**		
	⟦3⟧ ⟦🐕⟧ ⟦📶⟧ ⟦🚗⟧		Other info:
Beach Head Bunkhouse Wadebridge, PL27 7UU 📞 0344 335 1296 ✉ bunkhouses@nationaltrust.org.uk 🌐 www.nationaltrust.org.uk/holidays/beach-head-bunkhouse-cornwall	GR: SW852708	DP: 1 mile	
	N: **WADEBRIDGE**		
	⟦🚗⟧		Other info:
Mariners Lettings Ltd Rock Road, Rock, PL27 6JN 📞 01208 869257 ✉ carla@marinersrock.com 🌐 www.marinerslettings.co.uk	GR: SW933756	DP: 0 miles	
	N: **ROCK**		
	⟦🐕⟧ ⟦📶⟧ ⟦🚗⟧		Other info:
Cornish Horizons 19 New Street, Padstow, PL28 8EA 📞 01841 533331 ✉ cottages@cornishhorizons.co.uk 🌐 www.cornishhorizons.co.uk	GR: SW918752	DP: 0.3 miles	
	N: **PADSTOW**		
	Offers one night stays		
	⟦🐕⟧ ⟦📶⟧ ⟦🚗⟧		Other info: Open all year.
Cornish Traditional Cottages 3 Eddystone Court, Eddystone Road, Wadebridge, PL27 7FH 📞 01208 895354 ✉ bookings@corncott.com 🌐 www.corncott.com	GR: SW989724	DP: 0 miles	
	N: **PADSTOW**		
	⟦🐕⟧ ⟦📶⟧		Other info:

NAME	OTHER INFO	
Linhay Cornwall Trererthren Farm, Padstow, PL28 8LE ☎ 01237 426710 ✉ info@stayin.co.uk 🌐 www.stayincornwall.co.uk/cottages/padstow--the-linhay	GR: SW913742	DP: 0.25 miles
	N: **PADSTOW**	
	2 🐕 🛜 🚗	Other info:
The Red Bouy Glencoe, Porthcothan, PL28 8LW ☎ 01841 520393 ✉ janesdarke@gmail.com 🌐 www.janedarke.co.uk/holiday-accommodation-porthcothan	GR: SW858719	DP: 0 miles
	N: **PORTHCOTHAN**	
	Offers one night stays	
	2 🐕 🍴 🛒 🛜 🚗	Other info: Open all year.
The Village Watergate Bay, Newquay, TR8 4AA ☎ 01637 861005 ✉ life@beachretreats.co.uk 🌐 www.beachretreats.co.uk/developments/the-village-watergate-bay	GR: SW841649	DP: 0.5 miles
	N: **WATERGATE BAY**	
	2 🐕 🛜 🚗	Other info:
Newquay Bay Resort Trevelgue Road, Newquay, TR8 4AS ☎ 01637 851851 ✉ newquay@ariaresorts.co.uk 🌐 www.ariaresorts.co.uk/newquay-bay-resort	GR: SW839634	DP:
	N: **NEWQUAY**	
	120 🐕 🍴 🛒 🛜 🚗	

Getting Around

NAME	OTHER INFO	
Trev's Taxi Flat 2, St Catherines, 33 Downs View, Bude, EX23 8RG ☎ 07799 663217 ✉ trevstaxi3217@btinternet.com 🌐 www.trevstaxi.co.uk	GR: SW207071	DP: 0.25 miles
	N: **BUDE**	
	🐕 🛜	Other info:
Bayside Taxis 2 The Grange, Lymstone, Bude, EX23 0PR ☎ 07769 313654 ✉ baysidetaxis.bude@gmail.com 🌐 www.baysidetaxis.co.uk	GR: SS206051	DP: 0.5 miles
	N: **BUDE**	
	🐕	

Activities

NAME	OTHER INFO	
Newquay Zoo Trenance Gardens, Newquay, TR7 2NL ☎ 01803 697500 🌐 www.newquayzoo.org.uk	GR: SW820613	DP: 0.6 miles
	N: **NEWQUAY**	
	🛜 🚗	Other info: Open 10am daily except Christmas Day

Eat and Drink

NAME	OTHER INFO	
Rectory Farm Tea Rooms Crosstown, Morwenstow, Bude, EX23 9SR ☎ 01288 331251 ✉ jill@rectory-tearooms.co.uk 🌐 www.rectory-tearooms.co.uk	GR: SS205152	DP: 0.25 miles
	N: **BUDE**	
		Other info:
Brendon Arms Falcon Terrace, Bude, EX23 8SD ☎ 01288 354542 ✉ enquiries@brendonarms.co.uk 🌐 www.brendonarms.co.uk	GR: SS206061	DP: 0 miles
	N: **BUDE**	
	Offers one night stays	
	10 🍴 🛜 🚗	Other info: Open all year except Christmas day.
The Break Bar, Beach House Marine Drive Widemouth Bay, Bude, EX23 0AW ☎ 01288 361256 ✉ enquiries@beachhousewidemouth.co.uk 🌐 www.beachhousewidemouth.co.uk	GR: SS199028	DP: 0 miles
	N: **BUDE**	
	Offers one night stays	
	🐕 🍴 🚗	Other info: Stay at the Beach House B&B. Seasonal - see website.

Walking breaks by the sea

Discover the West Country your way!

Whatever your'e searching for we can help you create your perfect break in Devon and Cornwall. Providing tailor-made getaways that embrace every aspect of group travel, themed breaks and last minute deals that can all be experienced whilst staying in luxurious handpicked hotels.

NEW
WEBSITE
COMING
SOON

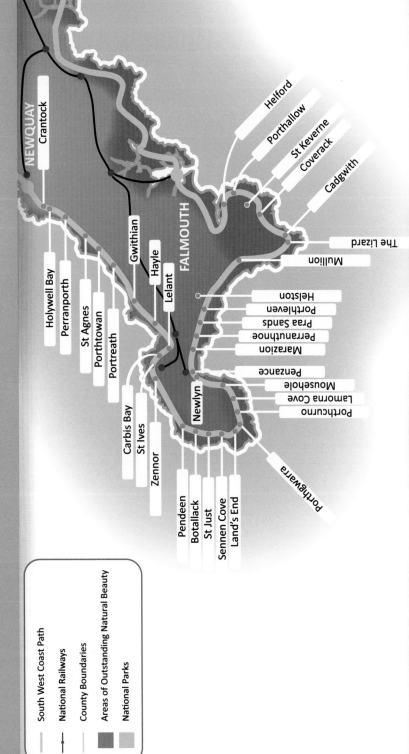

NEWQUAY

Crantock

Holywell Bay
Perranporth
St Agnes
Porthtowan
Portreath
Gwithian
Hayle
Lelant

FALMOUTH

Carbis Bay
St Ives
Zennor

Newlyn

Pendeen
Botallack
St Just
Sennen Cove
Land's End

Porthcurno
Lamorna Cove
Mousehole
Penzance
Marazion
Perranuthnoe
Praa Sands
Porthleven
Helston

Mullion

The Lizard

Helford
Porthallow
St Keverne
Coverack
Cadgwith

Porthgwarra

South West Coast Path
National Railways
County Boundaries
Areas of Outstanding Natural Beauty
National Parks

Map not to scale. For illustrative purposes only.

West Cornwall
Newquay to Falmouth

(Sections 22-37)

The cliffs to the west of Newquay give way to the scenic and sandy St Ives Bay. Beyond St Ives, an old fishing port of medieval origin, the coast encircles two great peninsulas: Penwith, the westernmost part of England, and the Lizard, the southernmost. Both are composed of hard, resistant rocks, making for a rugged cliff coastline, but their characters differ. Penwith is largely granite and inland of its impressive cliffs, frequently marked by rock pinnacles and solid jointed slabs, is a rough semi-moorland landscape. Along a length of Penwith's north coast, the Coast Path passes a number of old cliff-face tin mines. The Lizard has a much smoother profile, with its inland landscape an unusual flat-topped plateau. The exposed locations of these two peninsulas result in harsh, weather-beaten coastlines with a lack of large-scale tree cover, though both are superbly dramatic. Between these two magnificent peninsulas is the iconic Mount's Bay, site of the fairytale-like setting of St Michael's Mount, surmounted by its castle. The bay is the site of a number of coastal towns; Penzance, the main centre for this far western part of Cornwall, Marazion, with its ancient origins, the fishing port of Newlyn and picturesque Mousehole, once of great importance until burned by the Spanish in the wars of the 16th century. East of the Lizard, the quiet wooded estuary of the Helford River is followed by the extensive estuary of the River Fal, which marks the end of this length.

All of the locations on the map illustration to the left, have at least 1 facility including toilets, a cafe/restaurant, shop or pub.

Godrevy looking back across Gwithian

OS Maps: Landranger 200; Explorer 104

	This Walk	Cumulative	This Walk	Cumulative	Grading	Timing
Ascent	1,145ft	39,071ft	349m	11,909m	Moderate	3.5 hours
Distance	8.1mi	197.9mi	13.0km	318.5km		

For detailed directions see our Walking Guide no. 22, Newquay (Harbour) to Holywell Bay.

This Section includes some superb viewpoints from headlands in and around Newquay, the panoramas quite unspoiled by the proximity of the large town. Beyond Newquay, a range of landscapes is experienced, from wide sandy beaches to exposed cliff tops to small sandy bays, to dune systems. In addition, unexpectedly, the wooded estuary valley of the river known as The Gannel is crossed at the edge of Newquay. This variety, and the proximity to a range of facilities and accommodation, make this a popular, well-used length.

Directions

A regular bus service links Newquay with Holywell Bay, and also serves Crantock, between the two. This gives a number of bus-walk possibilities.

Newquay is the biggest town on Cornwall's north coast. Although usually busy, being especially popular with surfers and also with groups of young holidaymakers, it is in a very attractive setting of beaches and headlands. All the facilities are here, and there is a branch railway linking to the main line to Penzance.

From Newquay Harbour the Coast Path climbs past the old Huer's Hut to Towan Head. From Towan Head the Path then follows the back of Fistral Beach. This is probably the country's most popular surfing beach and international competitions are held here. The Path climbs to the cliffs at the southern end and then crosses the road to go along Pentire Crescent, which leads into Penmere Drive. The Path then arrives above the Gannel Estuary. However, this misses the major headland of Pentire Point East, which is well worth the diversion to the end. (If following the diversion round the headland, on returning from the end, aim for the far bottom of the car park at the neck of the headland. From here head along the suburban road parallel to the Gannel. Follow this to the Fern Pit Cafe.)

There are four options from here for crossing the Gannel, depending on the tide and time of year.

OPTION 1: FERN PIT FERRY (deduct 2 miles/3 kilometres from total mileage)

The first option is to use the Fern Pit Ferry from behind the cafe. The cafe is approximately 0.7 mile/1.1 kilometres west of Penmere Drive. The ferry operates continuously, 7 days a week, 9.30-18.00 mid May until mid September weather dependent . For further details see page 22.

OPTION 2: PENPOL CROSSING (official route)

Go along Penmere Drive then turn right into Trevean Way. Follow the waymarks right and go downhill across a grassy area. At the foot of the grass bank turn right along the footpath, then take the steps on the left down to the tidal Penpol Footbridge across the Gannel Estuary. This can be used 3-4 hours either side of low water. Cross the Gannel here. (If coming from the headland circuit, continue past the Fern Pit Cafe and on along Riverside Avenue, then ahead and right. At a junction where there is a footpath to the right, keep ahead, ignoring the footpath. Bear right into Penmere Drive, again ignoring another footpath on the right. Go along Penmere Drive and re-join the route detailed on previous page.)

OPTION 3: TRENANCE FOOTBRIDGE (add 3 miles/4.8km to total mileage)

This route is usable at most states of the tide. From the Newquay side of the Penpol crossing, continue upstream on the Path parallel to the river until it arrives at the A392 Gannel Road. There is a footbridge on the right just before the junction with the A3058 Trevemper Road. Cross the bridge and continue ahead. Do not follow the creekside path to Penpol, but instead take the bridleway on the left towards Trevemper. Turn right just before reaching the tarmac, and follow the footpath through Treringey to arrive at the south side of the Penpol tidal footbridge.

OPTION 4: MAIN ROAD ROUTE (add 4.5 miles/7.2km to total mileage)

Continue past the Trenance footbridge and along the A392 Trevemper Road from the roundabout. At the next roundabout turn right and after about 100 yards/90 metres take the little unsigned lane on the right. This leads to Trevemper, going forward and right as the lane goes left. After the gate turn left on the route described under Option 3 through Treringey.

Options 2, 3 and 4 come together at Penpol. Cross the ford to follow the lane then take the waymarked Path on the right above the estuary. After passing the ferry landing for Option 1, this path leads to Crantock Beach car park. Crantock village with its facilities and bus stop is a little way inland. Cross the car park and climb the steps through the gate opposite; bear left at the junction of grassy paths on entering the dune area and follow this inland of the main dune area, to re-emerge at a coastal path which leads to the cliffs of Pentire Point West where the Bowgie Inn among others, provide meals and refreshments. The Path goes round Porth Joke (known locally as Polly Joke), then on around Kelsey Head to Holywell Bay, descending across more dunes either into the village or to cross the river on a seaward footbridge. There are facilities, some seasonal here.

Holywell Bay

OS Maps: Landranger 200; Explorer 104

	This Walk	Cumulative	This Walk	Cumulative	Grading	Timing
Ascent	755ft	39,826ft	230m	12,139m	Moderate	2 hours
Distance	4.5mi	202.4mi	7.2km	325.7km		

For detailed directions see our Walking Guide no. 23, Holywell Bay to Perranporth.

The theme of this Section is sand, in the form of both dunes and beaches, although it begins by rounding headlands at Penhale and Ligger Points. However, even at Penhale the inland vista is dominated by dunes, although the adjacent former Army Camp is also prominent. For the bulk of this Section sand is everywhere around, on the seemingly endless length of Perran Beach and the dunes which back it. Both ends, Holywell and Perranporth, are busy holiday settlements, but the more remote areas of Perran Beach can be surprisingly quiet.

Directions

Holywell Bay and Perranporth are both served by regular bus services from Newquay, making a bus walk along this length using Newquay as a base an option.

Holywell Bay has all facilities, some seasonal. From Holywell Bay the Path rounds Penhale Point, skirting the seaward edge of the somewhat unattractive former Penhale army camp. It then goes on out to Ligger Point, where there is a panoramic view of the length of Perran Beach. The Path heads towards the dunes then descends behind the cliff quarry to the beach. It now follows the back of the beach for some 1.5 miles/2.5 kilometres. At the very highest tides it may not be possible to use the beach route. In this case do not descend to the beach but turn left uphill for a short distance, to follow the path on your right through the dunes next to a line of red and white posts, and then seaward of a holiday park, parallel to the sea. Join a track which leads to the top of steps from the beach. Even at lower tides it is often necessary to climb these steps from the beach. Coming up from the beach, at the top of the steps turn right following the slate Coast Path waymarks. The Path descends back to the beach on the south side, and then crosses the stream by the footbridge when nearly at Perranporth, where there are all needed facilities. Again at the very highest tides, the beach and footbridge may not be available, in which case follow a path around the lip of the dunes to the rear of the Surf Lifesaving Club, to a sandy track which leads to a road. Follow the road right then turn right at the mini-roundabout into Perranporth.

Holywell Bay

OS Maps: Landranger 200 (Perranporth); Landranger 203 (remainder); Explorer 104

	This Walk	Cumulative	This Walk	Cumulative	Grading	Timing
Ascent	2,250ft	42,076ft	686m	12,825m	Moderate then strenuous	5.75 hours
Distance	12.4mi	214.8mi	20.0km	345.7km		

For detailed directions see our Walking Guide no. 24, Perranporth to Portreath.

This section is one in which Cornwall's coastal mining heritage is paramount. There is much evidence of former mining activity, including somewhat stark areas of spoil and sometimes slightly sad building relics, but also some grand and imposing engine houses and chimneys. In some locations, the large-scale level of the activity is difficult to imagine now. In any event, the scale and grandeur of the cliffs, the beaches and the surf mean that nature always re-asserts itself.

Directions

A regular bus service links Perranporth to St Agnes. A skeletal summer service links Perranporth to Portreath, also passing St Agnes and Porthtowan along the way, giving numerous bus-walk options.

Perranporth is a busy holiday centre with all facilities. The Coast Path goes west from the promenade car park and follows the hill up Cliff Road. Keep left of the castellated building then along Tregundy Lane. Go half left at the entrance to the Youth Hostel and on to the cliffs, the Path clinging to the cliff face out to Cligga Head. Here the Path enters quarry and mine workings, but is well signposted. There is then a level stretch alongside Perranporth Aerodrome before the steep descent to Trevellas Porth, a valley marked by many relics of the mining industry. Go upstream to cross at the road bridge, then back to the cliffs and back down again into Trevaunance Cove, where there are toilets and refreshments. The bus stop at St Agnes is a little way inland.

On reaching the road at Trevaunance Cove, go straight across passing the Driftwood Spars car park and a large tall house on the right. Follow the waymarked footpath immediately right along a metalled lane, then fork right along a footpath. Soon the Path climbs steeply to the cliff top. A long and scenic high-level Path now goes around St Agnes Head, giving superb views ahead, then past the iconic engine house at Towanroath before descending to Chapel Porth, a small and attractive cove with toilets and seasonal refreshments available at the Chapel Porth Beach Cafe. The toilets here are only unlocked when the cafe is open.

Follow the stream inland for 200 yards/185 metres then turn right and up to the cliffs, before heading back down again into Porthtowan. Again there are toilets and refreshments and a magnificent beach. There is a bus stop a little inland.

Follow the road inland then turn right up West Beach Road, then left up the narrow road 'West Cliff' to the cliff top. More mine workings are passed, then the Path runs alongside a prominent fence next to MOD land before reaching a road which descends into Portreath. This former industrial harbour town has all facilities.

OS Maps: Landranger 203; Explorer 104 (eastern half); Explorer 102 (western half)

	This Walk	Cumulative	This Walk	Cumulative	Grading	Timing
Ascent	1,362ft	43,438ft	415m	13,240m	Moderate/ easy	5.5 hours
Distance	11.7mi	226.5mi	18.8km	364.5km		

For detailed directions see our Walking Guide no. 25, Portreath to Hayle.

There are two distinct characters to the coast of this Section. Between Portreath and Godrevy it is one of high, level cliffs, the sea far below. In contrast, between Godrevy and Hayle the walk focuses on sand, either dunes or beach, on the focal view of Godrevy lighthouse and on the great colourful sweep of St Ives Bay. This is never a lonely or remote length, but it is a scenic, fascinating and rewarding one.

Directions

A summer bus service links Portreath and Hayle, and also passes Godrevy, half-way between the two. This allows for bus-walk options over the whole Section or over either of the two distinct character lengths.

Portreath has all facilities and a pleasant beach. Leave the town crossing the bridge next to the car park then right, up Battery Hill. Continue ahead, meandering between properties at the end, turning right just beyond them up steps to the top of Western Hill, with its excellent views. After a couple of steep valleys the Path then embarks on a long easy cliff-top walk along Reskajeague Downs, eventually arriving at Hell's Mouth, where there is the seasonal Hell's Mouth Cafe. The Path then narrows and turns right at an obvious T-junction. Cross a stile next to a gate and cross the seaward side of a field, before continuing easily round Navax and Godrevy Points, the lighthouse becoming a focal point offshore. Keep seaward of the car park and access road, and follow the signs along the low cliffs and over the dunes to another car park, at the Godrevy Cafe. Follow the boardwalk from the car park to cross the Red River. Turn left for 30 yards/29 metres then go right, following the large slate waymarks through the former quarry, now a nature reserve.

Keep ahead through the dunes, following the signposts. Note it is often possible to walk along the beach here, but beware the incoming tide which can mean being cut off below the cliffs. If the tide is right, leave the beach at the lifeguard hut near the foot of Black Cliff. If coming through the dunes, keep ahead above the hut. Then, with either option, turn left up some steps just before two chalets. Turn right towards a house, leaving it on the right, and walk along a line of chalets on the left. The Path opens out at a car park. Follow the access track ahead, then bear right onto the raised walkway parallel to the harbour and continue ahead on this level. Descend the steps at the far end and follow the pavement ahead, then cross the old swing bridge to the road. Turn right to reach the railway viaduct in the centre of Hayle.

OS Maps: Landranger 203; Explorer 102

	This Walk	Cumulative	This Walk	Cumulative	Grading	Timing
Ascent	617ft	44,055ft	188m	13,428m	Easy	2.5 hours
Distance	6.1mi	232.6mi	9.8km	374.3km		

For detailed directions see our Walking Guide no. 26, Hayle to St Ives.

This Section is never far from roads and houses, so often has a suburban air. However, this is outweighed by the views over the River Hayle estuary, and particularly, by the vistas over the great sweep of St Ives Bay with its vast sandy beaches and dunes, the iconic offshore Godrevy Lighthouse as a focal point, and the fabulous sea colours, turquoises, greens and blues, whenever the sun shines on this length.

Directions

A regular bus service links Hayle and St Ives, giving a bus-walk option. In addition, a branch-line railway plies between Lelant and St Ives, and this gives marvellous sea views. This makes for an unusual and especially scenic train-walk option.

Hayle has all facilities, including a railway station on the main line to Penzance. Walk to the viaduct and turn right on the Path immediately before it. Go ahead to Carnsew Road and continue on the pavement, turning right on a narrow Path between housing. Go left at the end then continue to arrive alongside a large lagoon. Keep on to the end, then bear left to the road. Continue as the road passes alongside the River Hayle estuary on The Causeway, a birdwatchers' delight. Cross to the far side of the road then back to the riverside again, before forking right at the Old Quay House. Under the bridge turn right, signed to St Ives Park and Ride. At the car park attendant's kiosk turn left to a lane, then turn right here. Follow the lane next to the railway and estuary all the way to Lelant Church. Go along the Path next to the church to pass under the railway. Just before the beach turn left along the seaward side of the railway through dunes. (NB. this is also the route of the St Michael's Way, a cross-peninsula path from Lelant to Marazion – a guide leaflet is available at St Ives Tourist Information Centre (TIC)).

Follow the clear Path parallel to the magnificent Porthkidney Beach. Approaching the headland of Carrack Gladden the Path forks – keep right then continue ahead. Descend the road to Carbis Bay, where there are toilets and seasonal refreshments, walking on the seaward side of the hotel. Climb over a railway bridge then continue as the Path becomes a minor road. Pass the path taking St Michael's Way inland, then at a little cross-roads go straight ahead, steeply downhill. (Turning right shortly after the St Michael's Way turning down a private, pedestrians only path gives a more scenic alternative to the official route, re-joining at the little cross-roads.) Cross the railway bridge and double back right, then left to arrive at Porthminster Beach, just below St Ives railway station.

OS Maps: Landranger 203; Explorer 102

	This Walk	Cumulative	This Walk	Cumulative	Grading	Timing
Ascent	3,428ft	47,483ft	1,045m	14,473m	Severe	7 hours
Distance	13.7mi	246.3mi	22.0km	396.4km		

For detailed directions see our Walking Guide no. 27, St Ives to Zennor and Zennor to Pendeen Watch.

There are no settlements on this Section and the character is lonely and remote. It is also tough going, with rocky scrambles and boggy lengths. But it can only be described as a magnificent length. Stark cliffs, rock pinnacles, tiny scenic coves with translucent water, rugged exposed headlands – all are here. Inland the view is often of empty moorland. This is the Coast Path at its most awe-inspiring. Prepare for its rigours, then enjoy the wonderful experience.

Directions

A regular summer bus service links St Ives and Pendeen village, a little inland of the Coast Path. It also passes through other inland settlements linked by footpath to the Coast Path, principally Zennor, Treen (Gurnard's Head) and Morvah, allowing for various bus-walks options.

A warning: this is a tough and deserted length of the Coast Path. There are no settlements or refreshment facilities, though there are some path links inland to small settlements. The terrain is often rough and rocky and in places can be boggy. But a compensation: this is a length of wonderfully dramatic coastal scenery.

From the Path below St Ives railway station, keep along as close as possible to the sea and harbour. The official route goes round the green St Ives Head, usually known as The Island. This is reached by following signs to the museum from the far end of the harbour, and on through a small car park. From The Island go through the old "Downlong" quarter to Porthmeor Beach and the Tate. There are also short cuts direct to here – follow signs to the Tate.

Go along the rear of Porthmeor Beach, then bear off right along the Path next to the putting green. The Coast Path now leads out to the rugged Clodgy Point and then on round Hor Point to Pen Enys Point, where it cuts across the neck of the headland. Pass the trig point on Carn Naun, where there are extensive views forward and back, then descend to cross the stream at River Cove. Just beyond, the Path passes the offshore Carracks, where seals are regularly seen. Approaching Zennor Head the Path forks – keep right to follow the seaward path round the headland. From Zennor Head the Path heads inland – look out for the signed Coast Path descending steeply to the right. If in need of refreshments, or for the bus, continue along the Path inland to Zennor, where there is a pub and seasonal cafe.

On the Coast Path, more ups and downs lead to the distinctive headland of Gurnard's Head. The Path cuts across its neck, but a diversion onto the headland, an Iron Age fortified site, is worth the effort. There are also diversions inland here to Treen, where refreshments are available at the Gurnard's Head Inn and there is a bus stop.

The Coast Path continues, generally easy to follow if not always an easy walk. Approaching Bosigran, another Iron Age fortification, head for the high point of the ridge, following Coast Path signs and keeping on the landward side of a low wall. At the crest of the ridge head inland and downhill, aiming for a stream and building.

Cross the stream on a small bridge near a ruined building, then follow the Path uphill, just seaward of an obvious stone wall. There is a diversion path inland here to a bus stop at Rosemergy. After heavy rain the Path round here can be boggy.

Further on the Coast Path, look out for a path inland to Morvah for another bus stop, if needed. Otherwise keep on the obvious Coast Path round the back of Portheras Cove, and on to the lighthouse at Pendeen Watch. Pendeen village, with its pubs, cafe, shop, toilets and bus stop, is about 1 mile/1.5 kilometres inland.

Cape Cornwall

OS Maps: Landranger 203; Explorer 102

	This Walk	Cumulative	This Walk	Cumulative	Grading	Timing
Ascent	1,683ft	49,166ft	513m	14,986m	Moderate	4.25 hours
Distance	9.1mi	255.4mi	14.6km	411.0km		

For detailed directions see our Walking Guide no. 28, Pendeen Watch to Sennen Cove.

This Section offers a wide range of walking experiences. Between Pendeen Watch and Botallack, the overriding experience is of Cornwall's coastal mining heritage. This ranges from unattractive early 20th century industrial relics to romantic stone-built cliff-face engine houses, all this next to sheer cliffs and often wild seas. Beyond Botallack is a superb length of scenic exposed cliffs, highlighted by the magnificent headland of Cape Cornwall. This Section has all that is best on the Cornish coast – rugged cliffs, mining relics, translucent water, turquoise coves, purple heather, rocky scrambles, the view of a lighthouse. Then, approaching Sennen Cove, there is a sweep of broad sandy beaches backed by dunes, and the length ends with a scenic harbour and a lifeboat station. A wonderful length.

Directions

A regular summer bus service links Pendeen village, a little inland of the Coast Path, with Sennen Cove. It also serves St Just, inland of Cape Cornwall, which is used as the centre of various Coast Path-based circular walks. Bus-walks are also possible from Geevor and Botallack, reached by the footpath from the coast.

From Pendeen Watch the Path goes along the road to the end of the row of cottages, then turns right at a granite marker. (The road continues into Pendeen village, with its range of facilities.) The Coast Path is clear and leads to the old mining area at Geevor. A diversion inland leads to refreshments and toilets at the mining museum, which is itself well worth a visit, if possible. Follow the signed track beyond Geevor to the National Trust's Levant Beam Engine House, open for steaming at certain times. From here the official Path follows the clear track parallel to the coast, but a narrower path to seaward with better views leads from the far end of the car park. The two options come together as more mines are passed at Botallack. Look to seaward to see the famous Crowns Mine engine houses, perched improbably on the cliff.

Beyond Botallack, as the mines give way, look for the signed Path to the right which leads to the headland at Kenidjack Castle. A lot of the waymarking in this area uses granite stones, perfect for the landscape setting. From the old building on the headland descend left to a track, go left then bear right on a path down to another track. Go left here then turn right to cross the floor of the Kenidjack Valley. Climb to the top and turn right. Ahead now is the distinctive shape of Cape Cornwall, surmounted by its chimney. Turn right immediately before the road and then bear right across a field past the ruins of a chapel to a stone stile. Cross this, turn left and then climb right to reach the top of the headland. Savour the views, then join the Path, which descends over the seaward side of the Cape by zigzags and steps to reach the National Coastwatch Institution watchhouse. This recent addition to the Coast Path provides a superb experience. Go to the left of the watchhouse, then down the steps and along a path past some stone buildings and through a gate, to reach another set of granite steps descending to the right. In the nearby car park are seasonal refreshments and toilets. St Just is about 1 mile/1.5 kilometres up the road.

At the bottom of the steps go left, then climb right on the track to a road at the top. Bear off right at the sign and follow the clear Path into the Cot Valley. A new route has been established down the valley. For this, turn left at the road and almost immediately right, over a footbridge and past old mine workings, climbing to reach a path which heads to the cove at Porth Nanven. Just before reaching the cove, climb left onto the cliffs. There is a good clear cliff-face path to the beach at Gwynver, although with one rocky climb. From Gwynver the Path continues through the dunes behind the sandy beaches, which can be walked at low tide, to the car park at Sennen Cove. This is a popular family and surfing spot with all facilities.

Sennen Cove

OS Maps: Landranger 203; Explorer 102

	This Walk	Cumulative	This Walk	Cumulative	Grading	Timing
Ascent	1,542ft	50,708ft	470m	15,456m	Moderate	3.25 hours
Distance	6.3mi	261.7mi	10.1km	421.1km		

For detailed directions see our Walking Guide no. 29, Sennen Cove to Porthcurno.

This is the most westerly length of coast in England. Much of it has the character of moorland meeting the sea, with great granite headlands and massive rock outcrops, interspersed with isolated coves with exquisite sea colours. Towards Porthcurno the moorland is replaced by a more pastoral landscape, but the cliffs and coves continue. Much of this Section has a quiet character, interrupted only by the visitor mecca of Land's End.

Directions

Sennen Cove and Porthcurno are linked by a regular bus service, which also goes to Land's End. This allows for a choice of bus-walks, and there are also numerous circuits possible based on the Land's End area.

Sennen Cove has all facilities. Leave the village passing the Round House gallery into the car park. Turn left up steps then right, towards the lookout. From here a range of parallel paths all lead to Land's End. Bear right to the First and Last House, at England's most westerly point, then keep seaward of the main complex to the outpost at Greeb Cottage. The complex has toilets and refreshments if needed. The Path goes behind Greeb Cottage; then again a choice of paths all lead towards the beautiful bay of Nanjizal. At the far end of the bay, head inland up the track then turn right steeply uphill on a stepped path. After passing through a gate, look out for the official, unsigned, Path leaving the main track to go seaward down some rocky steps. The Path descends then climbs to the Coastwatch station on Gwennap Head. The main track also leads here, but less scenically.

The official Path is clear from Gwennap Head down into Porthgwarra. An alternative, to be used in good conditions and for the sure-footed only, is to leave the main Path to the right some 150 yards/140 metres after the Coastwatch station, then pass the hole of Tol-Pedn-Penwith ("the holed headland of Penwith") before bearing left to re-join the main Path.

Porthgwarra is a charming little hamlet, with toilets and seasonal refreshments and unusual passages through the cliffs. Leave along a track next to some cottages, climbing again to the cliffs. The clear Path descends to Porth Chapel, passing St Levan's Holy Well. Continue straight ahead over the bridge, climbing again to arrive at the car park of the unique cliff-face Minack Theatre. Leave by the Path next to the theatre entrance. The Path drops very steeply, with deep steps, to Porthcurno Beach. If in doubt, because of the conditions or possible vertigo, follow the road. At the bottom of the steps, keep left above the beach to Porthcurno's facilities.

OS Maps: Landranger 203; Explorer 102

	This Walk	Cumulative	This Walk	Cumulative	Grading	Timing
Ascent	1,381ft	52,089ft	421m	15,877m	Strenuous	3.25 hours
Distance	5.4mi	267.1mi	8.7km	429.9km		

For detailed directions see our Walking Guide no. 30, Porthcurno to Lamorna Cove.

This is a quiet, remote and very scenic Section of cliffs and headlands, punctuated by some picturesque coves and a lighthouse. The larger coves, at each end, Porthcurno and Lamorna, are particularly attractive and are the only access points for cars, so are more popular, Otherwise, the sound of the sea and seabirds are likely to be the only disturbances in this beautiful length.

Directions

A regular bus service goes to Porthcurno and passes about 1 mile/1.5km inland of Lamorna Cove, making a bus-walk feasible. Many undertake one of a variety of circular walks between Porthcurno and Treen using the Coast Path.

Porthcurno has all facilities in summer. The Coast Path leaves at the back of the beach, climbing a steep track to Percella Point before turning to run parallel to the sea. A seaward loop gives a good view of the beautiful Pednvounder Beach, but requires a little scramble to return to the official route. The Path then reaches the neck of Treen Head, or Treryn Dinas, the site of an Iron Age fortification. A cul-de-sac diversion heads for the end and the Logan Rock. Continue on the clear Path over the cliff to descend into Penberth Cove, a superb little fishing hamlet with an old capstan. There are toilets but no refreshments.

After climbing away from Penberth, the Path continues along the cliff top, with one steep descent and climb at Porthguarnon, then starts to head inland. After passing a seaward house look out for the signed Path to the right, which descends into the wooded valley of St Loy and on to the boulder beach. Keep along the top of the beach for 55 yards/50 metres before leaving up the Path. This climbs to pass above the lighthouse of Tater-du. Approaching Lamorna Point the Path crosses a length of tumbled rocks, making for slow going, until it suddenly descends to the car park at Lamorna Cove. Here are toilets and seasonal refreshments.

Penberth Cove

OS Maps: Landranger 203; Explorer 102

	This Walk	Cumulative	This Walk	Cumulative	Grading	Timing
Ascent	725ft	52,814ft	221m	16,098m	Strenuous then easy	3.5 hours
Distance	9.2mi	276.3mi	14.8km	444.7km		

For detailed directions see our Walking Guide no. 31, Lamorna Cove to Penzance to Marazion.

West of Mousehole this Section is one of lushly vegetated cliffs, but most of it is urban or semi-urban in character as it passes through Newlyn and Penzance. However, it is really defined by its views over the magnificent Mount's Bay, dominated by the iconic sight of St Michael's Mount and its castle, which give this coast a magical character.

Directions

A regular bus service passes about 1 mile/1.5km inland of Lamorna Cove and also serves Newlyn and Penzance, with links possible between Penzance and Marazion, giving a variety of possible bus-walk options.

Lamorna Cove has a seasonal cafe, toilets and, a little way inland, a pub. The Coast Path leaves the cove behind the harbour, bearing right to the cliffs. The well-marked path eventually leads to a road which descends into Mousehole. The road leads to the harbour; however, the official route turns right opposite "Lowena" then continues towards the sea, turning left, along a terrace to a car park. It briefly passes along the harbour before turning left then right to reach the main harbour-side road. Mousehole has all facilities and is very picturesque.

At the far end of the harbour go through the car park, on along a concrete walkway then up some steps. Turn right along the road, then along a seaward track to arrive at Newlyn. Follow the road round the harbour and past the fish market, turning right just after the Seamen's Mission to cross a bridge. Bear right past the Tolcarne Inn then follow the promenade to Penzance. Pass the harbour, then go right through the large car park to where a walkway leaves from its far right-hand end. Penzance has all facilities, is the end stop of the main-line railway, and is the hub of local bus services. The train and bus stations are next to the car park.

The walkway follows the sea wall to the edge of Marazion. At the end of the walkway and cycle route, either cross over and follow the road or cross the dunes to a large car park, cross this and continue behind the sea wall into Marazion.

Marazion is the centre for access to St Michael's Mount, and is the southern end of the cross-peninsula St Michael's Way from Lelant. The little town of Marazion has all facilities.

OS Maps: Landranger 203; Explorer 103 (Porthleven); Explorer 102 (remainder)

	This Walk	Cumulative	This Walk	Cumulative	Grading	Timing
Ascent	1,916ft	54,730ft	584m	16,682m	Moderate then strenuous	4.75 hours
Distance	10.8mi	287.1mi	17.4km	462.0km		

For detailed directions see our Walking Guide no. 32, Penzance to Marazion to Praa Sands and Praa Sands to Portleven.

Between Marazion and Cudden Point this Section is dominated by the sweep of Mount's Bay and its iconic focal point of St Michael's Mount. It is a charming length of low cliffs and small fields. East of Cudden Point the Mount is lost but the local landscape is bolder, with craggy headlands, long sandy beaches, inaccessible coves and picturesque cliff-top engine houses.

Directions

There are regular bus services which link Marazion and Porthleven and also serve Perranuthnoe and Praa Sands between the two, making a variety of bus-walks possible. Marazion is a pleasant little town with all facilities and the causeway to St Michael's Mount.

The Coast Path leaves along the main road, following it for some way to the speed restriction sign. Turn right before the cemetery, then bear left on a concrete path down steps and follow the Path to the beach. Cross the top of the beach to some metal steps, climb them and continue ahead. Just after Trenow Cove the Path turns inland. Look out for the signed right turn after 275 yards/250 metres, which goes back to the low cliffs and on to Perranuthnoe. There are toilets and seasonal refreshments here.

Take the lane on the seaward side of the car park, bearing right and then left into a field. The well-marked path leads to Cudden Point, with magnificent views over Mount's Bay. It descends past Little Cudden to Bessy's Cove, where it joins a track. Go ahead, bearing right at some granite gate posts, then through Prussia Cove on a lane between large stone buildings. Keep ahead on the Path which passes above Kenneggy Sand and then descends to Praa Sands, where there are toilets and seasonal refreshments. Go down the slipway to the beach then along in front of the shop, taking the steps up beside the cafe. Keep along the top of the grassy dunes, turning left when signed at the end, then right into a housing estate. At the end bear right and climb to the cliffs. The Path skirts behind Rinsey Head, then through a car park and down to a restored engine house. It continues to Trewavas Head, inland of more restored engine houses. Beyond there have been numerous cliff falls – be sure to follow the signed Path. This then enters Porthleven on a lane – fork right entering the town to pass alongside the harbour to its head. Porthleven has all facilities.

OS Maps: Landranger 203; Explorer 103

	This Walk	Cumulative	This Walk	Cumulative	Grading	Timing
Ascent	781ft	55,511ft	238m	16,920m	Moderate	3 hours
Distance	5.2mi	292.3mi	8.4km	470.4km		

For detailed directions see our Walking Guide no. 33, Porthleven to Poldhu Cove.

This is a Section mostly of low cliffs with cliff-face paths, long stretches being above extensive beaches. It harbours a couple of unexpected features, firstly in the shape of Loe Bar, a large strip of shingle barring the freshwater Loe Pool from the sea, and secondly in the unusual position of Gunwalloe Church, hidden away in the corner of a sandy cove. Add a cliff-top monument to Marconi, a couple of picturesque coves, and the rocky and atmospheric harbour at Mullion Cove, and it makes for a fascinating length.

Directions

Porthleven and Mullion village, which is some 0.5 mile/1 kilometre from the Coast Path, are both served by regular but separate bus routes, which meet at Helston. The Mullion bus also serves Poldhu Cove, allowing various bus-walks.

Porthleven has all facilities. The Coast Path goes alongside the harbour towards the clock-tower at the end near the pier. Follow the road past this building, going right at the fork and keep on out of the town to a car park. Climb the steps and continue ahead on the track to Loe Bar. Cross the bar to the far side, forking right, downhill, shortly after the memorial. After passing a renovated fishery building, the Path arrives at Gunwalloe Fishing Cove. Go ahead onto the National Trust's Baulk Head, then above Halzephron Cove to a road. Bear right to a small car park then go right again, away from the road, on the cliffs down to Gunwalloe Church Cove. There are toilets and seasonal refreshments here. The picturesque church is tucked away at the right-hand end of the cove.

Skirt the beach to a road, then take the signed Path over a footbridge and over the rear of the beach to the Path rising away. Immediately after the car park at the top, turn right along the cliff top before returning to the road and dropping into Poldhu Cove, where there is a bus stop, toilets and refreshments. A good path leads inland to Mullion village.

Chough

OS Maps: Landranger 203; Explorer 103

	This Walk	Cumulative	This Walk	Cumulative	Grading	Timing
Ascent	1,631ft	57,142ft	497m	17,417m	Moderate	4 hours
Distance	8.2mi	300.5mi	13.2km	483.6km		

For detailed directions see our Walking Guide no. 34, Poldhu Cove to The Lizard.

This is an exposed Section of high, flat-topped cliffs and spectacular coves and bays. The coastal landscape is superb throughout, but punctuated by some real scenic gems, of which Kynance Cove is probably the pick. The combination of steep cliffs, unusual geology and flora, beautiful sea colours and long stretches of easy walking make this a rewarding length. And watch out for choughs, Cornwall's iconic bird now returned to re-colonise this coast.

Directions

A regular bus service links Mullion village with Lizard Town, each settlement about 0.5 mile/ 1 kilometre inland from its respective end, thus giving a possible bus-walk. In addition, there are many easy local circuits based on the Coast Path in the Lizard-Kynance area.

From the road at Poldhu turn right up the driveway signed to the Marconi Centre, leaving this after 110 yards/100 metres for a path on the right. This passes the Marconi monument on the cliffs, then drops down into Polurrian Cove. Climb away past the Polurrian Hotel, then right along the Path to the Mullion Cove Hotel. Keep seaward and drop down to the harbour, where there are seasonal refreshments. There are toilets 110 yards/100 metres up the road.

The Coast Path leaves the cove slightly inland to the right, up the hill just after the cafe. Climb to the cliffs, keeping to the right to hug the coastline. There is an information board on the unique flora and fauna of the area here.

The easy and clear Path rounds Parc Bean Cove and Lower Predannack Cliff. Approaching Vellan Head, be sure to keep close to the coast for the official route – the more obvious track misses the views. After the deep valley at Gew Graze, the Path rounds Rill Point and descends to Kynance Cove. The steep descent leads to the beach by the seasonal cafe. There are also toilets here. If the sun is shining, the sea is brilliant turquoise.

From the cafe, either follow the main track up towards the car park or cross the little beach (at low tide) and climb a partly stepped path to the cliffs, leaving this at a sign pointing right. This passes adjacent to the car park, where the main track arrives, and the Coast Path then continues clearly and easily above Pentreath Beach at Caerthillian and round Old Lizard Head, and on to Lizard Point, England's most southerly point, where there are cafes, gift shops and toilets. The nearby lighthouse is open to visitors at certain times. A path leads inland to Lizard Town, which has all facilities including regular bus services.

OS Maps: Landranger 203 (Lizard); Landranger 204 (remainder); Explorer 103

	This Walk	Cumulative	This Walk	Cumulative	Grading	Timing
Ascent	2,293ft	59,435ft	699m	18,116m	Moderate, strenuous in places	5.75 hours
Distance	10.4mi	310.9mi	16.7km	500.3km		

For detailed directions see our Walking Guide no. 35, The Lizard to Coverack.

This is a Section of cliffs and coves, punctuated by headlands giving excellent views along the coastline. Here and there are areas of sandy beach at the foot of the cliffs, but only at Kennack are they very extensive. This coast is largely sheltered from the worst of the prevailing south-westerly winds, and consequently has a lush, well-vegetated character. This being a relatively unfrequented stretch, substantial lengths are quiet and remote.

Directions

Lizard Town, about 0.5 mile/1 kilometre inland of the Coast Path, has a bus service which also passes a little inland of Cadgwith, about half-way along this length, which presents a bus-walk possibility. In addition, there are numerous easy circuits based on The Lizard using the Coast Path, which are popular and attractive.

Lizard Point has cafes and toilets, while Lizard Town, inland, has all necessary facilities. Lizard Point has the distinction of being England's most southerly point and is a fine location. The Coast Path leaves the Point alongside the car parking area and on in front of the lighthouse. There is a Heritage Centre at the lighthouse, and both lighthouse and Heritage Centre are open to the public at certain times (www.trinityhouse.co.uk). After passing the lighthouse descend to cross a footbridge then climb, passing in front of the Housel Bay Hotel and on past the Lloyds Signal Station, bearing right here. The route passes Bass Point National Coastwatch Institution lookout, the first in the country to be established. At Kilcobben Cove the Path goes behind The Lizard lifeboat station with its boathouse, which was completed in 2011. It then arrives at Church Cove. Go left for a short distance, then take the Path through the gate on the right. There are some ups and downs to a Path junction just after a stone stile at Polgwidden Cove; keep right here. A little further on, the Path skirts the dramatic collapsed cave of the Devil's Frying Pan. Follow the signed Path past the cottages and down into the picturesque little fishing hamlet of Cadgwith.

Cadgwith has a pub, shop, refreshments and toilets. There is a superb little beach here where the fishing boats are hauled up. This is overlooked by a convenient grassy knoll with seats known as The Todn (Cornish for lawn). Walk through Cadgwith and up the hill, turning right on the signed path a little way up. The Path then descends to Poltesco, crossing a footbridge. There is a diversion to the right leading to the attractive and interesting cove, complete with old serpentine works, where the local colourful rock was made into useful items. Climbing out of Poltesco, the Path then joins a road which leads to the beach at Kennack Sands. There are toilets here and seasonal refreshments.

Follow the Path behind the beaches and on to the cliffs to reach the neck of the long promontory of Carrick Lûz, the site of an Iron Age cliff fort. The Path cuts across the neck and then negotiates the steep valley at Downas Cove. Another, shallower valley crossing leads to the end of Black Head and its lookout hut. The Path now descends over the cliffs towards Chynhalls Point, going amongst the natural rock outcrops which can be slippery in wet weather. Beyond the Point the Path soon reaches Coverack.

An alternative inland path avoids the slippery Chynhalls Cliff. At the top of the Coast Path descent, the wide alternative path goes through gorse and passes a Sculpture Park, then the edge of a caravan park before arriving at a bungalow on a tarmac road. Turn right towards the hotel and then almost immediately bear left down a narrower path to rejoin the Coast Path, at Chynhalls Point.

Reaching the road at Coverack, the Path soon veers off right down some steps to arrive at a car park at the end of the village. Follow the road past the harbour. Coverack, a pretty place, has all facilities, including a regular bus service into Helston.

The lifeboat slipway at Church Cove

OS Maps: Landranger 204; Explorer 103

	This Walk	Cumulative	This Walk	Cumulative	Grading	Timing
Ascent	2,192ft	61,627ft	668m	18,784m	Moderate	5.75 hours
Distance	12.9mi	323.8mi	20.8km	521.1km		

For detailed directions see our Walking Guide no. 36, Coverack to Helford.

This is a sheltered Section of the Coast Path. It includes low cliffs facing away from the prevailing winds, but also lengths of pleasant rural field paths, a little inland, necessary to avoid inaccessible coastal working and former quarries. In addition, this Section has substantial lengths which fringe a tidal creek and wooded estuary-side paths passing pretty beaches where the Coast Path reaches the Helford River. While not as dramatic as some Sections, it is an attractive stretch with a quiet charm of its own.

Directions

Separate bus routes from Helston serve Coverack and Helford Passage, across the river via ferry (Good Friday or 1st April to October) from Helford, allowing a bus-walk based on Helston. There is an attractive local circuit using the Coast Path between Helford and Gillan Creek.

There are all necessary facilities at Coverack. The Coast Path follows the road away from the pub and past the harbour, continuing straight ahead on a narrow lane when the road goes left. Look out for the sign pointing right, just before the end of the lane. The Path goes over sometimes boggy ground next to the coast to arrive at Lowland Point. Next, the old workings at Dean Quarry are passed on their seaward side. The well-signed path then arrives at the open area at Godrevy Cove. The next length of coast is inaccessible due to operating quarries, so the Coast Path heads across the open area inland to pick up a signed path going uphill between fields. This leads to the little hamlet of Rosenithon. At the T-junction, turn right on the lane, uphill, turning left into a field just after the right-hand bend. Cross three fields in the same direction, stone stiles between them, to emerge on a lane. Go left then, at a junction, right, which leads to Porthoustock, a coastal hamlet with public toilets.

The route of the next stretch, to another coastal hamlet, Porthallow, is also a rural inland walk. It leaves Porthoustock past the telephone box and up the hill. Where the road bears right go straight ahead on a narrower lane. Go past a row of thatched cottages and over a little grassy bank at the end next to a greenhouse to a kissing-gate. Just past the gate there is a fork in the Path. Bear right and follow the Path climbing to the far top corner of the field to cross a lifting-bar stile and a Cornish stile (a sort of stone cattle grid) into another field. Turn right in this field alongside the hedge, then bear away left at the top to cross another Cornish stile to a road. At the road go left, passing through the tiny hamlet of Trenance. Here the route follows the road round to the right to a T-junction. At the junction go slightly right and immediately left onto an enclosed path, which leads to a track between buildings. At the road turn right to arrive at Porthallow.

Porthallow has a pub, toilets and seasonal refreshments. Look out for the marker indicating the half-way point of the Coast Path, equidistant (at 315 miles) from Minehead and Poole. Leave Porthallow along the back of the beach and up the steps. The Path now follows the coastline, keeping close to the edge round Nare Point and then past a couple of pretty beaches. Moving into the mouth of the Helford River, the Path continues alongside its tidal tributary, Gillan Creek. A tidal ferry crosses the creek.

Use the signal board to request the ferry. See page 22 for ferry details.

Otherwise (and for the official Coast Path route), take the lane left from the creekside up the hill to a sharp left-hand bend. Here go straight ahead along the field edge, then bear right over two further fields to a road. Turn right to Carne, at the head of the creek, then right again along the north side of the creek to St Anthony Church. Past the church turn left uphill, then shortly right on a farm track which leads into a field. Cross diagonally left to the top of the field to a kissing-gate.

For a short, direct route from here go through the gate and turn left. However, the Coast Path includes an optional extra of a circuit of Dennis Head. For this circuit do not pass through the gate but turn right, then almost immediately left over a stile. At the next junction continue straight ahead to reach the end of the headland. The Path circles around the headland, re-joining the outward route to the stile and then the kissing-gate.

Go through the gate and continue along the top of the field. The route now heads up the estuary side of the Helford River through woods and past coves. Towards the end the Path reaches a track – follow to the road and go right here then quickly left. The Path then emerges next to the main car park at Helford. Go down the hill into the village. Helford has a pub and shop and there are toilets at the car park.

Helford Estuary

OS Maps: Landranger 204; Explorer 103

	This Walk	Cumulative	This Walk	Cumulative	Grading	Timing
Ascent	1,397ft	63,024ft	426m	19,210m	Moderate	4.5 hours
Distance	10.3mi	334.1mi	16.6km	537.7km		

For detailed directions see our Walking Guide no. 37, Helford to Falmouth (Ferry).

There are two contrasting parts to this Section. Between Helford and Rosemullion Head, it is a sheltered walk alongside the mouth of the beautiful Helford River, with undulating, relatively low cliffs alternating with charming little beaches. Between Rosemullion Head and Falmouth, the walk flanks the sweep of Falmouth Bay, with rather larger coves overlooked by the great headland of Pendennis Point at the Falmouth end, crowned by its castle. Over the bay is St Anthony Head lighthouse. None of this is a lonely or remote walk, and the Falmouth end is decidedly urban, but it is never uninteresting and always very scenic.

Directions

Helford Passage and Falmouth are linked by a regular bus service, giving numerous bus-walk options. The short circular walk round Pendennis Head in Falmouth is a great local favourite.

Helford has pub, shop and toilets; Helford Passage, over the river, has a pub and seasonal refreshments. There is a seasonal ferry link. For ferry details see page 22.

Walk around Helford River

If the ferry is not operating, a 13 miles/21 kilometre walk around the Helford River is possible. This will add another day to the itinerary. For this route, from Helford take the Path up the hill to arrive at Penarvon Cove. Go round the back of the cove and turn inland up a track to a road. Turn right, then left on a track to the permissive path along the atmospheric Frenchman's Creek. At the end take the Path on the right signed to Withan, past Frenchman's Pill Cottage, crossing a footbridge. Follow the Path through the woods and aim for the far left corner of the field, taking the stile on the left. Follow the boundary on the left past Withan Farm, then head west over the fields to a lane. Here turn left to a crossroads, turning right here towards Mawgan. The lane joins a larger road; turn right past Gear then down and up into Mawgan-in-Meneage village. Turn right just after the church on the Path towards Gwarth-an-drea, then left behind a bungalow to a road. Turn right, and at the junction bear right and continue downhill to the bridge at Gweek. There is a shop and pub here. Take the road opposite the Gweek Inn, and at Tolvan Cross turn right along a bridleway to a road junction. Go straight ahead, towards Porth Navas. After crossing the stream, take the footpath on the left along the field edge to the road.

Follow the road ahead to Nancenoy and Polwheveral. At the crossroads after Polwheveral turn right, then after 140 yards/128 metres take the Path on the left along the field edge, then across the field corner to a road junction. Take the Porth Navas road opposite, through the village to Trenarth Bridge, then turn right towards Falmouth. At the junction at Trebah turn right, then right again into Bar Road. At the end turn left on a footpath which leads to the Helford River, turning left to the Ferryboat Inn at Helford Passage, the landing place for the ferry from Helford.

Ferry users start from here

Coast Path, Helford Passage - Falmouth

From the Ferryboat Inn, facing the pub, turn right along the river and up to a grassy hill. Keep on to a concrete track and follow this, passing behind Trebah Beach at Polgwidden Cove. Continue on the riverside then through woods to meet a track. Turn right to descend to the little village of Durgan. Go up the road, ignoring one path to the right, until the road turns left and the Path continues straight ahead. Follow this path, arriving at Porth Saxon Beach behind a building, and then through a field to Porthallack Beach. The Path then climbs round Toll Point to arrive at a wooded area. At the fork keep right and follow the Path onward to Rosemullion Head, leaving the Helford River behind.

Keep seaward round the headland, then descend to go through a small wood and then on, the Path becoming suburban now, to reach Maenporth where there are toilets and refreshments and a bus stop. Turn right behind the cafe and continue to Swanpool, with more toilets and refreshments and another bus stop. Take the Path from the far end of the beach to arrive at Gyllyngvase, then keep along Falmouth's promenade to the far end. The official Path goes around the magnificent Pendennis Point – keep to the seaward road all the way to the end, then at the car park descend on the signed Path up the river, parallel to the road above. The Path emerges from woods and passes the Leisure Centre, descending above the docks to a T-junction. Turn right then go ahead under the railway bridge, passing the Maritime Museum and along Falmouth's main shopping street to arrive at the Prince of Wales Pier at the far end. Falmouth, of course, has all facilities, including a rail link to the main line at Truro.

Pendennis Castle Falmouth

If you enjoy sleeping, eating or drinking at any business on the Path please suggest they join us as Business Members so that we can share their brilliance!

The businesses listed here are all supporters and members of the South West Coast Path Association. Please find more details on our website www.southwestcoastpath.org.uk

- **GR** Grid Reference
- **DP** Distance from the Path
- **N** Nearest Town/Village with facilities
- **3** Number Of Rooms
- Dogs Welcome
- Evening Meal Available
- Wifi
- Parking
- Grocery Shop On Site

Bed & Breakfast and Hotels

NAME	OTHER INFO	
White Horses B&B and APT Ramoth Way, Reen Sands, Perranporth, TR6 0BY 📞 01872 573425 ✉ whitehorses@talktalk.net 🌐 www.gocoastal.co.uk/det.asp?ch=1265	GR: SW762543 — DP: 0.2 miles N: **PERRANPORTH** Offers one night stays [2] [🚗] [📶]	Other info:
St George's Country House Hotel St George's Hill, Perranporth, TR6 0ED 📞 01872 572184 ✉ contact@stgeorgescountryhousehotel.com 🌐 www.stgeorgescountryhousehotel.com	GR: SW746533 — DP: 0.25 miles N: **PERRANPORTH** Offers one night stays [8] [🍽] [📶] [🚗]	Other info:
Cliff House B&B Cliff Terrace, Portreath, TR16 4LE 📞 01209 843847 ✉ cliffhousebookinginfo@gmail.com 🌐 www.cliffhouseportreath.co.uk	GR: SW656453 — DP: 0 miles N: **PORTREATH** Offers one night stays [5] [🐕] [📶] [🚗]	Other info: Vegetarian & Vegan option on request.
Portreath Arms The Square, Portreath, TR16 4LA 📞 01209 842259 ✉ email@theportreatharms.co.uk 🌐 www.theportreatharms.co.uk	GR: SW657453 — DP: 0 miles N: **PORTREATH** Offers one night stays [7] [🐕] [🍽] [📶] [🚗]	Other info:
Nanterrow Farm Gwithian, Hayle, TR27 5BP 📞 01209 712282 ✉ nanterrow@hotmail.com 🌐 www.nanterrowfarm.co.uk	GR: SW599412 — DP: 1.25 miles N: **GWITHIAN** Offers one night stays [2] [📶] [🚗]	Other info: Open Easter -End Oct
Sandbank House B&B 51 Upton Towans, Hayle, TR27 5BL 📞 01736 752820 ✉ info@sandbank-holidays.co.uk 🌐 www.sandbankhouse.co.uk	GR: SW582400 — DP: 2 miles N: **HAYLE** Offers one night stays [3] [📶] [🚗]	Other info:
Creekside B&B 34 Penpol Terrace, Hayle, TR27 4BQ 📞 01736 753969 ✉ valsherris@hotmail.com 🌐 www.southwestcoastpath.org.uk/creekside-bb-hayle	GR: SW558374 — DP: 0 miles N: **HAYLE** Offers one night stays [3] [📶]	Other info: Open all year
The Painters Cottage The Cottage Talland Road, St Ives, TR26 2DF 📞 01736 797626 ✉ madie28@btinternet.com 🌐 www.thepainterscottagestives.com	GR: SW518401 — DP: 0.25 miles N: **ST IVES** Offers one night stays [5] [🍽] [📶] [🚗]	Other info:

NAME	OTHER INFO		
Cohort Hostel The Stennack, St Ives, TR26 1FF ☎ 01736 791664 ✉ hello@stayatcohort.co.uk 🌐 www.stayatcohort.co.uk	GR: SW516403 DP: 0.5 miles N: **ST IVES** Offers one night stays [60] [📶] Other info:		
The Western Hotel Gabriel Street, St Ives, TR26 2LU ☎ 01736 795277 ✉ enquiries@hotelstives.com 🌐 www.hotelstives.com	GR: SW516403 DP: 0.5 miles N: **ST IVES** Offers one night stays [17] [🛒] [📶] Other info: Luggage transfer available. Please enquire.		
Boswednack Manor B&B Zennor, St Ives, TR26 3DD ☎ 01736 794183 ✉ boswednack@btinternet.com 🌐 www.boswednackmanor.co.uk	GR: SW443378 DP: 0.5 miles N: **ZENNOR** Offers one night stays [5] [📶] [🚗] Other info: Evening food at Zennor and Treen pubs.		
The Gurnard's Head Zennor, St Ives, TR26 3DE ☎ 01736 796928 ✉ enquiries@gurnardshead.co.uk 🌐 www.gurnardshead.co.uk	GR: SW435377 DP: 1 mile N: **ZENNOR** Offers one night stays [7] [🐕] [🍴] [📶] [🚗] Other info: Open all year except Christmas.		
St Johns House B&B Boscaswell Downs, Pendeen, Penzance, TR19 7DW ☎ 01736 786605 ✉ moriakeogh@btinternet.com 🌐 www.stjohnshousebedandbreakfast.co.uk	GR: SW384344 DP: 1 mile N: **PENDEEN** Offers one night stays [3] [📶] Other info:		
The Old Post House B&B 24 Bosorne Road, St Just, TR19 7LU ☎ 07931 139603 ✉ moylefiona@gmail.com 🌐 www.theoldposthousebandb.co.uk	GR: SW368312 DP: 0.4 miles N: **ST JUST** Offers one night stays [3] [📶] Other info: Yoga Room available. Close to pubs, hotel, cafes & grocery stores.		
Bosavern House St Just, TR19 7RD ☎ 01736 788301 ✉ info@bosavern.com 🌐 www.bosavern.com	GR: SW370304 DP: 0.5 miles N: **ST JUST** Offers one night stays [8] [🐕] [📶] [🚗] Other info: Walking holiday packages available, free drop off/collection service.		
Sennen Rise Mayon Farm, Sennen, TR19 7AD ☎ 01736 871376 ✉ info@sennenrise.co.uk 🌐 www.sennenrise.co.uk/our-house	GR: SW357256 DP: 0.5 miles N: **SENNEN COVE** Offers one night stays [4] [🍴] [📶] [🚗] Other info:		
Sea View House The Valley, Porthcurno, Penzance, TR19 6JX ☎ 01736 810638 ✉ paulinewillows@hotmail.co.uk 🌐 www.seaviewhouseporthcurno.com	GR: SW382228 DP: 0 miles N: **PORTHCURNO** Offers one night stays [7] [📶] [🚗] Other info: Open Jan-Nov.		
Lamorna Pottery B&B Lamorna, Penzance, TR19 6NY ☎ 01736 810330 ✉ potterylamorna@gmail.com 🌐 www.lamornapottery.co.uk	GR: SW441257 DP: 1.25 miles N: **LAMORNA COVE** Offers one night stays [2] [🐕] [🍴] [📶] [🚗] Other info: Evening meals, for your room, can be requested from our Cafe before 5pm.		

NAME	OTHER INFO	
Castallack Farm Lamorna, Penzance, TR19 6NL 📞 01736 731969 ✉ info@castallackfarm.co.uk 🌐 www.castallackfarm.co.uk	GR: SW453253 DP: 1 miles N: **LAMORNA COVE** Offers one night stays [2] 🐾 🍴 📶 🚗	Other info:
Glencree House 2 Mennaye Road, Penzance, TR18 4NG 📞 01736 362026 ✉ stay@glencreehouse.co.uk 🌐 www.glencreehouse.co.uk	GR: SW469297 DP: 0.5 miles N: **PENZANCE** [7] 📶	Other info:
Keigwin House Alexandra Road, Penzance, TR18 4LZ 📞 01736 363930/07557 057773 ✉ fran@keigwinhouse.co.uk 🌐 www.keigwinhouse.co.uk	GR: SW466299 DP: 0.25 miles N: **PENZANCE** Offers one night stays [9] 📶 🚗	Other info: Packed lunches available by prior arrangement
The Tremont Hotel Alexandra Road, Penzance, TR18 4LZ 📞 01736 362614 ✉ info@tremonthotel.co.uk 🌐 www.tremonthotel.co.uk	GR: SW466299 DP: 0.5 miles N: **PENZANCE** Offers one night stays [10] 📶	Other info:
Number Nine B&B 9 Regent Square, Penzance, TR18 4BG 📞 01736 369715 / 07855427764 ✉ janeclayton27@gmail.com 🌐 www.numberninepenzance.jimdo.com	GR: SW473299 DP: 0.25 miles N: **PENZANCE** Offers one night stays [2] 📶	Other info: Complimentary cream tea on arrival
Honeydew Guesthouse 3 Leskinnick Street, Penzance, TR18 2HA 📞 01736 364206 ✉ info@honeydewguesthouse.co.uk 🌐 www.penzance-bed-breakfast.co.uk	GR: SW475306 DP: 0.2 miles N: **PENZANCE** Offers one night stays [4] 🐾 🚗	Other info: Open all year.
Mount View Hotel Longrock, Penzance, TR20 8JJ 📞 01736 710416 ✉ mountviewhotel@hotmail.co.uk 🌐 www.mountviewhotelcornwall.com	GR: SW499313 DP: 0 miles N: **PENZANCE** Offers one night stays [5] 🐾 🍴 📶 🚗	Other info: Full Board deals are available.
Mount Haven Turnpike Road, Marazion, TR17 0DQ 📞 01736 719937 ✉ reception@mounthaven.co.uk 🌐 www.mounthaven.co.uk	GR: SW527306 DP: 0.1 miles N: **MARAZION** Offers one night stays [19] 🐾 🍴 📶 🚗	Other info: Open all year
Mzmia Penlee Close, Praa Sands, Penzance, TR20 9SR 📞 01736 763856 ✉ marianfoy@hotmail.com 🌐 www.southwestcoastpath.org.uk/mzima-praa-sands	GR: SW581287 DP: 0.5 miles N: **PRAA SANDS** Offers one night stays [2] 📶 🚗	Other info:
Wellmore End Cottage Methleigh Bottoms, Porthleven, TR13 9JP 📞 01326 569310 ✉ wellmoreend-bandb@tiscali.co.uk 🌐 www.wellmoreend.com	GR: SW627259 DP: 0.2 miles N: **PORTHLEVEN** Offers one night stays [2] 📶 🚗	Other info: Grocery shop, pubs, eateries&bakery 2 minutes away.

NAME	OTHER INFO	
PJ's Bed & Breakfast Mullyon Cottages, 13 The Crescent, Porthleven, TR13 9LU 📞 01326 722907 📧 info@pjsbedandbreakfast.co.uk 🌐 www.pjsbedandbreakfast.co.uk	GR: SW629262 DP: 0.25 miles N: **PORTHLEVEN** **2** 🐕 🛜 🚗 **Other info:** We arrange transport around the Lizard for walkers staying up to 4 nights.	
The Old Vicarage, Mullion Nansmellyon Road, Mullion, TR12 7DQ 📞 01326 240898 📧 bandbmullion@hotmail.com 🌐 www.facebook.com/TheOldVicarageHolidayAccomodation	GR: SW677189 DP: 0.5 miles N: **MULLION COVE** Offers one night stays **4** 🛜 🚗 **Other info:** Family rooms available.	
Polurrian on the Lizard Polurrian Road, Mullion, TR12 7EN 📞 01326 240421 📧 info@polurrianhotel.com 🌐 www.polurrianhotel.com	GR: SW670186 DP: 0.5 miles N: **MULLION COVE** Offers one night stays **41** 🐕 🍴 🛜 🚗 **Other info:** Open all year	
Mullion Cove Hotel Mullion, Helston, TR12 7EP 📞 01326 240328 📧 sarah@mullion-cove.co.uk 🌐 www.mullion-cove.co.uk	GR: SW667180 DP: 0 miles N: **MULLION COVE** Offers one night stays **30** 🐕 🍴 🛜 🚗 **Other info:**	
Penmenner House Bed & Breakfast Penmenner Road, The Lizard, TR12 7NR 📞 01326 290315 📧 sgnegus@btinternet.com 🌐 www.penmenner-house.co.uk	GR: SW701120 DP: 0.3 miles N: **LIZARD** Offers one night stays **4** 🛜 🚗 **Other info:** Open March - November	
Haelarcher Farmhouse Penmenner Road, The Lizard, Helston, TR12 7NN 📞 01326 291188 📧 info@haelarcher.co.uk 🌐 www.haelarcher.co.uk	GR: SW701123 DP: 0.5 miles N: **LIZARD** Offers one night stays **5** 🐕 🛜 🚗 **Other info:**	
The Top House Inn The Lizard, Helston, TR12 7NQ 📞 01326 290974 📧 mail@thetophouselizard.co.uk 🌐 www.thetophouselizard.co.uk	GR: SW702125 DP: 0.3 miles N: **LIZARD** Offers one night stays **8** 🛜 🚗 **Other info:** Dogs in the pub not rooms	
Housel Bay Hotel The Lizard, Helston, TR12 7PG 📞 01326 567500 📧 stay@houselbay.com 🌐 www.houselbay.com	GR: SW708121 DP: 0 miles N: **LIZARD** Offers one night stays **20** 🐕 🍴 🛜 🚗 **Other info:**	
Chyheira B&B Grade Ruan, Helston, TR12 7LQ 📞 01326 290343 📧 info@chyheira.co.uk 🌐 www.chyheira.co.uk	GR: SW709143 DP: 0.5 miles N: **CADGWITH** Offers one night stays **2** 🐕 🛜 🚗 **Other info:** Around 15 mins walk to pub. 2 rooms ensuite.	
Penmarth House Coverack, TR12 6TQ 📞 01326 280240 / 07779 221951 📧 enquiries@coverack-bandb.co.uk 🌐 www.coverack-bandb.co.uk	GR: SW780185 DP: 0.15 miles N: **COVERACK** Offers one night stays **3** 🛜 🚗 **Other info:** All bedrooms have ensuite.	

NAME	OTHER INFO	
The Five Pilchards Inn Porthallow, TR12 6PP ☎ 01326 280256 ✉ fivepilchards@btinternet.com 🌐 www.thefivepilchards.co.uk	GR: SW797231 — DP: 0.12 miles N: **PORTHALLOW** Offers one night stays [4] [🍴] [📶] [🚗]	Other info: Pack lunches available
The Sail Loft B&B Point, Helford, Nr Helston, TR12 6JY ☎ 01326 231083 ✉ pamroyall@btinternet.com 🌐 www.southwestcoastpath.org.uk/sail-loft-point-helford	GR: SW758263 — DP: 0 miles N: **HELFORD** Offers one night stays [1] [📶] [🚗]	Other info:
Trevarn B&B Carninion Road, Mawnan Smith, Falmouth, TR11 5JD ☎ 01326 251245 ✉ enquiries@trevarn.co.uk 🌐 www.trevarn.co.uk	GR: SW779284 — DP: 0.75 miles N: **MAWNAN SMITH** Offers one night stays [3] [📶] [🚗]	Other info:

Campsites and Holiday Parks

NAME	OTHER INFO	
Newperran Holiday Park Hendra Croft, Newquay, TR8 5QJ ☎ 0333 370 0555 ✉ newperran@ariaresorts.co.uk 🌐 www.ariaresorts.co.uk/newperran	GR: SW794546 — DP: 0 miles N: **PERRANPORTH** [150] [🐕] [🍴] [📶]	Other info:
Perran View Holiday Park Trevellas, St Agnes, TR5 0XH ☎ 01872 552 623 🌐 www.johnfowlerholidays.com/cornwall-holiday-park/ perran-view-holiday-park	GR: SW738515 — DP: 1 mile N: **ST AGNES** [113] [🐕] [🍴] [🛒] [📶]	Other info: Choice of 2&3 bedroom houses & bungalows. Open Mar-Nov.
Presingoll Farm Caravan & Camping Site Penwinnick Road, St Agnes, TR5 0PB ☎ 01872 552333 ✉ pam@presingollfarm.co.uk 🌐 www.presingollfarm.co.uk	GR: SW722493 — DP: 1.5 miles N: **ST AGNES** [🐕] [🚗]	Other info:
Tolroy Manor Holiday Park Tolroy Road, Hayle, TR27 6HG ☎ 01736 753 082 🌐 www.johnfowlerholidays.com/cornwall-holiday-park/ tolroy-manor-holiday-park	GR: SW565358 — DP: 1 miles N: **HAYLE** [202] [🐕] [🍴] [🛒] [📶] [🚗]	Other info: Wide range of accommodation including Tudor style houses and bungalows.
St Ives Holiday Village Lelant, St Ives, TR26 3HX ☎ 01736 752000 🌐 www.johnfowlerholidays.com/cornwall-holiday-park/st- ives-holiday-village	GR: SW527362 — DP: 3 miles N: **CARBIS BAY** [292] [🐕] [🍴] [🛒] [📶] [🚗]	Other info: Luxury lodges set in 100 acres of woodland.
Ayr Holiday Park Alexandra Road, St Ives, TR26 1EJ ☎ 01736 795855 ✉ recept@ayrholidaypark.co.uk 🌐 www.ayrholidaypark.co.uk	GR: SW510405 — DP: 0.5 miles N: **ST IVES** Offers one night stays [🐕] [📶] [🚗]	Other info:

NAME	OTHER INFO	
Trevaylor Camp Site Botallack, St Just, TR19 7PU 01736 787016 trevaylor@cornishcamping.co.uk www.cornishcamping.co.uk	GR: SW369324	DP: 0.3 miles
	N: **ST JUST**	
	Offers one night stays	
		Other info: Open March - January
Teneriffe Farm Campsite Predannack, Mullion, Helston, TR12 7EZ 01326 240293 TeneriffeFarmCampsite@nationaltrust.org.uk www.nationaltrust.org.uk/holidays/teneriffe-farm-campsite	GR: SW672167	DP: 1 mile
	N: **MULLION**	
		Other info: 20 pitches
Little Trevothan Holiday Park Coverack, TR12 6SD 01326 280260 holidays@littletrevothan.co.uk www.littletrevothan.co.uk	GR: SW770178	DP: 0.5 miles
	N: **COVERACK**	
	Offers one night stays	
		Other info:

Self Catering

NAME	OTHER INFO	
Rosehill Lodges Rosehill, Porthtowan, TR4 8AR 01209 891920 reception@rosehilllodges.com www.rosehilllodges.com	GR: SW693473	DP: 0.3 miles
	N: **PORTHTOWAN**	
		Other info: 10 luxury lodges with private hot tubs.
Sandbank Holidays 51 Upton Towans, Hayle, TR27 5BL 01736 752594 info@sandbank-holidays.co.uk www.sandbank-holidays.co.uk	GR: SW582400	DP: 2 miles
	N: **HAYLE**	
		Other info:
St Ives Holidays 9 High Street, St Ives, TR26 1RS 01736 794686 mail@stivesholidays.com www.stivesholidays.com	GR: SW517404	DP: 0 miles
	N: **ST IVES**	
		Other info:
Bosigran Cottage Penzance, TR20 8YX 0345 800 2070 cottages@nationaltrust.org.uk www.nationaltrust.org.uk/holidays/bosigran-cottage-cornwall	GR: SW426369	DP: 0 miles
	N: **PENDEEN**	
		Other info:
Land's End Hostel, Trevescan Mill Barn, Trevescan, Sennen, Penzance, TR19 7AQ 07585 625774 lou@landsendholidays.co.uk www.landsendholidays.co.uk	GR: SW355248	DP: 0.7 miles
	N: **LANDS END**	
	Offers one night stays	
		Other info: Need to book continental breakfast in advance. Dogs on request.
The Studio 3 Coastguard Cottages, Treen, Porthcurno, St Levan, TR19 6LQ 01736 810504 jeffrey_hardman@sky.com www.sennencornwall.com	GR: SW392232	DP: 0.1 miles
	N: **PORTHCURNO**	
	Offers one night stays	
		Other info: Sleeps 4 in the family room. Double bed and 2 "Put me Ups."

NAME	OTHER INFO	
Logan Rock Holidays Glencoe Farm, Treen, Penzance, TR19 6LG 01736 810340 nmzgibbs@gmail.com www.loganrockholidays.com/self-catering/little-barn-kiji	GR: SW393230 DP: 0.25 miles N: **PORTHCURNO** Offers one night stays [1] 📶 🚗	Other info:
Porthgwarra Holiday Cottages Estate Office, Kings Road, Marazion, TR17 0EL 01736 888515 info@staubynestatescottages.co.uk www.staubynestatescottages.co.uk	GR: SW371217 DP: 0.1 miles N: **MARAZION** 🐕 📶 🚗	Other info:
Penrose Bunkhouse Helston, TR12 7PY 0344 335 1296 bunkhouses@nationaltrust.org.uk www.nationaltrust.org.uk/holidays/penrose-bunkhouse-cornwall	GR: SW653234 DP: 0 miles N: **HELSTON** [2] 🐕 📶 🚗	Other info: Sleeps 16.
Berepper Barns Berepper Farm, Gunwalloe, Helston, TR12 7PZ 07443522064 berepperbarns@gmail.com www.berepperbarns.co.uk	GR: SW656228 DP: 0.25 miles N: **HELSTON** [1] 🐕 📶 🚗	Other info: Minimum stay 2 nights. A pub with great food is a 5 min walk.
Trenance Farm Cottages Mullion, Helston, TR12 7HB 01326 240639 info@trenancefarmholidays.co.uk www.trenancefarmcottages.co.uk	GR: SW672184 DP: 0.5 miles N: **MULLION COVE** [26] 🐕 📶 🚗	Other info: Open all Year, short break available
Wireless Cottage Housel Bay, Lizard, Helston, TR12 7AP 0345 800 2070 cottages@nationaltrust.org.uk www.nationaltrust.org.uk/holidays/wireless-cottage-cornwall	GR: SW714119 DP: 0 miles N: **THE LIZARD** [1] 🐕 📶 🚗	Other info: Parking nearby - Meals on arrival by prior notice.
Townplace Helston, TR12 7LA 0345 800 2070 cottages@nationaltrust.org.uk www.nationaltrust.org.uk/holidays/townplace-cornwall	GR: SW720144 DP: 0 miles N: **CADGWITH** [1] 🚗	Other info:
Silversands Holiday Park Gwendreath, Ruan Minor, Lizard, TR12 7LZ 01326 290631 info@silversandsholidaypark.co.uk www.silversandsholidaypark.co.uk	GR: SW729169 DP: 0.62 miles N: **CADGWITH** [15] 🐕 📶 🚗	Other info:
Wych Elm Glamping Ponsongath, Coverack, TR12 6SQ 07887 298314 wychelmyurts@gmail.com www.wychelmyurts.co.uk	GR: SW756179 DP: 0.4 miles N: **COVERACK** Offers one night stays [5] 🐕 🚗	Other info:
Cedarwood Holidays Tregellast Barton, St Keverne, TR12 6NX 07375 509966 kirstie@cedarwoodholidays.co.uk www.cedarwoodholidays.co.uk	GR: SW794207 DP: 1 mile N: **ST KEVERNE** Offers one night stays [1] 🚗	Other info: Cabin with ensuite, heating & kitchenette. Close to pubs & village store.

NAME	OTHER INFO		
Powders Helston, TR12 6JZ ☏ 0345 800 2070 ✉ cottages@nationaltrust.org.uk ⊕ www.nationaltrust.org.uk/holidays/powders-cornwall	GR: SW754262 DP: 0 miles N: **HELFORD** 2 🐕 📶 Other info:		
Falmouth Lodge Backpackers 9 Gyllyngvase Terrace, Falmouth, TR11 4DL ☏ 01326 319996 / 07525 722808 ✉ judi@falmouthlodge.co.uk ⊕ www.falmouthbackpackers.co.uk	GR: SW810318 DP: 0.1 miles N: **FALMOUTH** Offers one night stays 6 📶 Other info: Small dorms plus twin/doube rooms available; 5 mins from railway sation.		

Eat and Drink

NAME	OTHER INFO		
Bowgie Inn Ltd West Pentire, Crantock, Newquay, TR8 5SE ☏ 01637 830363 ✉ enquiries@bowgie.com ⊕ www.bowgie.com	GR: SW776606 DP: 0 miles N: **CRANTOCK** 🍴 🚗 Other info: Open from 11am till late all year.		
Tideline Cafe 2 The Square, Portreath, Redruth, TR16 4LA ☏ 01209 844882 ✉ hello@tidelinecafe.com ⊕ www.facebook.com/tidelinecafe	GR: SW657453 DP: 0.5 miles N: **PORTREATH** 🐕 📶 Other info:		
The Hoxton Special Cafe The Former Life Guard Hut, Beach Road, Marazion, TR17 0EW ☏ 07572432402 ✉ info@thehoxtonspecial.com ⊕ www.thehoxtonspecial.com	GR: SW504312 DP: 0 miles N: **MARAZION** 🐕 📶 Other info: 10am - 8pm summer all week 10am - 5 pm winter wed -sun.		
Godolphin Arms West End, Marazion, TR17 0EN ☏ 01736 888510 ✉ enquiries@godolphinarms.co.uk ⊕ www.godolphinarms.co.uk	GR: SW517305 DP: 0.1 miles N: **MARAZION** 10 🐕 🍴 📶 🚗 Other info: Open all year.		
Glenbervie Bar at the Mullion Cove Hotel Mullion, Helston, TR12 7EP ☏ 01326 240328 ✉ enquiries@mullion-cove.co.uk ⊕ www.mullion-cove.co.uk	GR: SW667180 DP: 0 miles N: **MULLION** 🐕 🍴 📶 🚗 Other info: All day menu.		
Housel Bay Hotel and Restaurant The Lizard, Helston, TR12 7PG ☏ 01326 567500 ✉ eat@houselbay.com ⊕ www.houselbay.com	GR: SW708121 DP: 0 miles N: **LIZARD** 🐕 🍴 📶 🚗 Other info: Open all year		

Getting Around

NAME	OTHER INFO	
St Agnes Taxis China Palace Peterville, St Agnes, TR5 0QU 📞 01872 553795 ✉ stagnestaxis@gmail.com 🌐 www.stagnestaxis.com	GR: SW723506　DP: 0 miles N: **ST AGNES**	
		Other info:
Meneage Taxis 10 Cunnack Close, Helston, TR13 8XQ 📞 01326 560530 ✉ meneagetaxis@yahoo.com 🌐 www.meneagetaxis.co.uk	GR: SW663281　DP: 0 miles N: **HELSTON**	
	Other info: Luggage transfers and one way taxi trips welcomed.	
Telstar Taxi & Private Hire Telstar House, Goonhilly Downs, Helston, TR12 6LQ 📞 01326 221007 ✉ traveltelstar@yahoo.com 🌐 www.telstartravel.co.uk	GR:　DP: N: **HELSTON**	
	Other info:	

Activities

NAME	OTHER INFO	
Nomadic Camping Cornwall Sanderling, 92 Alexandra Road, Illogan, Redruth, TR16 4EN 📞 01209 311332 ✉ info@nomadiccampingcornwall.co.uk 🌐 www.nomadiccampingcornwall.co.uk	GR: SW662437　DP: 0 miles N: **PORTREATH**	
	Other info:	
Explore In Cornwall Treassowe Barton, Ludgvan, Penzance, TR20 8XQ 📞 01736 740234 ✉ info@exploreincornwall.co.uk 🌐 www.exploreincornwall.co.uk	GR: SW497337　DP: 1 mile N: **MARAZION**	
	Other info: Open all year	
Western Discoveries Walking Holidays Chynoey, Newmill, Penzance, TR20 8XW 📞 01736 362763 ✉ info@westcornwallwalks.co.uk 🌐 www.westcornwallwalks.co.uk	GR: SW456341　DP: 0 miles N: **PENZANCE**	
	Other info:	
The Hoxton Special Watersports The Former Life Guard Hut, Beach Road, Marazian, TR17 0EW 📞 07572 432402 ✉ info@thehoxtonspecial.com 🌐 www.thehoxtonspecial.com	GR: SW504312　DP: 0 miles N: **MARAZION**	
	Other info: 10 am - 8 pm Summer all week 10 am - 5 pm Winter weds - sun.	
St Michael's Mount Marazion, TR17 0EL 📞 01736 710265 ✉ enquiries@stmichaelsmount.co.uk 🌐 www.stmichaelsmount.co.uk	GR: SW514300　DP: 0.1 mile N: **MARAZION**	
	Other info:	
Trebah Gardens Mawnan Smith, Falmouth, TR11 5JZ 📞 01326 252200 ✉ mail@trebah-garden.co.uk 🌐 www.trebahgarden.co.uk	GR: SW768276　DP: 0.1 mile N: **FALMOUTH**	
	Other info: A world renowned garden minutes from the coast path with cafe facilities.	

St Michaels Mount

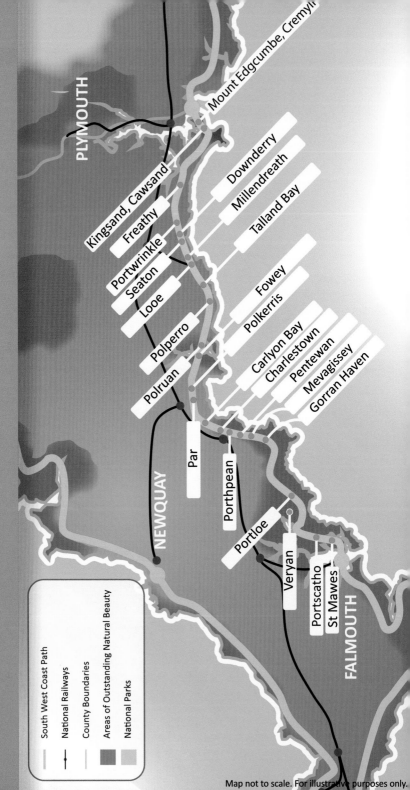

PLYMOUTH

Mount Edgcumbe, Cremyll

Kingsand, Cawsand

Freathy

Downderry

Millendreath

Talland Bay

Portwrinkle

Seaton

Looe

Fowey

Polkerris

Polperro

Carlyon Bay

Charlestown

Pentewan

Mevagissey

Gorran Haven

Polruan

NEWQUAY

Par

Porthpean

Portloe

Veryan

Portscatho

St Mawes

FALMOUTH

South West Coast Path

National Railways

County Boundaries

Areas of Outstanding Natural Beauty

National Parks

122

South Cornwall
Falmouth to the River Tamar

(Sections 38-46)

The South Cornwall stretch of coast is relatively sheltered, being either south-east or south-facing with much of it in the lee of the large peninsula of the Lizard. Cliffs of moderate height are found along most of the length, and there are numerous intimate little bays and some quite prominent headlands. In the west the main feature is the superb estuary of the River Fal. Also known as Carrick Roads, this forms one of the largest natural harbours in the world. Walkers will need to take two ferries to cross this superb estuary, which contains the maritime centre of Falmouth. St Austell Bay comprises the central part of this length, the only stretch that lacks the otherwise ubiquitous cliffs. The bay also has the only major length of coastal development on the south coast of Cornwall, based around the town of St Austell. It includes the wonderfully preserved Georgian port of Charlestown, as well as the picturesque traditional fishing town of Mevagissey. To the east, there are attractive estuaries at Fowey and Looe, drowned mouths of river valleys. The great sweep of Whitsand Bay, again backed by cliffs, then leads to the mouth of Plymouth Sound.

All of the locations on the map illustration to the left, have at least 1 facility including toilets, a cafe/restaurant, shop or pub.

Path to Polperro

OS Maps: Landranger 204; Explorer 105

	This Walk	Cumulative	This Walk	Cumulative	Grading	Timing
Ascent	974ft	63,998ft	297m	19,507m	Easy	2.75 hours
Distance	6.2mi	340.3mi	10.0km	547.7km		

For detailed directions see our Walking Guide no. 38, St Mawes (Ferry) to Portscatho.

This Section includes a trip on the ferry across the mouth of the River Fal, a treat of scenery and interest in its own right. Beyond, the walk round St Anthony Head is one of superb estuarine and coastal views, followed by an easy but charming Path on low cliffs, sheltered from the westerlies, while passing some fine sandy beaches and giving excellent views up the South Cornwall coast.

Directions

A regular bus route serves Portscatho and St Mawes from Truro, which is also linked to Falmouth by bus and train. There is also a very popular circular walk using the Coast Path in the St Anthony Head area and another from Portscatho.

Two ferries are required to cross between Falmouth and the Coast Path at Place, east of the large estuary. The first goes between Falmouth and St Mawes, across the mouth of the main Fal Estuary, sometimes referred to as Carrick Roads. The ferry operates all year from Prince of Wales Pier (year round) and Custom House Quay (summer only). For ferry details see page 22.

The second leg of the crossing is the ferry between St Mawes and Place, crossing the mouth of the Fal's tributary, the Percuil River. For ferry details see page 23. In winter an alternative may be offered by a water taxi service. See page 22 for details..

There is also Falmouth Water Taxi service which operates between Falmouth and St Mawes or Place, weather permitting. If needed, it is advisable to telephone 2-3 days in advance in the summer. See page 22 for further details.

Information is also available from the Fal River Visitor Information Centre at Prince of Wales Pier, or visit www.falriver.co.uk

If arriving at St Mawes and wishing to proceed to Place when the Place ferry is not operating it is possible to take the regular bus service from St Mawes to Gerrans, walking from here to Place (2.5 miles/4 kilometres). For this option, go to Gerrans Church and pick up the walking route described below. Local taxi firms will carry walkers around the peninsula.

Walk between St Mawes and Place

A walking route also exists between St Mawes and Place, via Gerrans. This adds 9 miles/14 kilometres to the overall route, effectively an extra day to the itinerary. Leaving the ferry point in St Mawes, turn left along the road. Approaching the castle, take the minor lane left, which leads to a footpath at the end. This becomes a scenic path alongside the Carrick Roads – the Fal Estuary. At the minor road go right then bear left in front of the boatyard and then on a bank above the shore. This leads to the churchyard of St Just in Roseland, a beautiful spot. Pass the church and keep to the Path next to the shore. Follow the Path as it bears right up the hill, signed St Just Lane, to emerge on a road. Turn left, ignoring the first footpath on the right, but take the second a little afterwards. Follow the Path alongside field boundaries, first to the right, then to the left, then to the right again. Go down to the road at the end of the fourth field and turn right to the A3078 at Trethem Mill. Turn left and immediately right after the bridge up some steps and through a small wood. Out of the wood, cross the field diagonally right (bearing 110°) then in the next field bear diagonally right again (bearing 140°), leaving it by a wooded track. Cross the stile at the top and bear diagonally right again (bearing 137°) to meet a hedge, which is followed to a road. Turn right on the road. At the next junction follow the road curving to the right past Polhendra Cottage then turn left through the second gate. Descend towards the bottom of the hedge visible on the opposite side of the valley (bearing 123°). Cross the bridge and climb as close as possible with the hedge to the left. Cross the stone steps behind the gorse at the top and bear slightly left across the next two fields (bearing 125°) to emerge on a road. Turn right to arrive at Gerrans Church. (Those who have taken the bus from St Mawes will join here – see above.)

At the church fork left into Treloan Lane, keeping ahead past the buildings. Go through the gate at the end of the lane, crossing an open field ahead into another enclosed track, which leads to Porth Farm. At the road turn right then go left at the sign indicating "Footpath to Place by Percuil River". Follow this very scenic path which leads to the ferry landing point then on to Place itself.

Coast Path, Place - Portscatho

At Place, walk up the lane past the gates to the grand house. Turn right into the churchyard of St Anthony Church, passing behind the church and up into a wooded area. Turn right at the track then at the creek look for the sign on the left taking the Path alongside the plantation. The Path now gives superb views over Carrick Roads to Falmouth. Approaching St Anthony Head keep to the Coast Path to the right until passing through the gate towards the lighthouse. Just after the gate climb the steps to the left to the car parking area. There are also toilets here. Leave the car park next to the coast and the superb and easy Path then leads to Portscatho, which has a shop, toilets and pubs, as well as a bus service to St Mawes and Truro.

OS Maps: Landranger 204: Explorer 105

	This Walk	Cumulative	This Walk	Cumulative	Grading	Timing
Ascent	1,674ft	65,672ft	510m	20,017m	Strenuous	3.75 hours
Distance	7.4mi	347.7mi	11.9km	559.6km		

For detailed directions see our Walking Guide no. 39, Portscatho to Portloe.

This is a very quiet Section for the most part. Cliffs are relatively low at first, but increase in height as the great promontory of Nare Head, with its superb views, is approached. The long sandy beaches below the cliffs passed west of Nare Head are replaced by tiny isolated and inaccessible coves east of the headland. This length has a wonderfully remote atmosphere.

Directions

Portscatho and Portloe are both served by regular, but different, bus services, both linking with Truro. There are some local circular walks using the Coast Path around Nare Head, based on the inland village of Veryan.

Portscatho has a shop, pubs, toilets and bus service. The Coast Path leaves past the Harbour Club; keep right just after leaving the village at the footpath junction. The Path goes round the back of Porthcurnick Beach, then up the road on the far side, turning right along the coastal edge. The Path continues to undulate along the coast until it turns inland to reach a road. Turn right, past Pendower Court and down the road to its end at Pendower Beach. Cross the rear of the beach and head for the public toilets, going up the hill and turning right. The Path soon diverts around the rear of the Nare Hotel to a road, descending to Carne Beach. Follow the road round the bend and up the hill for a short way, turning right to return to the cliffs. The Path now heads for Nare Head, via a steep descent and ascent at Tregagle's Hole and past an old fisherman's cottage. A short diversion at the top of Nare Head reveals some stunning coastal views.

The Path now goes round the seaward edge of Rosen Cliff and over the valley behind Kiberick Cove to Blouth Point. At this point enter a field and keep left for a short way before bearing right, downhill, towards some trees. The Path zigzags upward to pass Broom Parc and then goes through a field to round Manare Point. After this it is downhill going over a short uneven section before joining a tarmac path which descends into Portloe. The village is very picturesque and has pubs and toilets as well as a bus service.

Portloe

OS Maps: Landranger 204; Explorer 105

	This Walk	Cumulative	This Walk	Cumulative	Grading	Timing
Ascent	2,841ft	68,513ft	866m	20,883m	Strenuous then easy	5.75 hours
Distance	12.2mi	359.9mi	19.6km	579.2km		

For detailed directions see our Walking Guide no. 40, Portloe to Mevagissey.

This is a quiet Section of mostly high cliffs, often covered in lush vegetation. Towards Gorran Haven these cliffs reduce in height. The section includes the great headland of Dodman Point, from where there are views to the Lizard in one direction and Devon in the other on a clear day. Below the cliffs are some sandy beaches, often all but inaccessible. This is a coastline for those preferring remoteness.

Directions

There are some excellent circular walks using the Coast Path at Dodman Point and linking to Gorran Haven, giving a variety of options here.

The scenic little harbour village of Portloe has toilets, pubs and a bus service. The Coast Path leaves behind the Lugger Hotel, leaving the road to reach a prominent converted chapel. Pass this then climb steeply to the cliffs. After a quite strenuous length the Path arrives at West Portholland. Follow the road above the shore to a junction, then turn right to East Portholland. There are toilets here and a seasonal cafe and shop. Pass the cottages at the far end and climb behind them on a clear path to a field, turning right down the field edge. The Path leads to a road which descends to Porthluney Cove. Here are toilets and seasonal refreshments and the picturesque setting is enhanced by the presence of Caerhayes Castle just inland. Walk behind the beach and turn right into parkland. Climb behind the field-edge trees then go to the right and follow the field edge to the woods. After crossing the rocky ridge at Greeb Point the Path descends to a road behind Hemmick Beach. Cross the bridge and go right, climbing to the headland of Dodman Point ("The Dodman"), with its memorial cross and superb views. The Path stays clear above the lovely sands of Bow or Vault Beach, then rounds the headland of Pen-a-maen to enter Gorran Haven. This little harbour village has a shop, pub and toilets. There is a Gorran community bus which runs 4 days a week (www.gorranbus.org) which walkers have recommended and can be hailed anywhere along its route.

Leave Gorran Haven up Church Street, turning right into Cliff Road. At the top of the hill, follow to the end of the road and a small wooden bridge will lead to a stile into the field, which leads to the cliffs. The clear Path leads to Chapel Point, where it crosses the tarmac access road to follow the Path along the coast into Portmellon. Follow the road uphill and go down through the park on the right on entering Mevagissey. Steps descend to the harbour. Mevagissey is the archetypal Cornish fishing village and has all facilities.

OS Maps: Landranger 204; Explorer 105 (western half); Explorer 107 (eastern half)

	This Walk	Cumulative	This Walk	Cumulative	Grading	Timing
Ascent	2,434ft	70,947ft	742m	21,625m	Strenuous then easy	5 hours
Distance	10.7mi	370.6mi	17.2km	596.4km		

For detailed directions see our Walking Guide no. 41, Mevagissey to Charlestown.

The western half of this Section has a relatively remote feel, enhanced by some quite strenuous climbs and some attractive cliffs and headlands. To the east the coastline is more urbanised but with beaches and the lovely Georgian docks of Charlestown found among the houses, golf courses and clay industry. The cliff-top Path between Porthpean and Charlestown was reinstated in late 2011, avoiding two miles of road diversion.

Directions

There are bus routes from St Austell to Charlestown and Par, one of these routes also serving Mevagissey, so that a range of bus-walks is possible.

The attractive fishing village of Mevagissey has all facilities. The Coast Path goes along the back of the harbour and then turns right along its eastern side before forking left steeply uphill. After crossing some playing fields, pass seaward of the houses then continue along the undulating cliffs to descend behind the ruined fish cellars at Portgiskey Cove. Continue uphill along the seaward and far field boundaries to a fenced path at the top. Turn right here, parallel to the road. At the entrance to Pentewan Sands Holiday Park follow the B3273 road pavement and turn first right before the petrol station, signposted to Pentewan. There are a few shops, toilets, pub and café in the village. The official route then follows the road through Pentewan and up the hill for about 100 yards/90 metres, taking the first turn sharp right along The Terrace and along a narrow path at the end to arrive at the cliffs. A more interesting alternative turns right, away from the road into the harbour area just after the public toilets then, immediately after the last cottage, goes left steeply uphill, through gardens, to arrive at the official route on the cliffs.

After some 1.25 miles/2 kilometres the Path descends through a wood and reaches a track. Turn right here to arrive at another track just behind the remote Hallane Mill Beach. Turn left here then quickly right, climbing back up the cliffs to arrive at Black Head. A diversion from the memorial stone goes to the tip of this atmospheric location. Continuing from Black Head the Path enters Ropehaven Woods with some confusing paths – it is important to follow the waymarking. Entering the wood turn right down a rocky and sometimes slippery path, then left. Go left again onto a walled path, ignoring descending paths on the right, to arrive beside a cottage and emerge onto a track. Go right here then leave the road to the right just after a parking area and follow the cliff-top path down, up and down again to Porthpean. Walk along the promenade to the far end and climb the steps to rejoin the newly reinstated cliff-top Path all the way to Charlestown.

Charlestown has a fascinating Georgian harbour, the home of a group of tall ships, and has refreshments, toilets, pubs and buses. Note that the official Coast Path does not cross the dock gate at the mouth of the harbour, though many people use that route. On the east side climb the Path and on to reach a suburban road for a short way, soon forking off right over a long grassy area. Arriving at a large car park above Carlyon Bay Beach keep seaward then cross the beach access road where a new resort is being developed and continue ahead on the low cliffs. Keep seaward of the golf course to approach the old china clay works at Par Docks. At the little beach at Spit Point turn inland and follow the narrow path past the works and then turn right alongside a railway line to emerge on a road. Turn right along the pavement past the docks entrance and under a railway bridge. Turn right at the junction, signposted to Fowey, over a level crossing and then under another railway bridge before forking right on the road, Par Green.

To continue beyond Par on the Coast Path, walk along Par Green, looking for house no.52 and follow the Path signed on the right. Par has all facilities, including a mainline railway station; for the station turn left at the far end of Par Green along Eastcliffe Road.

Mevagissey Spring

OS Maps: Landranger 200 or 204; Explorer 107

	This Walk	Cumulative	This Walk	Cumulative	Grading	Timing
Ascent	1,132ft	72,079ft	345m	21,970m	Moderate	3 hours
Distance	6.8mi	377.4mi	10.9km	607.4km		

For detailed directions see our Walking Guide no. 42, Charlestown to Fowey.

This Section goes out to the prominent Gribbin Head. The west side of the headland is relatively exposed, mostly on high cliffs, with views west over St Austell Bay. The east side is more indented and sheltered, the cliffs lower, and the Path passes numerous scenic little sandy coves. At its eastern end the Path enters the lovely part-wooded estuary of the River Fowey, culminating in the atmospheric little town of Fowey.

Directions

Par and Fowey are linked by two bus routes giving a half-hourly service, making this a bus-walk option. In addition, a popular local circular walk from Fowey takes in Gribbin Head, using the waymarked Saints' Way path with the Coast Path.

Par has all facilities, including a mainline railway station. For the Coast Path walk along the road called Par Green and follow the Path which leaves the road next to no.52. After crossing the private clay haul road, fork right along a grassy path immediately before the chalet park. Follow this path before turning left then quickly right along the road to a small car park at the western end of the sands of Par Beach. Walk along the back of the beach to another car park at the far, eastern end. This is Polmear; a pub and buses are to be found on the road outside the car park.

The Coast Path crosses the car park to a footbridge and then up the cliffs and continues on to the little harbour village of Polkerris. Here are a pub, toilets and restaurant. The Path continues from the back of the beach, up a ramp to join a zigzag path through woods to the top. The Path now continues to the Daymark on Gribbin Head (or "The Gribbin"). The tower is open to visitors on some summer Sundays. From the Daymark follow the Path downhill to the scenic cove at Polridmouth ("Pridmouth"), said to have inspired the setting for Daphne du Maurier's "Rebecca". Cross behind the beach on the stepping stones and turn right into the woods, then on over cliff-top fields and past a couple of small coves to arrive at another woodland. Look out for the Path on the right, which goes past St Catherine's Castle and gives superb views upriver to Fowey. Now follow the Path down the woodland track and behind Readymoney Cove before following the road into Fowey.

Note that it is possible to walk Coast to Coast across Cornwall between Fowey and Padstow on the north coast using the Saints' Way. A guidebook is available from Fowey Tourist Information Centre ("Enjoy Fowey").

OS Maps: Landranger 200 or 204 (Fowey); Landranger 201 (remainder); Explorer 107

	This Walk	Cumulative	This Walk	Cumulative	Grading	Timing
Ascent	1,939ft	74,018ft	591m	22,561m	Strenuous	3.5 hours
Distance	7.1mi	384.5mi	11.4km	618.8km		

For detailed directions see our Walking Guide no. 43, Fowey to Polperro.

This is a connoisseur's Section – it is quiet and remote; it is scenic, with beautiful large sandy bays and smaller coves plus impressive headlands; it is started and finished at superbly picturesque locations, the Fowey estuary at one end and Polperro at the other; and it is quite hard work, emphasising that nothing this good should come too easily.

Directions

Polruan and Polperro are linked by a bus service, giving a bus-walk option, though unfortunately it does not operate at weekends. There is a popular scenic circular walk (the Hall Walk) taking in Fowey and Polruan and using two ferries, an estuary tributary valley and the Coast Path.

Fowey is a charming little town, well worth exploring, with all facilities. The crossing of the river to Polruan on the opposite bank is by foot ferry. In summer it usually operates from Whitehouse Quay, below the Esplanade opposite Fowey Hotel, while in winter and in summer early mornings and evenings it operates from Town Quay (centre of Fowey). See page 23 for further details.

At Polruan, a picturesque little place, go up the steps next to The Lugger. Turn right at the top in West Street then turn left up Battery Lane. At the grassy area keep left by the wall then through the car park parallel to the coast to a signed path on the right. After around 2 miles/3 kilometres the Path passes above and behind the impressive Lantic Bay, climbing steeply at the far end. There is a higher path here, going to the top of the hill and turning right, or a lower one, turning off right 30 yards/28 metres before the top, dropping then climbing again to meet the higher path (ignore beach turnings to the right). The Path goes out around Pencarrow Head then behind an old watch house to descend and pass behind two charming and remote coves at Lansallos West and East Coombes. After climbing past a marker warning shipping of an offshore rock, more ups and downs follow until the Path approaches the almost hidden inlet of Polperro. Follow the waymarked path to arrive at a rocky outlook point – go left here then fork right to descend to the harbour. Polperro, an impossibly picturesque harbour village which figures justifiably in most picture books and calendars of Cornwall, has all facilities.

OS Maps: Landranger 201; Explorer 107

	This Walk	Cumulative	This Walk	Cumulative	Grading	Timing
Ascent	774ft	74,792ft	236m	22,797m	Moderate	2.25 hours
Distance	5.0mi	389.5mi	8.0km	626.8km		

For detailed directions see our Walking Guide no. 44, Polperro to Looe.

The cliffs on this Section, never really lofty, tend to decrease in height towards the east. This is a relatively sheltered length passing around lush bays, while offshore, Looe Island is a seaward focal point from the eastern end. Here, also, extensive rocky platforms are exposed at low tide. These factors, and the popularity of Polperro and Looe, have made this a justifiably popular length of coast.

Directions

There is a bus route between Polperro and Looe, making a bus-walk a popular option here.

Polperro is a popular visitors' destination with all facilities. The Coast Path crosses the stone bridge behind the harbour then turns right along The Warren. Climb out of the village, keeping left at the first fork and right at the second, which leads to the war memorial on it's headland. Continue along the Path towards Talland Bay. The Talland Bay Hotel a short walk up the hill is open all the year round.Cafes and toilets by the beaches are open here from Easter to the end of October. Pass behind the first beach, going left then right by the public toilets and behind a second beach to a small car parking area. The Path climbs back to the cliffs from here – keep well back from the crumbling edge. It then continues very clearly (ignore all turnings towards the beach) eventually arriving at the end of a suburban road at Hannafore, the western end of Looe. Continue along the road, or the lower promenade; there are toilets and seasonal refreshments along here. At the end a short stretch of road with no pavement turns alongside the mouth of the Looe River. Take steps down on the right to the riverside of West Looe. There is a seasonal and tidal ferry from here to East Looe, the main part of the town, as an option. Otherwise continue along the West Looe riverside and over the bridge, turning right into East Looe's main street. Looe has buses to Plymouth and a branch to the mainline railway at Liskeard - for the station turn left after the bridge. Between them, East and West Looe have all necessary facilities.

Looe

OS Maps: Landranger 201; Explorer 107 (western half); Explorer 108 (eastern half)

	This Walk	Cumulative	This Walk	Cumulative	Grading	Timing
Ascent	1,965ft	76,757ft	599m	23,396m	Strenuous, moderate in places	4.5 hours
Distance	7.7mi	397.2mi	12.4km	639.2km		

For detailed directions see our Walking Guide no. 45, Looe to Portwrinkle.

Quiet and relatively remote cliff lengths in the western and eastern parts of this Section are separated by a low-level, suburban length, or by an optional route via sea wall and beach between Seaton and Downderry. The western cliffs are covered in lush vegetation, scrub and woodland, and there are stretches where the sea is only glimpsed through the trees. The eastern cliffs are more open and give some superb views along the coast in both directions, with the distinctive Rame Head a focal point.

Directions

A bus service connects Seaton, Downderry and Portwrinkle, making a bus-walk option possible over the eastern end of this section. Further bus-walk options may be possible with a change of bus from Looe at Hessenford (inland of Seaton).

From East Looe's town centre, turn up Castle Street (Ship Inn on the corner) and keep climbing until it becomes a footpath above the sea. Continue, then at a road turn right, passing Plaidy Beach, and continue until just after the road veers left inland. Here go right, up a steep tarmac path then ahead at the top until the road turns left. The Coast Path descends steps between houses to Millendreath Beach. Café with toilets open all year here. On the far side go up the cul-de-sac road and climb the sunken lane to reach another road. After 50 yards/45 metres turn right and take the signed route left through twin gates across a drive. Follow the Path ahead through woods to rejoin the road. Turn right on the road and keep ahead past the Monkey Sanctuary onto a narrow lane. At the crest of this lane turn right and cross the field, going left on the far side to follow the Path until it arrives at the lane again. Turn right to descend to Seaton beach.

Turn right, where there are Cafés, Pub and public toilets. Although the official Path follows the narrow and busy road up the hill to Downderry, if the tide is not high it is preferable to walk along the top of the sea wall from Seaton and then the beach, taking one of the choice of footpath links into Downderry, where there are pubs, café, shops and public toilets.

Follow the road to the eastern end of Downderry, where it turns inland, and take the signed path right, which zigzags steeply upward. A superbly scenic cliff-top Path, with several ups and downs, continues until it arrives at a road just above Portwrinkle. Turn right to descend to the village and the quiet sea-front road. The Jolly Roger Cafe and Bistro is open all year in Portwrinkle or other facilities are at Crafthole, a 10 minute walk uphill inland

OS Maps: Landranger 201; Explorer 108

	This Walk	Cumulative	This Walk	Cumulative	Grading	Timing
Ascent	2,169ft	78,926ft	661m	24,057m	Moderate	5.75 hours
Distance	13.2mi	410.4mi	21.2km	660.5km		

For detailed directions see our Walking Guide no. 46, Portwrinkle to Cawsand and Cawsand to Cremyll (Plymouth Ferry).

This is a Section of great interest rather than spectacular drama. There is a golf course, a gunnery range, a cliff face of wooden chalets and an historic Country Park. It also includes the magnificent and atmospheric Rame Head, which is a significant landmark for many miles along the coast in both directions, the charming twin villages of Cawsand and Kingsand and some superb views, including Plymouth Sound and, indeed, the city itself.

Directions

A bus route links Cawsand to Cremyll, part-way along the section, and also runs along the coast road adjacent to the Coast Path between Tregantle and Rame Head, giving various bus-walk options. There are a number of popular circular walks using the Coast Path based on Mount Edgcumbe Country Park, next to Cremyll, and also around Rame Head.

From Portwrinkle walk up the road, past the first footpath, which leads to the beach, then turn right on the signed path opposite the golf club. After climbing, the Path goes along the seaward side of the golf course. After leaving the golf course the Path begins to rise towards the Tregantle Firing Ranges. When firing is not taking place it is possible to walk an excellent, well-signed permissive path through the ranges. Please note that live firing may still take place on weekends if operational requirements demand. In addition there is no live firing on Bank Holiday weekends nor on any day in August. Other non-firing days are known up to two weeks in advance - telephone The Ranges on 01752 822516 during office hours to check. If live firing is in progress red flags will be raised and the access gates locked - do not proceed into the range. If open, keep closely to the marked path and, at the far end of the range path, emerge through another security gate onto the National Trust's cliff-top path.

If the range path is closed, continue on the official Coast Path through a field to a road, where the Path initially continues inside the hedge before joining the road further along. The road is usually quite busy so take care. There is the compensation of a magnificent view up the Tamar to Plymouth from the car parking area here, where there is often a refreshment van. Follow the road (past Tregantle Fort entrance) then turn right at the first road junction and continue along the road to the cliffs (passing where the range path emerges).

The Coast Path is then off-road, along National Trust land, before it rejoins the road for about 1.25 miles/2 kilometres. The signed Path then leaves the road again to descend onto the sloping cliff face, although this cliff length had to be closed in 2013 because of subsidence, the Coast Path continuing on the road. There is a cafe just off the Path down the cliff at this point. The Path undulates quite steeply and meanders unexpectedly among chalets and gardens – keep alert for the waymarking – climbing back to the road. The route then descends gently across the cliff slope to Polhawn Cove at the base of Rame Head. After crossing a private access road for Polhawn Fort the Path climbs to reach the headland. The official Coast Path route omits the very end, with its medieval chapel, but the easy climb is worthwhile for the views and the atmosphere. Just inland is a public toilet and car park adjacent to the Coastwatch lookout.

A good cliff path then goes to Penlee Point, where there are the first views of Plymouth Sound. Bear left to reach a road then fork off to the right on the signed Path through woods to descend to the charming little village of Cawsand, with pubs, toilets, shops and refreshments. Go through the village square to Garrett Street and continue, turning right in front of the Post Office having, imperceptibly, crossed into Kingsand. At The Cleave turn left then first right up Heavitree Road, which leads to a gate on the right into Mount Edgcumbe Country Park. Continue through the park to a road, turning right then almost immediately left, forking uphill through woods. After a woodland drive there is a waymarked diversion to avoid a cliff fall, the route climbing left to a higher level path before continuing parallel to the coast. Once around the fallen cliff the Path descends to the foreshore of Plymouth Sound. Keep on the signed Path up and through a deer gate then back down towards the shore to follow into an Italian Ornate garden, past the Orangery of Mount Edgcumbe House (refreshments), and out through the park gates to the ferry point. Cremyll has a pub and toilets, but most will use it as the staging point for the ferry across the Tamar to Plymouth, an interesting excursion in its own right.

Wild ponies at Rame Head

If you enjoy sleeping, eating or drinking at any business on the Path please suggest they join us as Business Members so that we can share their brilliance!

The businesses listed here are all supporters and members of the South West Coast Path Association. Please find more details on our website www.southwestcoastpath.org.uk

GR Grid Reference
DP Distance from the Path
N   Nearest Town/Village with facilities

3   Number Of Rooms
🐕 Dogs Welcome
🍴 Evening Meal Available

📶 Wifi
🚗 Parking
🛒 Grocery Shop On Site

Bed & Breakfast and Hotels

NAME	OTHER INFO
Braganza B&B 4 Grove Hill, St Mawes, TR2 5BJ ☎ 01326 270281 ✉ braganzak@googlemail.com 🌐 www.braganza-stmawes.co.uk	GR: SW846331 DP: 0.25 miles N: **ST MAWES** Offers one night stays [5] 🐕 📶 🚗 Other info:
The Rosevine Portscatho, Truro, TR2 5EW ☎ 01872 580206 ✉ info@rosevine.co.uk 🌐 www.rosevine.co.uk	GR: SW879362 DP: 0.2 miles N: **PORTSCATHO** Offers one night stays [15] 🐕 🍴 📶 🚗 Other info: Michelin guide restaurant on site. Closed 2wks in Jan.
Trenona Farm Holidays Ruan High Lanes, Truro, TR2 5JS ☎ 01872 501339 ✉ pam@trenonafarmholidays.co.uk 🌐 www.trenonafarmholidays.co.uk	GR: SW915411 DP: 3 miles N: **VERYAN** Offers one night stays [5] 🐕 📶 🚗 Other info: Can collect guests from/return them to Coast Path for small charge.
Broom Parc B&B Veryan, Truro, TR2 5PJ ☎ 01872 501803 ✉ lindsay@broomparc.co.uk 🌐 www.broomparc.co.uk	GR: SW930389 DP: 0 miles N: **PORTLOE** Offers one night stays [3] 📶 🚗 Other info:
Corfingle B&B Portloe, TR2 5QU ☎ 01872 501388 ✉ carol_sherwood@hotmail.co.uk 🌐 www.southwestcoastpath.org.uk/corfingle-bb-portloe	GR: SW937393 DP: 0 miles N: **PORTLOE** Offers one night stays [2] 📶 Other info:
Jen's B & B 13 Treviskey Hill, Portloe, Truro, TR2 5RH ☎ 01872 501846 ✉ jburley805@btinternet.com 🌐 www.southwestcoastpath.org.uk/jens-b-b	GR: SW940398 DP: 0.4 miles N: **PORTLOE** Offers one night stays [1] 📶 🚗 Other info: 10 mins from local pubs. Open Mar-End of Oct.
Carradale Portloe, TR2 5RB ☎ 01872 501508 ✉ barbara495@btinternet.com 🌐 www.carradale-bnb.co.uk	GR: SW934394 DP: 0.25 miles N: **PORTLOE** Offers one night stays [2] 📶 🚗 Other info: Offer pick-up & drops-off to the Path.
SeaSpray Cottage & Cabin East Portholland, St Austell, PL26 6NA ☎ 01872 501187 ✉ seaspraycornwall@gmail.com 🌐 seaspraycornwall.co.uk	GR: SW962412 DP: 0 miles N: **PORTLOE** Offers one night stays [1] 🍴 📶 🚗 Other info: Right on the Path! Open all year.
Mevagissey Bay Hotel Polkirt Hill, Mevagissey, PL26 6UX ☎ 01726 843453 ✉ info@mevagisseybayhotel.co.uk 🌐 www.mevagisseybayhotel.co.uk	GR: SX016444 DP: 0 miles N: **MEVAGISSEY** Offers one night stays [11] 📶 🚗 Other info:

NAME	OTHER INFO	
Honeycombe House 61 Polkirt Hill, Mevagissey, PL26 6UR ☎ 01726 843750 ✉ enquiries@honeycombehouse.co.uk 🌐 www.honeycombehouse.com	GR: SX016445 DP: 0 miles N: **MEVAGISSEY** [3] 📶 🚗	**Other info:** Open February - October.
Carlyon Bay Hotel Sea Road, St Austell, PL25 3RD ☎ 01726 812304 ✉ reservations@carlyonbay.com 🌐 www.carlyonbay.com	GR: SX051520 DP: 0 miles N: **CHARLESTOWN** Offers one night stays [86] 🍴 📶 🚗	**Other info:** Spa & golf course.
The Strand 61 B&B 61 Tehidy Road, Tywardreath, PL24 2QD ☎ 07792 062471 ✉ j.askew439@btinternet.com 🌐 www.thestrandbnb.com	GR: SX083542 DP: 1 mile N: **FOWEY** Offers one night stays [3] 🐕 📶 🚗	**Other info:** Breakfast included in room rate.
The Old Quay House Hotel 28 Fore Street, Fowey, Pl23 1AQ ☎ 01726 833302 ✉ info@theoldquayhouse.com 🌐 www.theoldquayhouse.com	GR: SX126517 DP: 0.25 miles N: **FOWEY** Offers one night stays [13] 🍴 📶 🚗	**Other info:** Closed 2nd - 19th January
Fowey Harbour Hotel The Esplanade, Fowey, Pl23 1HX ☎ 01726 832551 ✉ fowey@harbourhotels.co.uk 🌐 www.harbourhotels.co.uk/fowey	GR: SX122514 DP: 0 mile N: **FOWEY** Offers one night stays [37] 🐕 🍴 📶 🚗	**Other info:** Dogs in rooms only. All day dining.
Fowey Hall Hotel Hanson Drive, Fowey, PL23 1ET ☎ 01726 833866 ✉ info@foweyhallhotel.co.uk 🌐 www.foweyhallhotel.co.uk	GR: SX120514 DP: 0.5 miles N: **FOWEY** Offers one night stays [36] 🐕 🍴 📶 🚗	**Other info:** Open all year.
Hormond House B&B 55 Fore Street, Polruan, PL23 1PH ☎ 01726 870853 ✉ bellacornwall@outlook.com 🌐 www.hormondhouse.com	GR: SX126508 DP: 0.5 miles N: **POLRUAN** Offers one night stays [3] 🐕 📶	**Other info:** Dogs allowed with notice. Open all year.
Gypsy Wagon Tidal Waters, Penpol, PL22 0NG ☎ 07966 284592 ✉ alisonfogg100@hotmail.com 🌐 https://bit.ly/2s5kteB	GR: SX146544 DP: 3 miles N: **POLRUAN** Offers one night stays [1] 🐕 📶 🚗	**Other info:** Electric vehicle charger available. Open 01/03-31/09.
Landaviddy Farm Landaviddy Lane, Polperro, PL13 2RT ☎ 01503 273302 ✉ enquiries@landaviddyfarm.co.uk 🌐 www.landaviddyfarm.co.uk	GR: SX205510 DP: 0.4 miles N: **POLPERRO** Offers one night stays [2] 📶 🚗	**Other info:** Open all year.
The House On The Props B&B Talland Street, Polperro, PL13 2RE ☎ 07855 265268 ✉ houseontheprops@yahoo.com 🌐 www.houseontheprops.co.uk	GR: SX208509 DP: 0 miles N: **POLPERRO** Offers one night stays [3] 🐕 🍴 📶	**Other info:** Washing/Drying facilities, Free WiFi.
Hendersick Farm House Portlooe, Looe, PL13 2HZ ☎ 01503 263207 ✉ hendersick@gmail.com 🌐 www.hendersickfarmhouse.com	GR: SX239523 DP: 0.3 miles N: **TALLAND BAY** [3] 📶 🚗	**Other info:** Ideal for small groups (up to 6). Own kitchen & lounge.

NAME	OTHER INFO	
2 Pendennis B&B Barbican Hill, Looe, PL13 1BE 📞 07989 037699 / 01503 598124 ✉ marian.cole@ymail.com 🌐 www.southwestcoastpath.org.uk/2-pendennis-bb	GR: SX256533	DP: 0 miles
	N: **LOOE**	
	Offers one night stays	
	1 🛜	**Other info:** Open all year, eateries nearby.
Bridgeside Guest House Fore Street, Looe, PL13 1HH 📞 01503 263113 ✉ bridgesideguesthouse@googlemail.com 🌐 www.bridgeside.cornwall.uk.net	GR: SX254535	DP: 0.5 miles
	N: **LOOE**	
	Offers one night stays	
	8 🐕 🛜	**Other info:** Dogs by arrangement.
The Anchorage Seaton Park Road, Seaton, Torpoint, PL11 3JF 📞 01503 250445 / 07864 104732 ✉ angelastidwell6@gmail.com 🌐 www.southwestcoastpath.org.uk/anchorage	GR: SX304546	DP: 0.2 miles
	N: **SEATON**	
	Offers one night stays	
	1 🛜 🚗	**Other info:** Open all year.
Coombe House B&B Fourlanesend, Cawsand, PL10 1LR 📞 01752 823925 ✉ info@coombehouse-cawsand.co.uk 🌐 www.coombehouse-cawsand.co.uk	GR: SX429512	DP: 0.5 miles
	N: **KINGSAND/CAWSAND**	
	Offers one night stays	
	5 🍴 🛜 🚗	**Other info:**

Campsites and Holiday Parks

NAME	OTHER INFO	
Highertown Farm Campsite Lansallos, Looe, PL13 2PX 📞 0354 800 1895 ✉ enquiries@nationaltrust.org.uk 🌐 www.nationaltrust.org.uk/holidays/highertown-farm-campsite	GR: SX173517	DP: 1 mile
	N: **POLPERRO**	
	Offers one night stays	
	🐕 🚗	**Other info:** 30 pitches
Great Kellow Farm Caravan & Campsite Lansallos, Polperro, PL13 2QL 📞 01503 272387 ✉ enquiries@greatkellowfarm.co.uk 🌐 www.greatkellowfarm.co.uk	GR: SX203520	DP: 1 mile
	N: **POLPERRO**	
	Offers one night stays	
	🐕	**Other info:** Open March - January
Killigarth Manor Holiday Park Polperro, PL13 2JQ 📞 01503 272216 🌐 www.johnfowlerholidays.com/cornwall-holiday-park/ killigarth-manor-holiday-park	GR: SX214519	DP: 1.5 miles
	N: **POLPERRO**	
	230 🐕 🍴 🛒 🛜 🚗	**Other info:** Caravans and lodges.
Trelawne Manor Holiday Park Trelawne, Looe, PL13 2NA 📞 01503 272151 🌐 /www.johnfowlerholidays.com/cornwall-holiday-park/ trelawne-manor-holiday-park	GR: SX220539	DP: 0 mile
	N: **LOOE**	
	Offers one night stays	
	322 🐕 🍴 🛒 🛜 🚗	**Other info:** Caravan Holiday Accommodation, Holiday Apartments and Lodges
Camping Caradon Touring Park Trelawne, Looe, PL13 2NA 📞 01503 272388 ✉ enquiries@campingcaradon.co.uk 🌐 www.campingcaradon.co.uk	GR: SX217541	DP: 2 miles
	N: **LOOE**	
	Offers one night stays	
	🐕 🍴 🛒 🛜 🚗	**Other info:**

Self Catering

NAME	OTHER INFO	
The Major's Quarter St Anthony, Porscatho, Truro, TR2 5HA 📞 0345 800 2070 ✉ cottages@nationaltrust.org.uk 🌐 www.nationaltrust.org.uk/holidays/the-majors-quarter-cornwall	GR: SW847312 DP: 0 miles N: **ST MAWES**	2 🛜 🚗 Other info:
Portscatho Holidays Ltd 4 The Quay, St Austell, PL26 6NY 📞 01326 270900 ✉ info@portscathoholidays.co.uk 🌐 www.portscathoholidays.co.uk	GR: SX002410 DP: N: **GORRAN HAVEN**	2 🛜 🚗 Other info:
Eden's Yard Backpackers 17 Tregrehan Mills, St Austell, PL25 3TL 📞 01726 814907 ✉ info@edensyard.uk 🌐 www.edensyard.uk	GR: SX43544 DP: 2 miles N: **FOWEY** Offers one night stays	14 🍽 🛜 🚗 Other info: Open Easter - mid Oct.
4 Degrees West 13 Par Green, Par, PL24 2AF 📞 01726 253545 / 07766135867 ✉ kay@4degreeswest.online 🌐 www.4degreeswest.online	GR: SX076536 DP: 0 miles N: **PAR** Offers one night stays	2 🛜 🚗 Other info: Open all year
Hemmick Cottage Lansallos, Looe, PL13 2PX 📞 0345 800 2070 ✉ cottages@nationaltrust.org.uk 🌐 www.nationaltrust.org.uk/holidays/hemmick-cottage-cornwall	GR: SX173517 DP: N: **POLPERRO** Offers one night stays	🐕 🚗 Other info: 30 pitches
Riverview Farm Looe, PL13 1PW 📞 01503 262454 ✉ angela@riverviewfarm.co.uk 🌐 www.riverviewfarm.co.uk	GR: SX250850 DP: 2.5 miles N: **LOOE**	2 🐕 🛜 🚗 Other info: Open all year
House by the Beach Trewollock Lane, Looe, PL13 1PW 📞 01726 843122 ✉ info@housebythebeach.co.uk 🌐 www.housebythebeach.co.uk	GR: SX250850 DP: 2.5 miles N: **LOOE**	2 🐕 🛜 🚗 Other info: Offering several adjacent properties by the beach.
Mount Edgcumbe Cottages and Glamping Cremyll, Torpoint, PL10 1HZ 📞 01752 822236 ✉ mt.edgcumbe@plymouth.gov.uk 🌐 www.mountedgcumbe.gov.uk	GR: SX453527 DP: N: **CREMYLL**	Other info:

Eat and Drink

NAME	OTHER INFO	
Coast Path Cafe Gorran Haven, St Austell, PL26 6JN 📞 07512 543735 ✉ geoff.cooke@icloud.com 🌐 www.facebook.com/Coast-Path-Cafe-287587094719036	GR: SX14416 DP: 0 miles N: **GORRAN HAVEN**	🛜 🚗 Other info: Limited opening - check facebook prior to visit.

Activities

NAME	OTHER INFO	
Walk Kernow Nordic Walking New Haven, Trewedna Lane, Perranwell Station, Truro, TR3 7PG 📞 07540 478919 ✉ info@walkkernow.co.uk 🌐 www.walkkernow.co.uk	GR: SW770388	DP: 0 miles
	N: **TRURO**	
	🐕	**Other info:** Open all year
Meadow View Guided Hikes 6 Long Meadow Views, Fowey, PL23 1ES 📞 07736 066319 ✉ info@foweybedandbreakfast.co.uk 🌐 www.meadow-view-guided-hikes.eventbrite.com	GR: SX119521	DP: 0.75 miles
	N: **FOWEY**	
	Offers one night stays	
	1 📶 🚗	**Other info:** All dietry requirements catered for
Mount Edgcumbe House and Country Park Cremyll, Torpoint, PL10 1HZ 📞 01752 822236 ✉ mt.edgcumbe@plymouth.gov.uk 🌐 www.mountedgcumbe.gov.uk	GR: SX453527	DP:
	N: **CREMYLL**	
		Other info:

Getting Around

NAME	OTHER INFO	
Barries Taxis Taxi Rank, Looe, PL13 1HL 📞 07792 722549 ✉ barrie48@icloud.com	GR:	DP: 0 miles
	N: **LOOE**	
	🐕	

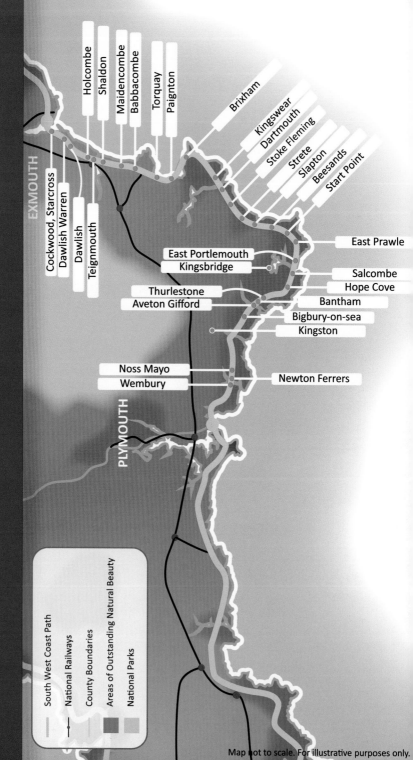

Holcombe
Shaldon
Maidencombe
Babbacombe
Torquay
Paignton
Brixham
Kingswear
Dartmouth
Stoke Fleming
Strete
Slapton
Beesands
Start Point

EXMOUTH

Cockwood, Starcross
Dawlish Warren
Dawlish
Teignmouth

East Prawle

East Portlemouth
Kingsbridge

Salcombe
Hope Cove

Thurlestone
Aveton Gifford

Bantham

Bigbury-on-sea
Kingston

Noss Mayo
Wembury

Newton Ferrers

PLYMOUTH

South West Coast Path
National Railways
County Boundaries
Areas of Outstanding Natural Beauty
National Parks

Map not to scale. For illustrative purposes only.

South Devon
Plymouth to the Exe

(Sections 47-57)

At the west of this length is the estuary of the River Tamar with the major naval port of Plymouth, the biggest urban area on the South West Coast Path but full of historic interest. East of Plymouth the coast is largely characterised by cliff scenery cut by attractive estuaries, the drowned mouths of wooded river valleys – the Yealm, Erme, Avon, Kingsbridge and Dart estuaries. As well as the ups and downs of the cliffs these estuaries present the walker with a number of ferry crossings (some seasonal and with limited timetables) and one (low-tide only) ford. This southernmost part of Devon forms the area known as the South Hams and includes the attractive and historic town of Dartmouth. Following the dramatic cliffs that lead to to the limestone headland of Berry Head, the coast becomes an area of low, mostly red sandstone cliffs. This length, the "Riviera", is largely occupied by towns based on tourism such as Paignton, Torquay, Teignmouth and Dawlish. The major estuary of the River Exe forms the eastern boundary of this length.

All of the locations on the map illustration to the left, have at least 1 facility including toilets, a cafe/restaurant, shop or pub.

Wembury Bay

OS Maps: Landranger 201; Explorer 108

	This Walk	Cumulative	This Walk	Cumulative	Grading	Timing
Ascent	463ft	79,389ft	141m	24,198m	Easy	3.5 hours
Distance	7.5mi	417.9mi	12.1km	672.5km		

For detailed directions see our Walking Guide no. 47, Admiral's Hard (Plymouth) to The Barbican and The Barbican to Mount Batten.

This is an urban walk along the waterfront of one of the country's prime historical maritime cities. It is therefore quite different to the vast majority of the Coast Path, but is nevertheless well worth doing. The view over Plymouth Sound, flanked on both sides by cliffs, is inspiring, and often referred to as the finest urban vista in the country. Elsewhere are lengths of waterside industry, historic quays and modern marinas, making this a fascinating excursion.

Directions

A range of urban bus services runs throughout Plymouth, including to and from Admiral's Hard, the ferry point for Cremyll, and Mount Batten. Though not on the same route, they link in the city centre. There is also a ferry link across the mouth of the River Plym between the historic Sutton Harbour and Mount Batten. These links make a range of public transport-walks possible.

The Coast Path from Cremyll uses the ferry across the Tamar. The ferry operates all year, weather, tide and other circumstances permitting, generally at 30 minute intervals. For ferry details see page 23.

Plymouth's Waterfront Walk is enhanced by a variety of information plaques and pieces of artwork relating to the city's history. A companion guidebook "Plymouth's Waterfront Walkway" is available free of charge from the association with a small fee to cover postage.

The route through Plymouth is waymarked by white bands on lamp-posts, red metal marker signs and pavement signs.

From the ferry walk up the road and turn right, going round the car park into Cremyll Street and on to the gates of the Royal William Yard. Enter the Yard via the walkway to the right of the main entrance and go through the Yard following the sea wall. (There is a ferry from the Royal William Yard to the Barbican that will also stop at Mount Batten on request for those who want a short cut). At the far corner of the Yard's sea wall climb the Eric Wallis Memorial Steps to Devil's Point Park. Follow the Path around the Park, overlooking Drake's Island and Plymouth Sound to reach the Artillery Tower, now a restaurant. At this point bear inland into Durnford Street and continue past the Royal Marines Barracks, turning right immediately after them. Continue along Millbay Road then, after the entrance to Millbay Docks, turn right into West Hoe Road. Fork right off here into Great Western Road, then bear off right down a narrow path along the shoreline. The Path returns to the road; here turn right to walk along the Hoe promenade all the way to The Barbican and Sutton Harbour, Plymouth's original harbour. Above on the left, away from the Coast Path but worth a visit, are the lighthouse of Smeaton's Tower, Drake's statue and other points of interest.

At The Barbican on the right are the Mayflower Steps, marking the site of the Pilgrim Fathers' embarkation. The large pontoon on nearby Commercial Wharf is the ferry point for Mount Batten, an unofficial short cut direct to the end of the Section.

The ferry operates all year. For ferry details see page 23.

Continuing on the Coast Path Waterfront Walk, walk across the lock gates at the entrance to Sutton Harbour, past the Marine Aquarium and then along Teat's Hill Road past the entrance to Queen Anne's Battery. At Breakwater Road, just after the entrance to Victoria Wharves, turn right up a narrow hill and footpath and down to the industrial Cattedown Wharf area. Continue past warehouses, then turn right into Neptune Park, keep to the right of the car parks and exit left just beyond the TR2 building up a slope and right onto Finnigan Road to Laira Bridge. Turn right to cross the River Plym then, at the first roundabout, turn right (at the rhinoceros!). Go right, into Breakwater Road, and continue for about 500 yards/450 metres then turn left, still in Breakwater Road, to the entrance to Yacht Haven Quay Boatyard. To the left of a mesh fence is a path, signed as the Coast Path, which is followed to Oreston Quay. At the quay walk past the grassy area into Marine Road then left into Park Lane. Turn left at the top of the hill, and this path descends to Radford Lake. From here a Coast-to-Coast walk goes to Lynmouth on the north coast, following the Erme-Plym Trail and the Two Moors Way. Guidebooks are available at Ivybridge Tourist Information Centre (TIC).

Go across the causeway with its old mini castle folly and turn right. Follow the Path along then left and at a junction turn right down Hexton Hill Road to Hooe Lake. Skirt the lake, going along Barton Road skirting Hooe Lake and Turnchapel Wharf to Turnchapel. Go through the village, bearing left at the Clovelly Bay Inn, up the hill then turn right down steps to the marina and over the slipway and along the shoreline to Mount Batten and the Sutton Harbour ferry. There are toilets, refreshments and a pub here. The short walk along the breakwater is very popular, although not part of the Coast Path.

Plymouth

OS Maps: Landranger 201; Explorer OL20

	This Walk	Cumulative	This Walk	Cumulative	Grading	Timing
Ascent	1,260ft	80,649ft	384m	24,582m	Easy	3 hours
Distance	7.5mi	425.4mi	12.1km	684.6km		

For detailed directions see our Walking Guide no. 48, Mount Batten to Warren Point (Yealm Ferry).

This is a Section of low cliffs, much of it overlooking Plymouth Sound. Below the cliffs are extensive areas of rock platform and offshore the Great Mew Stone becomes a focal point. Caravan and chalet sites and suburban villages are never far away and this is never a lonely Section. Towards its eastern end, as the cliffs rise somewhat, is the picturesque mouth of the River Yealm, forming a dramatic wooded gap in the cliffs.

Directions

Separate bus routes serve Mount Batten and Wembury village, and also Heybrook Bay, midway along this section, all from Plymouth city centre, allowing bus-walk options. There is a popular circular walk using the Coast Path between Wembury and Warren Point and a longer, full-day circular using the Erme-Plym Trail between Wembury and Mount Batten plus the Coast Path.

Mount Batten has toilets and refreshments, as well as a direct ferry link to and from Plymouth's Sutton Harbour. From Mount Batten the Coast Path heads over the little hill and past the old fort tower to the grassy area at Jennycliff, where there are more toilets and refreshments. Stay to the lower side of the field and at the end of the grass, from the stone "doormat" to Plymouth, use the renovated steps down and stairs up again to access woodland. The Path then undulates and emerges above Fort Bovisand; there are seasonal refreshments here. Cross the carpark and follow the Path down to Bovisand beach, then up to the chalet park road; follow round to the right to pass seaward of the chalets, past a cafe and toilets and on round the point and so to Heybrook Bay. There is a pub a little way up the road here, as well as a bus stop. Keep right and follow the Path above the shore around Wembury Point and on to Wembury Beach. Yet more toilets and refreshments await here and the bus stop, together with pub and shop, are in the village a little way inland.

From Wembury Beach a Coast-to-Coast walk goes to Lynmouth on the north coast, following the Erme-Plym Trail and the Two Moors Way. Guidebooks are available from Ivybridge Tourist Information Centre (TIC).

Continuing on the Coast Path, climb seaward of the church and along the now higher cliffs to a junction of paths at the Rocket House. The Path going inland from here leads to Wembury village and its facilities. For the Coast Path, bear right, downhill, to reach the ferry point. Note that operating times on this ferry can be limited – see page 23 and Walk 49.

OS Maps: Landranger 201 (western end); Landranger 202 (remainder); Explorer OL20

	This Walk	Cumulative	This Walk	Cumulative	Grading	Timing
Ascent	1,466ft	82,115ft	447m	25,029m	Easy then strenuous	4 hours
Distance	10.3mi	435.7mi	16.6km	701.2km		

For detailed directions see our Walking Guide no. 49, Noss Mayo (Yealm Ferry) to Mothecombe.

This is a fine Section of high-level coastal cliffs, cut mid-way by the substantial and extremely picturesque estuary of the River Erme. The western end is a particularly good length, since the superb cliff coastline is easily accessed by a scenic former carriage route. Beyond that a series of descents and ascents, some quite steep, accentuate the dramatic landscape of the coastline. At the eastern extremity is the tidally insular Burgh Island, a focal point on this part of the coast. Because of its remoteness and strenuous nature, much of this section has a quiet character which will specially appeal to those in search of a lonely coastline.

Directions

A once-daily bus service links Noss Mayo, near the western end of this length, with Battisborough cross, a little way inland from the eastern end, making a bus-walk feasible. There is a very popular local walk using the Coast Path on the carriage drive from Noss Mayo.

The ferry at Wembury's Warren Point operates three ways over the River Yealm and its tributary Newton Creek. Warren Point is thus linked with both Newton Ferrers and Noss Mayo, and these two points with each other. For the Coast Path the link between Warren Point and Noss Mayo is needed. The ferry operates seasonally and at limited times. For ferry details see page 23.

There is a signal board to summon the ferryman by the steps at Warren Point or the slipway at Noss Mayo. Alternatively, telephone beforehand.

Because of the somewhat limited nature of the ferry it may be necessary to make alternative arrangements to reach Noss Mayo. Both Wembury and Noss Mayo have a regular bus service to and from Plymouth, so it is possible to use these services as a link, perhaps combining with an overnight stop in Plymouth. Alternatively, local taxi companies are available.

It is also possible to walk round the Yealm Estuary from ferry point to ferry point. This is a distance of some 9 miles/14.5 kilometres, effectively adding an extra day or half day to the itinerary.

Walk around the Yealm Estuary

Walk uphill inland from the ferry steps to the house at the top, the Rocket House. Continue inland along the track, which in turn becomes a road. Where the road bears sharp right go ahead along a public footpath into a field, then keep ahead alongside a high wall. At the end of the wall, after two gates, bear left (bearing 330˚) across fields, then go down a few steps. The now enclosed path goes left then right to arrive at a road. This is Knighton, on the outskirts of Wembury. The bus stop for Plymouth is a little way to the left, just before the pub.

To continue the walking route around the estuary cross the road at Knighton to a minor lane, following it left to another junction. Turn right here and continue until the road meets another, more major, road. Cross this road, going ahead and left for a short way then turn right on a signed footpath. This is part of a waymarked route, the Erme-Plym Trail, and is shown on the OS Explorer OL20 map. Follow the waymarked route across fields, over Cofflete Creek, next to a lane and on to the village of Brixton. Turn right and follow the road through the village to Brixton Church then back on the Erme-Plym Trail up Old Road, along a suburban road, over fields, along a minor lane then over more fields to arrive at another village, Yealmpton. On reaching the A379 road at Yealmpton the Erme-Plym Trail is now abandoned. Here, turn right along the A379 then quickly left, into Stray Park. At the bottom bear right along a tarmac path then, when it arrives at a road, turn left along a stony track. At the footpath sign continue ahead, eventually emerging at a road by a car park. Turn left along the road to cross Puslinch Bridge then follow the road up the hill. Take the footpath on the right near the top of the hill, crossing a couple of fields to a road. Turn right and continue to meet a more major road, which is followed ahead to Newton Ferrers. At the edge of the village turn left down the road signed to Bridgend and Noss Mayo, and at the junction at the head of the creek keep to the right. Follow the riverside road, forking right into Noss Mayo. Keep on the road round Noss Creek and continue on the creekside road out of the village until this becomes a track. A signed path on the right leaves the track for the ferry point.

Coast Path, Noss Mayo-River Erme

From the ferry point, follow the Path westward through the woods as it climbs to meet a track, an old carriage drive. (NB if refreshments are needed here, turn left and continue for about a mile to Noss Mayo village, where there are two pubs and seasonal toilets). The drive continues through woods, past a row of former coastguard cottages, into more woods, then on a superb cliff-face shelf round Mouthstone Point. Further on keep right where the more obvious path bears left inland to a car park, the drive continuing round Stoke Point and on to Beacon Hill. A series of ups and downs now ensues as the Path approaches the estuary of the River Erme, which has been fairly described as England's most unspoiled river estuary, and is possibly the most attractive. The Path crosses the top of a small beach then passes through a short woodland stretch to arrive at Mothecombe slipway on the Erme. There are seasonal refreshments a little way inland.

There is no ferry at the River Erme. It is usually possible to wade the river 1 hour either side of low water along the old ford and, under normal conditions, at low tide the water is about knee deep and the river bed is of sand with pebbles. The crossing is between grid references 614 476 and 620 478, ie the road by the row of coastguard cottages at Mothecombe and the end of the inland road to Wonwell Beach. However, great care should be taken as heavy rains or high seas can make conditions dangerous. Low water is approximately at the same time as at Devonport; see tide tables on pages 25-31.

Alternatively, it is possible to walk round the estuary. There are no riverside rights of way and for the most part minor roads must be used. The distance is approximately 8 miles/13 kilometres, adding extra time to the itinerary.

Walk round the Erme Estuary

From the slipway follow the road inland, following signs to Holbeton. Go through the village and leave on the minor lane to Ford and then Hole Farm. At the sharp bend after this farm follow the waymarked Erme-Plym Trail to the A379 and across the River Erme at Sequer's Bridge. Then leave the waymarked trail, continuing very carefully along the A379 for a couple of hundred yards/metres, before turning right on the lane signed to Orcheton. Follow this for about 2 miles/3 kilometres then turn right, following signs for Wonwell Beach. Follow the lane downhill to arrive at the estuary.

OS Maps: Landranger 202; Explorer OL20

	This Walk	Cumulative	This Walk	Cumulative	Grading	Timing
Ascent	1,860ft	83,975ft	567m	25,596m	Moderate	4 hours
Distance	9.3mi	445.0mi	15.0km	716.2km		

For detailed directions see our Walking Guide no. 50, Mothecombe to Thurlestone.

While the western end of this Section is relatively remote, in the east it is a well-used and popular Section, never far from residential and holiday accommodation. It is a length of low cliffs and sandy beaches, the coastline providing some interesting seascapes. These include views of the tidal Burgh Island, the estuary of the River Avon, the distinctive holed Thurlestone Rock and the headland of Bolt Tail. At the end of the Section, Hope Cove is a charming little settlement with a picturesque harbour and an old centre of historic cottages.

Directions

A regular, if infrequent, bus service links Thurlestone and Hope Cove, making a bus-walk option possible on the eastern part of this Section. There are popular short circular walks using the Coast Path between Bantham and Thurlestone.

For details of crossing the River Erme, see Section 49. On the eastern side, just inland of Wonwell slipway a path leaves the lane into the woods then continues above the shore, emerging on cliffs which rollercoaster up and down to the holiday park at Challaborough and then Bigbury-on-Sea. There are toilets here and also the year-round café. On Burgh Island offshore, reached by walking across the sands or by unusual sea tractor, is a pub.

From the main facilities at Bigbury-on-Sea, the Coast Path goes along the road, turning right immediately after the car park entrance to follow a short cliff-top length which re-joins the road further up. Cross the road and follow the Path along the field edge next to the road, climbing Folly Hill. Leave the field where signed and cross the road, passing through Folly Farm and down the cliffs to the flat open area of Cockleridge Ham. At the edge is the ferry point for the crossing of the mouth of the River Avon.

Arrangements for the ferry crossing on the Avon are changing for 2020 onwards. Details are not available at the time of print and so please check the website for details at www.southwestcoastpath.org.uk/walk-coast-path/trip-planning/estuaries-and-ferries or phone 01752 896237.

Alternatively, there is a waymarked walk round the estuary between Bigbury-on-Sea and Bantham. This route, the Avon Estuary Walk, is signed with blue waymarks and adds about 8 miles/13 kilometres to the route, or another half day to a day to the itinerary. The route is shown on OS Explorer map OL20 and can be followed from the top of Folly Hill.

Avon Estuary Walk

Continue up the road, without turning into Folly Farm, for a further 60 yards/55 metres and then turn right. The Path reaches the golf course, turning left on a track then off this to the right, down another track past Hexdown Farm. Follow this track to the bottom then go left along a drive which eventually arrives at a road. There is a permissive path alongside the road and at the end of this a path goes right over a field, through the top of a wood then downhill over another field to a road alongside the estuary. This tidal road is then followed to Aveton Gifford on the A379.

At high tide there is a waymarked diversion which crosses the tidal road on arriving at it and re-joins it next to the village. From Aveton Gifford cross the Avon on the A379 then take the first lane on the right, which becomes a track and continues to Stadbury Farm. Bear left approaching the farm onto a footpath, following field edges towards the valley bottom to cross Stiddicombe Creek. Enter the wood on the right and climb to leave at the far top corner. Follow the top edge of fields then cross a farm track and a stream to a junction of paths. Turn right and continue to Bantham village, where there is a pub, shop, toilets and seasonal refreshments.

Coast Path, Bantham-Hope Cove

From the ferry point go through the car park and round the edge of the dunes of Bantham Ham. Follow the shore, leaving the dunes to climb the hill and reach the undulating track around Thurlestone Golf Club, passing the small Leas Foot Sand beach, and continuing on to Thurlestone Sands. Cross a long footbridge at an inland lagoon (South Milton Ley), pass public toilets and seasonal refreshments then join a road for a short stretch before turning back to the shoreline and over low cliffs to Outer Hope, where there are all facilities in season. Follow the Path behind the little harbour and down to the old lifeboat station at Inner Hope, where the bus stop is situated. Buses to Kingsbridge leave from here. A little inland is the old village centre of Inner Hope, at The Square, a picture-postcard location worth seeing before leaving.

Sunset at Hope Cove

OS Maps: Landranger 202; Explorer OL20

	This Walk	Cumulative	This Walk	Cumulative	Grading	Timing
Ascent	1,506ft	85,481ft	459m	26,055m	Strenuous	4 hours
Distance	8.1mi	453.1mi	13.0km	729.2km		

For detailed directions see our Walking Guide no. 51, Thurlestone to Salcombe.

This is a very scenic Section of the coast, largely comprising quite spectacular high cliffs soaring above tiny, mostly inaccessible coves. Near both ends are dramatic headlands, Bolt Tail in the west and Bolt Head in the east, offering superb coastal views in their respective directions. At the eastern end this Section turns into the mouth of the estuary of Salcombe Harbour, and there is the contrast of softer, sandy bays. This is a length which is never really remote, but never really busy.

Directions

Separate bus routes serve Hope Cove and Salcombe from Kingsbridge and Malborough, a few miles inland, making a bus-walk feasible from there. There are numerous local circuits using the Coast Path based on Hope Cove and Salcombe, as well as Bolberry and Soar.

Leave Hope Cove from the old lifeboat station at Inner Hope up the signed Coast Path and out to the magnificent viewpoint of Bolt Tail, where the ramparts of an Iron Age cliff fort are crossed to reach the end. The Path doubles back along the cliff top over Bolberry Down and then down to the splendid Soar Mill Cove (there are seasonal refreshments inland from here). Climbing from the cove a long level stretch of easy walking follows. Keep along the cliff top and as the Path approaches Bolt Head pass through a couple of gates, staying on the closest path to the cliff top as possible. A steep descent will then lead to the headland, where a sharp turn to the north leads to the cliff-face path round Starehole Bay and then on to the Courtenay Walk below rocky pinnacles. Passing into woodland at the National Trust's Overbecks property the Path joins a road which is followed past South Sands and North Sands – toilets and seasonal refreshments at both – and then on into Salcombe town centre. For a variation, there is a summer ferry service between South Sands and Salcombe. The town is a renowned yachting centre and has all facilities.

Salcombe Estuary

OS Maps: Landranger 202; Explorer OL20

	This Walk	Cumulative	This Walk	Cumulative	Grading	Timing
Ascent	2,251ft	87,732ft	686m	26,741m	Strenuous	6.75 hours
Distance	12.6mi	465.7mi	20.3km	749.5km		

For detailed directions see our Walking Guide no. 52, Salcombe to Torcross.

This is a superb section of walking. Part of it is on exposed cliff faces, the sometimes stark cliffs contrasting with numerous tiny sandy coves below. A significant length in the middle is on an old "raised beach", a low shelf a little above the sea giving an easy passage. In the east the Path crosses the rocky spine of Start Point, behind its lighthouse, a dramatic stretch, before following a lush, sheltered length into Torcross.

Directions

Salcombe and Torcross are both on regular bus routes to and from Kingsbridge, a little inland, making a bus-walk possible from that town. There is also a popular local circuit using the Coast Path from the Salcombe Ferry.

Salcombe has all necessary facilities. The ferry across the estuary leaves from steps next to the Ferry Inn, a little way downstream from the town centre. The ferry operates all year. For ferry details see page 23.

From the ferry point on the eastern side, where there are toilets and seasonal refreshments, the Coast Path follows the road down the estuary side then, after crossing the rear of the beach at Mill Bay (toilets), passes the refreshment facilities at Gara Rock (call 01548 844810 for details), then follows a clear cliff Path to Prawle Point. The Path goes to the Coastwatch lookout at the very end, then descends to follow the "raised beach" shelf just above the waves before a short inland length to avoid a cliff fall leads to Lannacombe Beach. Beyond here a dramatic length goes along and up to the rocky ridge leading to Start Point, the Path dropping to the lighthouse access road. From the car park at the top the Path bears off right down the cliff face to Hallsands, passing above the old ruined village. A short diversion to the viewpoint is both instructive and interesting. The Path continues over low cliffs to Beesands, where there is a pub, toilets and seasonal refreshments. Continue along the shingle ridge then behind an old quarry to descend into Torcross, with a panoramic view of Slapton Ley ahead on the descent. Torcross has some facilities, and buses to Plymouth, Kingsbridge and Dartmouth.

Overlooking Beesands

OS Maps: Landranger 202; Explorer OL20

	This Walk	Cumulative	This Walk	Cumulative	Grading	Timing
Ascent	1,493ft	89,225ft	455m	27,196m	Easy then strenuous	4.75 hours
Distance	10.3mi	476.0mi	16.6km	766.0km		

For detailed directions see our Walking Guide no. 53, Torcross to Dartmouth.

Something like a quarter of this Section consists of the low shingle ridge known locally as the Slapton Line, cutting off the freshwater lake of Slapton Ley from the sea. Most of the remainder of the Section is cliffs and coves, partly looking to the sea and partly to the outer reaches of the picturesque wooded Dart Estuary.

Directions

A regular bus service runs along the coast road which is, for much of the Section, adjacent to the Coast Path. With stops at most obvious locations this gives numerous bus-walk options. There is also a very popular and scenic circular walk using the Coast Path between Dartmouth and the mouth of the Dart Estuary.

From Torcross, with all facilities, the Coast Path runs along the shingle ridge. The official route is on the landward side of the road. After the Strete Gate car park, look out for the fingerpost signing the new section of Coast Path, opened in summer 2015. Follow the Path along the cliff top and through the woods to the A379. It is now necessary to walk along this and for the next 400 yards/365 metres.

Follow the main road through Strete village (pub and shop) then, just after the village end, take the Path to the right which passes over fields and a footbridge to reach a high point above the sea. Continuing parallel to the coast for a while it then heads inland over a deep valley, crossing the main road and over more fields to a lane. Descend the lane then leave it across more fields until, after crossing the main road again, the picturesque cove of Blackpool Sands is reached. There are toilets and seasonal refreshments. Follow the Path uphill through the woods then the route enters and meanders along various paths in the village of Stoke Fleming (pub, shop and toilets), arriving at the village hall. Cross the main road again and follow a lane to a National Trust car park. From here a scenic cliff path proceeds, latterly through woods, to reach the Dart Estuary and arrive at Dartmouth Castle (toilets). An estuary-side path passes the adjacent church and joins the road which is followed into the town. Look out for some steps on the right just after the public toilets before reaching the centre; the steps lead down to Bayards Cove through its little castle and on to the Embankment at the town centre. Dartmouth, of course, has all facilities.

OS Maps: Landranger 202; Explorer OL20

	This Walk	Cumulative	This Walk	Cumulative	Grading	Timing
Ascent	2,992ft	92,217ft	912m	28,108m	Strenuous	5.75 hours
Distance	10.9mi	486.9mi	17.5km	783.6km		

For detailed directions see our Walking Guide no. 54, Dartmouth (Kingswear) to Brixham.

This is a Section of superb cliff scenery, tough going in places and often quite lonely. In the west, near the mouth of the Dart, are substantial wooded areas but further along the cliffs become higher and more open. This makes for a dramatic, steeply undulating landscape ending at the sea in steep cliff faces.

Directions

A regular bus service links Brixham and Kingswear, on the east side of the Dartmouth Ferry, making a bus-walk possible. There is also a bus service from Paignton to Kingswear. A popular circuit using the Coast Path exists based around Kingswear.

Walkers have two ferry options from Dartmouth town centre to cross the river, the Lower Car Ferry, which also carries foot passengers, and the Dartmouth Passenger Ferry. The Lower Car Ferry operates all year on a continuous service. The Dartmouth Passenger Ferry also operates all year on a continuous service telephone. For ferry details see page 23. The Lower Ferry is the easiest option for the Coast Path.

From either ferry landing point in Kingswear, follow the Coast Path signposts, turning left along Beacon Road then right up Church Hill and down Beacon Lane. Continue out of the village. After some 1.25 miles/2 kilometres turn right down some steps. The route then undulates, sometimes steeply, into and through woodland to the old Battery buildings at Froward Point. Here the Path descends steeply to the right from the corner of an old lookout building, passing World War II searchlight and gun positions before continuing along the cliffs. Pass Pudcombe Cove, by the National Trust Coleton Fishacre Gardens, and then on over Scabbacombe Head and past Scabbacombe Sands and Man Sands and over Southdown Cliff to Sharkham Point – this is a particularly strenuous length. Passing holiday accommodation the Path arrives at Berry Head, a Napoleonic fortified area. Divert to the end of the headland to see the unusually squat lighthouse. Berry Head has toilets and year round refreshments available at the Guardhouse Café. From here descend past an old quarry to a road, where there are further refreshment facilities. Turn right then go right again through the Shoalstone car park and along above the shoreline, returning to the road before descending steps to Brixham Breakwater. Follow the promenade to the harbour. Brixham has all facilities.

OS Maps: Landranger 202: Explorer OL20 (western half); Explorer 110 (eastern half)

	This Walk	Cumulative	This Walk	Cumulative	Grading	Timing
Ascent	1,972ft	94,189ft	601m	28,709m	Moderate	6 hours
Distance	13.2mi	500.1mi	21.2km	804.8km		

For detailed directions see our Walking Guide no. 55, Brixham to Paignton and Paignton to Babbacombe.

This is mostly an urban Section, passing along the shoreline of the "English Riviera", or Tor Bay. There is a mixture of grand terraces, open green parkland, amusement parks and the elegant white buildings overlooking the sea at Torquay. At the western end there is also the old fishing town of Brixham and at the other end the almost rural wooded cliffs around Babbacombe. All in all, this is a surprisingly diverse Section.

Directions

A range of bus routes runs throughout the Torbay area, including one which follows the coast road between Brixham and Torquay, and another linking Torquay to Babbacombe. As a result, a wide variety of bus-walks is possible. A pleasant alternative is the Torquay to Brixham ferry which runs regularly.

Leaving Brixham by the fish market, the Coast Path initially passes a car park and gardens before passing two small coves and climbing into woodland which takes the path to Elberry Cove. From here it passes behind the sweep of Broadsands, climbing by the railway viaduct at the far end to proceed alongside the steam railway line to the promenade at Goodrington. At the far end climb through ornamental gardens and go down a road to Paignton Harbour and so along the promenade. Paignton's railway station is inland of the pier. Turn inland at Hollicombe, at the far end of Preston Sands, going through a park to the main sea-front road which is followed to Torquay Harbour. Torquay Station is inland a little before the harbour.

Cross the pedestrian bridge across the harbour and climb the hill, turning right at the Imperial Hotel on the signed path which leads to the open area at Daddyhole Plain. Descend to the sea-front road at Meadfoot Beach, climbing again at Ilsham Marine Drive. Take the cliff path round Thatcher Point to Hope's Nose. A cul-de-sac path goes to the end of this low headland.

From Hope's Nose follow the Path inland of the road, crossing the road to the Bishop's Walk, which in turn arrives at a car park above Anstey's Cove. The Path now goes up and round the edge of the grassy downs on Walls Hill with excellent views across Lyme Bay, bearing off right to descend to Babbacombe Beach. Cross a wooden footbridge to Oddicombe Beach then climb by the cliff railway to reach Babbacombe's facilities at the top.

OS Maps: Landranger 202; Explorer 110

	This Walk	Cumulative	This Walk	Cumulative	Grading	Timing
Ascent	2,090ft	96,279ft	637m	29,346m	Strenuous	3.75 hours
Distance	6.4mi	506.5mi	10.3km	815.1km		

For detailed directions see our Walking Guide no. 56, Babbacombe to Teignmouth.

This is a tough Section of almost constant ups and downs. The characteristic red cliffs of this part of Devon are often quite high and quite sheer, though unfortunately the terrain is such that sea and cliff views are perhaps less frequent than would be hoped for as you pass through some attractive woods. Its strenuous nature makes it a relatively quiet Section, except for the two ends, although it is never far from roads or housing.

Directions

A regular bus service links Babbacombe and Teignmouth, making a bus-walk an option.

From Babbacombe, a pleasant suburb of Torquay with all facilities, the Coast Path descends next to the cliff railway and then soon climbs again to avoid a cliff fall. The Path goes up a grassy area to a main road where it turns right, then right again into Petitor Road. At the bottom turn left on the Coast Path again, which soon descends onto a cliff face before reaching the wooded valley at Watcombe. Cross the track running down the valley and on through a wooded length to a short rocky stretch, turning right at a junction before reaching the car park at Maidencombe. There is a pub and toilets here. Turn right after the car park and keep on the rollercoaster path which eventually climbs to go alongside the coast road, then quickly leaves it to pass alongside fields to a track. Turn right and go round the wooded Ness headland, with super views ahead, descending to the promenade at Shaldon, on the estuary of the River Teign. The ferry service across the River Teign operates throughout the year, weather permitting. For ferry details see page 24.

Walk, Shaldon-Teignmouth

If the ferry is not operating, continue inland along the riverside roads to Shaldon Bridge and cross the Teign. On the Teignmouth side turn right into Milford Park, through Bitton Sports Ground into Park Hill, cross into Bitton Avenue then into Clay Lane and right into Willow Street. At the end bear left then right into Quay Road, then right to go along the Strand and right to the Harbour Beach and the ferry point. Teignmouth has all facilities, including a mainline rail station and buses to Exeter.

OS Maps: Landranger 192; Explorer 110

	This Walk	Cumulative	This Walk	Cumulative	Grading	Timing
Ascent	488ft	96,767ft	149m	29,495m	Easy	3 hours
Distance	8.0mi	514.5mi	12.9km	828.0km		

For detailed directions see our Walking Guide no. 57, Teignmouth to Exmouth.

This Section primarily comprises two fairly large seaside towns, flanked by a coastline of high red cliffs at one end and marshes and a sand bar at the other. Running through it, often next to the Coast Path, is possibly the most scenic part of Brunel's GWR railway line, the embankment of which forms the sea wall for much of this length. This is a busy, largely urban and much used Section with an historic importance to the tourist trade.

Directions

A regular bus service links Teignmouth and Starcross, the ferry point for Exmouth, and also passes through Dawlish and Dawlish Warren. As there are also stations on the railway line at these places, bus or train-walks are options here.

From the ferry point at Teignmouth, or from the town centre, go to the car park at The Point, jutting out into the Teign Estuary, and begin by walking along the promenade. Leaving the town the Coast Path continues between railway and sea below the red cliffs to the end, where it descends steps to pass under the railway and then up Smugglers Lane to the A379 road at the top.

High water route, Teignmouth-Smugglers Lane

With a high sea and an onshore wind the far end of the promenade can become very wet, and at exceptionally high tides the steps at Smugglers Lane may become impassable. In these cases, immediately after leaving the town fork left and cross the railway on a footbridge on Eastcliff Walk, follow this lane around the outside of Eastcliff Park and then along a lane to Cliff Walk, eventually reaching the A379, which is then followed ahead to meet the official path at the top of Smugglers Lane.

Coast Path, Smugglers Lane-Dawlish Warren

Use the footway on the inland side of the A379 and walk for about 150 yards/135 metres before turning right into Windward Lane, going immediately left on a path which skirts fields before returning to the A379. Bear right into Old Teignmouth Road, which in turn returns to the A379 then, very soon, turn right into a park through some railings and follow the Path around its edge which then zigzags down to the shoreline. Follow the sea wall through Dawlish, past the station – all facilities are found beyond the railway here. The Coast Path then continues on the sea wall between railway and sea, again below the red cliffs, to Dawlish Warren. Just before the amusement area at Dawlish Warren, cross the obvious railway footbridge to a car park, turn right and follow to the main road.

High water route, Dawlish-Dawlish Warren

Occasionally, at the highest tides, it becomes impossible to proceed along the sea wall for a short stretch just beyond the station. In this case, from the sea wall, cross the footbridge immediately after the end of station platform and follow the Path up to the A379. Turn right and continue alongside the road until the Path reaches a path on the right between properties. Follow this path passing though a small park and up steps to a path locally known as Lady's Mile. This path follows the line of coast above the sea wall. Continue to follow this path until you reach the main road in Dawlish Warren to pick up the Coast Path here.

Coast Path, Dawlish Warren-Starcross

The Coast Path does not go around the large sand spit at Dawlish Warren itself, jutting out into the mouth of the River Exe, or the marshes behind it, but if there is time this can be an exhilarating experience. Otherwise continue along Warren Road on the pavement, then opposite the entrance to Dawlish Warren Sandy Park join the cycleway and footpath to Cockwood Harbour. After following the road around the harbour join the A379. Cross the road and follow the footpath and cycleway to Starcross, and the ferry point to Exmouth. Starcross has all facilities.

The ferry operates daily May – end October. For ferry details see page 24. If there is no ferry operating on arrival at Starcross, there are several options to reach Exmouth.

Option 1: Exeplorer Water Taxi – this runs daily from April until October. Check their web site before travelling as times vary: www.watertaxi.squarespace.com

Option 2: Bus or train from Starcross to Exeter, bus or train from Exeter to Exmouth.

Option 3: Walk from Starcross to Turf Lock following the waymarked Exe Estuary Trail on the riverside road and footpath (3 miles/5 kilometres), then ferry Turf Lock-Topsham and bus or train from Topsham to Exmouth.

Ferry operates seasonally. For ferry details see page 24.

Option 4: Walk from Starcross to Topsham Lock following the waymarked Exe Estuary Trail on the riverside road and footpath and Exeter Canal towpath (4.5 miles/7 kilometres), then ferry Topsham Lock-Topsham and bus or train from Topsham to Exmouth.

Ferry operates seasonally. For ferry details see page 24.

Dawlish beach huts

If you enjoy sleeping, eating or drinking at any business on the Path please suggest they join us as Business Members so that we can share their brilliance!

The businesses listed here are all supporters and members of the South West Coast Path Association. Please find more details on our website www.southwestcoastpath.org.uk

GR Grid Reference
DP Distance from the Path
N Nearest Town/Village with facilities

[3] Number Of Rooms
Dogs Welcome
Evening Meal Available

Wifi
Parking
Grocery Shop On Site

Bed & Breakfasts and Hotels

NAME	OTHER INFO
Mariners Guest House 11 Pier Street, West Hoe, Plymouth, PL1 3BS ☎ 01752 261778 ✉ marinersguesthouse@blueyonder.co.uk ⊕ www.marinersguesthouse.co.uk	GR: SX472538 ⋮ DP: 0.02 miles N: **PLYMOUTH** Offers one night stays [8] 🛜 **Other info:** Sauna available by request.
The Rusty Anchor Guest House 30 Grand Parade, Plymouth, PL1 3DJ ☎ 01752 663924 ✉ enquiries@therustyanchor-plymouth.co.uk ⊕ www.therustyanchor-plymouth.co.uk	GR: SX472536 ⋮ DP: 0 miles N: **PLYMOUTH** Offers one night stays [5] 🐕 🛜 **Other info:** Offers available, dog friendly eatery nearby.
Edgcumbe Guesthouse 50 Pier Street, West Hoe, Plymouth, PL1 3BT ☎ 01752 660675 ✉ enquiries@edgcumbeguesthouse.co.uk ⊕ www.edgcumbeguesthouse.co.uk	GR: SX473537 ⋮ DP: 0.1 miles N: **PLYMOUTH** Offers one night stays [7] 🐕 🛜 **Other info:** Special diets catered for.
Raleigh Stile B&B Hexton Hill Road, Hooe, Plymouth, PL9 9WA ☎ 01752 492232 ✉ enquiries@stormplymouth.co.uk ⊕ www.bedandbreakfastplymouth.uk.com	GR: SX499526 ⋮ DP: 0 miles N: **PLYMOUTH** Offers one night stays [3] 🛜 🚗 **Other info:**
Wembury Bay B&B 2 Warren Close, Wembury, PL9 0AF ☎ 01752 863392 ✉ pwgreenwood59@gmail.com ⊕ www.wemburybaybedandbreakfast.yolasite.com	GR: SX523488 ⋮ DP: 0.1 miles N: **WEMBURY** Offers one night stays [3] 🛜 🚗 **Other info:** 10 mins from the SWCP & The Odd Wheel pub.
Thorn House B&B Wembury, Plymouth, PL9 0EQ ☎ 01752 862494 ✉ bandb@thornhouse.co.uk ⊕ www.bit.ly/2O9cxkU	GR: SX541490 ⋮ DP: 1 mile N: **WEMBURY** Offers one night stays [3] 🍽 🛜 🚗 **Other info:** Stunning views. Extensive gardens.
Worswell Barton Farmhouse B&B Worswell Barton, Noss Mayo, Plymouth, PL8 1HB ☎ 01752 872977 ✉ info@worswellbarton.co.uk ⊕ www.worswellbarton.co.uk	GR: SX536471 ⋮ DP: 1 mile N: **NOSS MAYO** Offers one night stays [9] 🛜 🚗 **Other info:** 5 rooms B&B, 3 rooms static caravan, Camping Pods.
Sailaway Bridgend, Noss Mayo, PL8 1DX ☎ 01752 873556 ✉ sailawaystays@btinternet.com ⊕ www.sailawaystays.webs.com/contact-us	GR: SX554479 ⋮ DP: 0.3 miles N: **NEWTON FERRERS** Offers one night stays [2] 🛜 🚗 **Other info:**
Broadmoor Farmhouse Yealmpton, Plymouth, PL8 2NE ☎ 01752 880407 ✉ broadmoorfarmhouse@hotmail.com ⊕ www.broadmoorfarmhouse.co.uk	GR: SX570495 ⋮ DP: 2 miles N: **NEWTON FERRERS** Offers one night stays [2] 🐕 🛜 🚗 **Other info:** Pick up and drop off to Coast Path available.

NAME	OTHER INFO
The Ivy Barn B&B Fore Street, Holbeton, PL8 1NA 📞 01752 830484 ✉ theivybarn@gmail.com 🌐 www.theivybarnbnb.co.uk	GR: SX613501 DP: 2 miles N: **KINGSTON** Offers one night stays [6] 🐕 📶 🚗 **Other info:** Dietary needs catered (notify in advance). Packed lunch if pre-ordered.
Hooppells Torr Bed and Breakfast Kingston, Kingsbridge, TQ7 4HA 📞 07772 053919 ✉ info@hooppellstorr.com 🌐 www.hooppellstorr.com	GR: SX636484 DP: 1.6 miles N: **KINGSTON** [📶] **Other info:**
Summerwinds B&B Marine Drive Bigbury on Sea, Kingsbridge, TQ7 4AS 📞 01548 810669 / 07540 533854 ✉ tk.summerwinds@gmail.com 🌐 www.southwestcoastpath.org.uk/summerwinds-bigbury	GR: SX651442 DP: 0 miles N: **BIGBURY ON SEA** Offers one night stays [3] 📶 🚗 **Other info:** Rooms not available until 4pm.
Shute Farm South Milton, Kingsbridge, TQ7 3JL 📞 01548 560680 ✉ shutefarmdevon@gmail.com 🌐 www.shutefarm.co.uk	GR: SX699432 DP: 1.5 miles N: **HOPE COVE** Offers one night stays [3] 📶 🚗 **Other info:** Will help with lifts between Salcombe and Bantham.
Horsemans Close Bed and Breakfast West Alvington, Kingsbridge, TQ7 3PL 📞 07528 278506 ✉ ksrawlinson@hotmail.com 🌐 www.bit.ly/33gdjBf	GR: SX722438 DP: N: **KINGSBRIDGE** **Other info:**
Rocarno B&B Rocarno, Grenville Road, Salcombe, TQ8 8BJ 📞 01548 842732 ✉ rocarno@aol.com 🌐 www.rocarno.co.uk	GR: SX736388 DP: 0.25 miles N: **SALCOMBE** Offers one night stays [2] 📶 **Other info:**
Waverely B&B Devon Road, Salcombe, TQ8 8HL 📞 01548 842633 ✉ pauline@waverleybandb.co.uk 🌐 www.waverleybandb.co.uk	GR: SX738388 DP: 0.1 miles N: **SALCOMBE** Offers one night stays [5] 🐕 📶 🚗 **Other info:**
Salcombe Harbour Hotel and Spa Cliff Road, Salcombe, TQ8 8JH 📞 01548 844444 ✉ salcombe@harbourhotels.co.uk 🌐 www.harbourhotels.co.uk/hotels/salcombe	GR: SX739387 DP: 0.5 miles N: **SALCOMBE** Offers one night stays [50] 🐕 🍴 📶 🚗 **Other info:**
Welle House B&B East Prawle, Kingsbridge, TQ7 2BU 📞 01548 511151 ✉ enquiries@wellehouse.co.uk 🌐 www.wellehouse.co.uk	GR: SX778364 DP: 0.5 miles N: **EAST PRAWLE** Offers one night stays [4] 🐕 📶 🚗 **Other info:** Pub serving evening meals 5 minutes walk away.
Down Farm Start Point, Kingsbridge, TQ7 2NQ 📞 01548 511234 ✉ judy@downfarm.co.uk 🌐 www.downfarm.co.uk	GR: SX806377 DP: 0.25 miles N: **START POINT** Offers one night stays [3] 🍴 📶 🚗 **Other info:** Evening meals by prior arrangement. Dogs sleep in the front porch.
The Cricket Inn Beesands, Kingsbridge, TQ7 2EN 📞 01548 580215 ✉ enquiries@thecricketinn.com 🌐 www.thecricketinn.com	GR: SX819403 DP: 0 miles N: **BEESANDS** Offers one night stays [7] 🍴 📶 🚗 **Other info:**

NAME	OTHER INFO
Valseph The Green, Beesands, Kingsbridge, TQ7 2EJ ☎ 01548 580650 / 07890 197673 ✉ valseph@btinternet.com 🌐 www.beesandsbandb.co.uk	GR: SX819406 — DP: 0 miles N: **BEESANDS** Offers one night stays 1 📶 🚗 — Other info:
Roxburgh House Dartmouth Road, Strete, Dartmouth, TQ6 0RW ☎ 01803 770870 ✉ ingrid@roxburghhouse.co.uk 🌐 www.roxburghhouse.co.uk	GR: SX840468 — DP: 0 miles N: **STRETE** 3 🐕 📶 — Other info:
Eight Bells B&B South Embankment, Dartmouth, TQ6 9BB ☎ 07813 803472 ✉ lizhelyer20@gmail.com 🌐 www.dartmouthbandb.com	GR: SX878511 — DP: 0.15 miles N: **DARTMOUTH** Offers one night stays 2 📶 — Other info: From 2020, £80 double & £50 for a single, both to include breakfast.
Sea Tang Guest House 67 Berry Head Road, Brixham, TQ5 9AA ☎ 01803 854651 ✉ flames1@hotmail.co.uk 🌐 www.seatang-guesthouse.com	GR: SX930565 — DP: 0 miles N: **BRIXHAM** Offers one night stays 6 📶 🚗 — Other info:
Beacon House B&B Prospect Steps, South Furzeham Road, Brixham, TQ5 8JB ☎ 01803 428720 ✉ enquiries@beaconbrixham.co.uk 🌐 www.beaconbrixham.co.uk	GR: SX924563 — DP: 0 miles N: **BRIXHAM** Offers one night stays 4 📶 🚗 — Other info: Stunning Sea Views, 5 minutes to harbour.
Westbury Guest House 51 New Road, Brixham, TQ5 8NL ☎ 01803 851684 ✉ westburyguesthouse@gmail.com 🌐 westburyguesthouse.com	GR: SX920559 — DP: 0.2 miles N: **BRIXHAM** Offers one night stays 6 📶 🚗 — Other info: Open all year.
Brixham House 130 New Road, Brixham, TQ5 8DA ☎ 01803 853954 ✉ stay@brixhamhouse.co.uk 🌐 www.brixhamhouse.co.uk	GR: SX916555 — DP: 0.5 miles N: **BRIXHAM** Offers one night stays 6 🐕 📶 🚗 — Other info:
The Clifton at Paignton 9-10 Kernou Road, Paignton, TQ4 6BA ☎ 01803 556545 ✉ enquiries@cliftonhotelpaignton.co.uk 🌐 www.cliftonhotelpaignton.co.uk	GR: SX891607 — DP: 0.01 miles N: **PAIGNTON** Offers one night stays 12 🍴 📶 🚗 — Other info:
The Haldon Guest House 6 Beach Road, Paignton, TQ4 6AY ☎ 01803 551120 ✉ stay@haldonguesthouse.co.uk 🌐 www.haldonguesthouse.co.uk	GR: SX891608 — DP: 0.3 miles N: **PAIGNTON** 7 📶 — Other info: A Full English Breakfast Included. Fruit Cerals Tea and Coffee.
Palace Hotel Esplanade Road, Paignton, TQ4 6BJ ☎ 01803 555121 ✉ info@palacepaignton.co.uk 🌐 www.palacepaignton.com	GR: SX892610 — DP: 0 miles N: **PAIGNTON** Offers one night stays 55 🍴 📶 🚗 — Other info:
The Headland Hotel & Spa Daddyhole Road, Torquay, TQ1 2EF ☎ 01803 295666 ✉ reservations@headlandhotel.co.uk 🌐 www.headlandtorquay.com	GR: SX926629 — DP: 0 miles N: **TORQUAY** Offers one night stays 78 🍴 📶 🚗 — Other info:

NAME	OTHER INFO
The Imperial Park Hill Road, Torquay, TQ1 2DG ☏ 01803 294301 ✉ info@theimperialtorquay.co.uk ⊕ www.theimperialtorquay.co.uk	GR: SX920630 DP: 0 miles N: **TORQUAY** Offers one night stays 〔152〕🐕🍴📶🚗 Other info:
Morley Guest House 16 Bridge Road, Torquay, TQ2 5BA ☏ 01803 292955 ✉ themorleytorquay@gmail.com ⊕ www.themorleytorquay.co.uk	GR: SX906642 DP: 0.7 miles N: **TORQUAY** Offers one night stays 〔7〕🐕📶🚗 Other info: Evening meal at certain times of year. Dog friendly room. Open Oct - April.
Garway Lodge Guest House 79 Avenue Road, Torquay, TQ2 5LL ☏ 01803 293126 ✉ info@garwaylodge.co.uk ⊕ www.garwaylodge.co.uk	GR: SX904645 DP: 1.5 miles N: **TORQUAY** Offers one night stays 〔6〕🐕📶🚗 Other info:
Aveland House Aveland Road, Babbacombe, TQ1 3PT ☏ 01803 326622 ✉ enquiry@avelandhouse.co.uk ⊕ www.avelandhouse.co.uk	GR: SX921652 DP: 0.5 miles N: **BABBACOMBE** Offers one night stays 〔10〕🍴📶🚗 Other info: Contact us for 1 night stays during main holiday periods.
Coastguard Cottage 84 Babbacombe Downs, Babbacombe, Torquay, TQ1 3LU ☏ 01803 311634 ✉ sheila.besidethesea@gmail.com ⊕ www.babbacombebandb.co.uk	GR: SX927653 DP: 0.3 miles N: **BABBACOMBE** Offers one night stays 〔3〕📶 Other info:
Lynton House 7 Powderham Terrace, Teignmouth, TQ14 8BL ☏ 01626 774349 ✉ stay@lyntonhouseteignmouth.com ⊕ www.lyntonhouseteignmouth.com	GR: SX939725 DP: 0 mile N: **TEIGNMOUTH** Offers one night stays 〔12〕🐕📶 Other info:
The Thornhill Mere Lane, Seafront, Teignmouth, TQ14 8TA ☏ 01626 773460 ✉ stay@thethornhill.co.uk ⊕ www.thethornhill.co.uk	GR: SX944730 DP: 0 miles N: **TEIGNMOUTH** Offers one night stays 〔10〕🐕📶 Other info: Open all year.
The Blenheim 1 Marine Parade, Dawlish, EX7 9DJ ☏ 01626 862372 ✉ blenheimholidays@btconnect.com ⊕ www.theblenheim.uk.net	GR: SX962765 DP: 0 miles N: **DAWLISH** Offers one night stays 〔11〕🐕📶 Other info: Open all year.
Langstone Cliff Hotel Mount Pleasant Road, Dawlish Warren, Dawlish, EX7 0NA ☏ 01626 868000 ✉ info@langstone-hotel.co.uk ⊕ www.langstone-hotel.co.uk	GR: SX975783 DP: N: **DAWLISH WARREN** Offers one night stays 〔64〕🐕🍴📶🚗 Other info: All day dining available.
The Croft Guest House Cockwood Harbour, Starcross, Exeter, EX6 8QY ☏ 01626 890282 ✉ croftcockwood@aol.com ⊕ www.thecroftcockwood.com	GR: SX975808 DP: 0 miles N: **STARCROSS** Offers one night stays 〔8〕🐕📶🚗 Other info: 10% Discount on food at The Anchor Inn & The Ship.

Campsites and Holiday Parks

NAME	OTHER INFO	
Mount Folly Farm Bigbury on Sea, TQ7 4AR ☏ 01548 810267 ✉ info@bigburyholidays.co.uk ⊕ www.bigburyholidays.co.uk	GR: SX660446	DP: 0.1 miles
	N: **BIGBURY-ON-SEA**	
	Offers one night stays	
	🐕 🚗	Other info:
Bolberry House Farm Caravan & Camping Park Bolberry, Marlborough, Nr Kingsbridge, TQ7 3DY ☏ 01548 561251 ✉ enquiries@bolberryparks.co.uk ⊕ www.bolberryparks.co.uk	GR: SX695391	DP: 0.25 miles
	N: **HOPE COVE**	
	Offers one night stays	
	🐕 🛒	Other info: Open Easter to October.
Higher Rew Touring Caravan & Camping Park Malborough, Kingsbridge, TQ7 3BW ☏ 01548 842681 ✉ enquiries@higherrew.co.uk ⊕ www.higherrew.co.uk	GR: SX713382	DP: 0.75 miles
	N: **SALCOMBE**	
	Offers one night stays	
	🐕 🛒 🛜 🚗	Other info:
South Bay Holiday Park St Mary's Road, Brixham, TQ5 9QW ☏ 01803 853 004 ⊕ www.johnfowlerholidays.com/devon-holiday-park/ south-bay-holiday-park	GR: SX926548	DP: 0.5 miles
	N: **BRIXHAM**	
	333 🐕 🍴 🛒 🛜 🚗	Other info: Set above Brixham - Caravans and chalets available.
Longmeadow Farm Coombe Road, Ringmore, Shaldon, TQ14 0EX ☏ 01626 872732 ✉ anne@longmeadowfarm.co.uk ⊕ www.longmeadowfarm.co.uk	GR: SX922721	DP: 1 mile
	N: **SHALDON**	
	Offers one night stays	
	🐕 🛜 🚗	Other info: Open Easter - End Sept.
Cofton Holidays Starcross, Dawlish, EX6 8RP ☏ 01626 890111 ✉ info@coftonholidays.co.uk ⊕ www.coftonholidays.co.uk	GR: SX967802	DP: 0.7 miles
	N: **DAWLISH**	
	Offers one night stays	
	🐕 🛒 🛜 🚗	Other info: Open all year

Self Catering

NAME	OTHER INFO	
Carswell Cottages Carswell Farm, Holbeton, PL8 1HH ☏ 01752 830020 ✉ enquiries@carswellcottages.com ⊕ www.carswellcottages.com	GR: SX589477	DP: 0.3 miles
	N: **NOSS MAYO**	
	5 🐕 🛜 🚗	Other info: We have 7 cottages available to rent for short breaks or week stays. Sleeps 2-14.
Bolberry Farm Cottages Bolberry, Kingsbridge, TQ7 3DZ ☏ 07718 187469 ✉ info@bolberryfarmcottages.co.uk ⊕ www.bolberryfarmcottages.co.uk	GR: SX690392	DP: 0.5 miles
	N: **HOPE COVE**	
	7 🐕 🛜 🚗	Other info: Dogs welcome free of charge, private enclosed gardens. Countryside views.
Ocean Reach Holiday Homes Bolberry Down, Salcombe, TQ7 3DY ☏ 07718 187469 ✉ info@oceanreachholidays.co.uk ⊕ www.oceanreachholidays.co.uk	GR: SX688385	DP: 0 miles
	N: **HOPE COVE**	
	6 🐕 🍴 🛜 🚗	Other info: Onsite Oceans Restaurant & Bar - Open all year.

NAME	OTHER INFO	
Kittiwake Cottage East Prawle, Kingsbridge, TQ7 2BY ☎ 07980 310696 ✉ kittiwakecottage@btinternet.com 🌐 www.kittiwakecottage.com	GR: SX781364 DP: 0.5 miles	
	N: **EAST PRAWLE**	
	2 🐕 🐾 📶 🚗	**Other info:** Village with shop and cafe (March -October) and year round pub.
Devon Coastal Cottages Lamacraft Farm, Start Point, Kingsbridge, TQ7 2NG ☎ 01548 288477 ✉ info@devoncoastalcottages.co.uk 🌐 www.devoncoastalcottages.co.uk	GR: SX811385 DP: 0.25 miles	
	N: **START POINT**	
	Offers one night stays	
	6 🐕 🐾 📶 🚗	**Other info:**
Compass Cottage Dartmouth, TQ6 0JN ☎ 0345 800 2070 ✉ cottages@nationaltrust.org.uk 🌐 www.nationaltrust.org.uk/holidays/compass-cottage-devon	GR: SX884504 DP: 1 miles	
	N: **DARTMOUTH**	
	Offers one night stays	
	3 🐕 🐾 🚗	**Other info:**
The Old Newsagent 28 Newcomen Road, Dartmouth, TQ6 9BN ☎ 01803 832842 ✉ jasminecwilliams@icloud.com 🌐 www.theoldnewsagent.co.uk	GR: SX878510 DP: 0.1 miles	
	N: **DARTMOUTH**	
	Offers one night stays	
	1 📶	**Other info:**
Blueriver Cottages 6 - 7 Hauley Road, Dartmouth, TQ6 9AA ☎ 01803 833682 ✉ info@bluerivercottages.co.uk 🌐 www.bluerivercottages.co.uk	GR: SX878512 DP: 0 miles	
	N: **DARTMOUTH**	
	🐾 📶	**Other info:**
Brixham Caravans South Bay Holiday Park St Mary's Road, Brixham, TQ5 9QW ☎ 01243 827179 ✉ sales@brixhamcaravans.com 🌐 www.brixhamcaravans.com	GR: SX926548 DP: 0.5 miles	
	N: **BRIXHAM**	
	Offers one night stays	
	7 🛒 📶 🚗	**Other info:** Great Value Caravan Holiday's In Devon.
Vane Tower Penthouse Vane Tower Vane Hill Road, Torquay, TQ1 2BZ ☎ 07751 827787 ✉ toweronthehill18@gmail.com 🌐 www.vanetower.co.uk	GR: SX920632 DP: 0.2 miles	
	N: **TORQUAY**	
	2 📶 🚗	**Other info:** We are ideally placed for walks from Dartmouth/Brixham/Teignmouth & beyond.

Eat and Drink

NAME	OTHER INFO	
The Odd Wheel Knighton Road, Wembury, PL9 0JD ☎ 01752 863052 ✉ theoddwheel@btconnect.com 🌐 www.theoddwheel.co.uk	GR: SX527496 DP: 0.7 miles	
	N: **WEMBURY**	
	🍴 📶 🚗	**Other info:**
The Old Mill Café Church Road, Wembury, Plymouth, PL9 0HP ☎ 01752 863280 ✉ m1llcafe@btconnect.com 🌐 www.oldmillwembury.co.uk	GR: SX520487 DP: 0 miles	
	N: **WEMBURY**	
	🐾 📶 🚗	**Other info:**

NAME	OTHER INFO	
The Guardhouse Café Berry Head Nature Reserve, Brixham, TQ5 9AW ☎ 01803 855778 ✉ info@guardhousecafe.com 🌐 www.guardhousecafe.com	GR: SX943564 N: **BRIXHAM**	DP: 0 miles
	🐕 📶 🚗	**Other info:** Open all year.
The Strand Cafe 1 Strand, Shaldon, TQ14 0DL ☎ 01626 872624 ✉ info@thestrandcafebistro.co.uk 🌐 www.thestrandcafebistro.co.uk	GR: SX934722 N: **SHALDON**	DP: 1 mile
	🐕	**Other info:** Licensed cafe serving breakfast, lunch & afternoon tea. Cream tea & cakes daily.
Salty Dog Kiosk Smugglers Lane, Holcombe, EX7 0JL ☎ 07850 243 292 ✉ tq14@icloud.com 🌐 www.saltydogkiosks.business.site	GR: SX957747 N: **TEIGNMOUTH**	DP: 0 miles
	🐕 🚗	**Other info:**

Activities

NAME	OTHER INFO	
Paignton Zoo Totnes Road, Paignton, TQ4 7EU ☎ 01803 697500 🌐 www.paigntonzoo.org.uk	GR: SX875599 N: **PAIGNTON**	DP: 1.5 miles
	📶 🚗	**Other info:** Open 10am daily except Christmas Day
Living Coasts Torquay Harbourside, Beacon Quay, Torquay, TQ1 2BG ☎ 01803 697500 🌐 www.livingcoasts.org.uk	GR: SX918631 N: **TORQUAY**	DP: 0 miles
	📶 🚗	**Other info:** Open 10am daily except Christmas Day

Information

NAME	OTHER INFO	
Kingsbridge Information Centre Kingsbridge, TQ7 1HS ☎ 01548 853195 ✉ info@hellokingsbridge.co.uk 🌐 www.hellokingsbridge.co.uk	GR: SX735440 N: **KINGSBRIDGE**	DP: 4.5 miles
	🐕 📶	**Other info:** Open all year. Mon-Sat 9-5pm

Mayflower Steps

South West Water

Proud to support the
South West Coast Path
Association

Transforming our region's bathing waters from polluted seas 25 years ago to some of the finest beaches in Europe today has been our focus for a quarter of a century.

We continue to make improvements to ensure our bathing waters meet stringent standards for bathing water cleanliness.

Nowadays, the region is reaping the benefits of that work: a booming tourist economy where visitors and locals alike enjoy the Coast Path, the beaches, the sea and all the opportunities afforded by our stunning coastline.

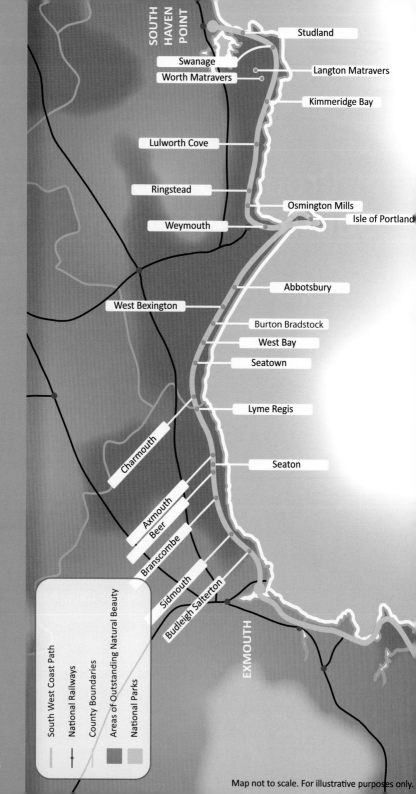

SOUTH
HAVEN
POINT

Studland

Swanage
Worth Matravers

Langton Matravers

Kimmeridge Bay

Lulworth Cove

Ringstead

Osmington Mills

Weymouth

Isle of Portland

Abbotsbury

West Bexington

Burton Bradstock

West Bay

Seatown

Lyme Regis

Charmouth

Seaton

Axmouth
Beer

Branscombe

Sidmouth

Budleigh Salterton

EXMOUTH

South West Coast Path
National Railways
County Boundaries
Areas of Outstanding Natural Beauty
National Parks

Map not to scale. For illustrative purposes only.

The Jurassic Coast
Exmouth to South Haven Point (Poole Harbour) (Sections 58-70)

Geology is both the curse and the boon of this part of the South West Coast Path. As a curse, the geology means the cliffs are vulnerable to slippage, especially in the Sidmouth area, in the Undercliffs and in West Dorset. This has meant that several diversions, necessary but hardly ideal, have had to be put in place for the Coast Path. However, as a boon, the Jurassic Coast's exposed and accessible layers of geological history have made it a textbook example for a wide range of coastal features. These features are also landscape highlights – the classic red cliffs of East Devon; the undisturbed nature reserve of the Axmouth to Lyme Regis Undercliffs; the great shingle bar of Chesil Beach backed by the semi-freshwater lagoon of the Fleet; the fortress-like monolith of the Isle of Portland, jutting into the English Channel; the familiar arch of Durdle Door; the erosion of soft rock once the harder limestone has been broken through forming hollowed-out bays, as at Lulworth Cove; the offshore Purbeck stone stacks at Handfast Point. In addition, the Jurassic Coast contains a number of classic holiday towns; Exmouth, Sidmouth, Lyme Regis, Weymouth and Swanage. This length also contains some taxing gradients for walkers including the climb to the highest point on the south coast of England, Golden Cap, as well as the challenge of the military firing ranges east of Lulworth Cove with its frequent closures.

All of the locations on the map illustration to the left, have at least 1 facility including toilets, a cafe/restaurant, shop or pub.

View of Clavell Tower and Kimmeridge Bay

OS Maps: Landranger 192; Explorer 115

	This Walk	Cumulative	This Walk	Cumulative	Grading	Timing
Ascent	722ft	97,489ft	220m	29,715m	Moderate	3 hours
Distance	5.4mi	519.9mi	8.7km	836.7km		

For detailed directions see our Walking Guide no. 58, Exmouth to Budleigh Salterton.

This is a well-used and popular Section, never far from houses and passing a large caravan site and golf course on the way. Most of this length is on relatively low cliffs and in the west these give excellent views over the mouth of the Exe and the great sandy bar of Dawlish Warren. Further east, the high point of West Down Beacon gives exceptionally fine panoramic views, while beyond the Beacon the Path becomes more enclosed. It is an easy-going Section of some variety, ideal for those not wishing to explore remote or strenuous lengths.

Directions

A regular bus service links Exmouth and Budleigh Salterton, making this a good bus-walk option. In addition, a summer service links Exmouth with Sandy Bay, approximately mid-way along the section, giving another, shorter bus-walk.

Exmouth has all facilities, including a railway station connecting to Exeter. The Coast Path follows the promenade from the redeveloped docks area at the mouth of the Exe, which is also the ferry landing point. Continue to the cliffs at Orcombe Point then climb the steps and continue on the cliff top, passing the Jurassic Coast marker and on to the Caravan Site at Sandy Bay. Follow the fence line inland of the Straight Point rifle range then climb to the high point at West Down Beacon. The Path then descends, seaward of the golf course though offering relatively few sea views on this stretch. Approaching Budleigh Salterton, a charming and traditional small town, the Path turns inland then almost immediately, at a junction, goes right to descend to the end of the promenade. The shops, pubs and other facilities are immediately inland of the Path, which continues towards the distinctive line of pine trees to the east of the town.

Near Exmouth

OS Maps: Landranger 192; Explorer 115

	This Walk	Cumulative	This Walk	Cumulative	Grading	Timing
Ascent	1,037ft	98,526ft	316m	30,031m	Moderate then strenuous	3.5 hours
Distance	7.1mi	527.0mi	11.4km	848.1km		

For detailed directions see our Walking Guide no. 59, Budleigh Salterton to Sidmouth.

Most of this pleasant Section is on relatively low red cliffs with attractive views inland over an undulating pastoral countryside as well as seaward. However, there are contrasts at both ends. The western end skirts the narrow, marsh-fringed estuary of the River Otter while the eastern end includes a wooded cliff top and high cliffs on the appropriately named High Peak and Peak Hill. This is a pleasant and quietly popular Section.

Directions

A regular bus service links Budleigh Salterton and Sidmouth, making a bus-walk a possible.

Budleigh Salterton, a town with something of an olde-world air, has all facilities. The Coast Path goes along the promenade to the car park at the eastern end. Progress east seems tantalisingly close, but the River Otter, with no bridge at its mouth, bars the way. The Path passes through a gate at the rear riverside corner of the car park and follows the riverside path until it meets a road. Turn right and cross the River Otter on the road bridge, then bear right to follow the Path back downriver to the sea.

The Path is clear to the caravan site at Ladram Bay, where there are toilets and seasonal refreshments. Here, descend across a field to the beach access track, going left then immediately right, past a pub and on to climb into woodland at High Peak. Here, the Path goes behind the very top, emerging on a track. Turn right and climb again to the open land at Peak Hill. Follow the Path down the cliff through woodland to a road, turn right then keep right along an old road then onto a large grassy area down to a zigzag Path next to the white Jacob's Ladder steps. At the bottom follow the seafront path to reach the main esplanade. Sidmouth is an elegant Regency town and has all facilities.

River Otter at Budleigh Salterton

OS Maps: Landranger 192; Explorer 115 (most); Explorer 116 (eastern end)

	This Walk	Cumulative	This Walk	Cumulative	Grading	Timing
Ascent	2,408ft	100,934ft	734m	30,765m	Severe then strenuous	5.5 hours
Distance	10.3mi	537.3mi	16.6km	864.7km		

For detailed directions see our Walking Guide no. 60, Sidmouth to Branscombe and Branscombe to Seaton.

This is a Section of lofty cliffs cut by deep and narrow valleys, making for a magnificent coastal landscape but a testing one to walk. In the west the cliffs are characteristically red, but this changes quite abruptly along the length as the Section reaches the most westerly chalk cliffs in England, appropriately bright white. Add an elegant Regency town, a charming picture-postcard village and a quaint fishing town and the result is a length of great attraction.

Directions

A regular bus service links Sidmouth with Seaton, making a bus-walk possible. There are also regular, if less frequent, bus links to Branscombe and Beer along the length giving further options.

The Coast Path passes along the elegant esplanade at Sidmouth to the footbridge over the mouth of the River Sid at the eastern end. Some dramatic cliff falls have occurred just east of Sidmouth and a well-signed diversion is necessary past housing until, at the top of Laskeys Lane, it turns back to the cliff top. A steep climb up Salcombe Hill is soon followed by an equally steep descent and climb through the Salcombe Regis valley. The Path skirts behind the hollow of Lincombe then descends to the beach at Weston Mouth. A short way along the beach the Path leaves to climb steeply back to the cliffs and a good level stretch, which eventually turns inland to meet a track. This descends to Branscombe Mouth, where there are refreshments and toilets. Beyond Branscombe the official Path passes among some holiday chalets then along an undercliff path, with imposing cliffs rearing above, before climbing to the cliff top at Beer Head. These are the most westerly chalk cliffs in England. An alternative route from Branscombe Mouth climbs up the valley side and proceeds directly along the cliff top to Beer Head.

Follow the signed Path from Beer Head, past a caravan site and into the village behind the beach. Beer, an attractive fishing village, has all facilities. Climb the Path on the east side of the beach to the cliff top, descending to a road and down to Seaton Hole. If the tide is low, walk along the beach to the end of the promenade at Seaton. If not, an inland diversion must now be taken. A cliff fall caused by the extreme wet weather in 2012 necessitated permanent closure of the previous Coast Path route. At Seaton Hole turn left on to Old Beer Road and walk approximately 220 yards/200 metres inland towards Beer. Turn right on a path through woodland to arrive at the B3172 Beer Road and turn right here. After approximately 875 yards/800 metres, leave Beer Road and take the Path on the right through the Chine and on to the promenade and into Seaton, which has all facilities, including bus services to Exeter and Lyme Regis.

OS Maps: Landranger 193; Explorer 116

	This Walk	Cumulative	This Walk	Cumulative	Grading	Timing
Ascent	1,401ft	102,335ft	427m	31,192m	Moderate then strenuous	3.5 hours
Distance	7.1mi	544.4mi	11.4km	876.1km		

For detailed directions see our Walking Guide no. 61, Seaton to Lyme Regis.

Some changes have occurred to part of this length following the storms of winter 2013-14. After crossing a golf course then cliff land the route now climbs to a superb viewpoint known as Goat Island, part of the old cliff top which was subject to a massive cliff fall in 1839. From here the path descends into the Axmouth-Lyme Regis Undercliff. This length, a National Nature Reserve, has been undisturbed since that cliff fall and is effectively a wilderness area of virtually virgin woodland and dense scrub, often with an almost eerie character. For most of this part the sea will not be visible. It is an odd and impressive experience, delighting some, but frustrating others.

Directions

Leave Seaton at the east end, using the old concrete bridge to cross the River Axe. Turn inland along the road then turn right up the golf course access road, past the club house then across the fairway to the end of a lane. Turn right off the lane to reach the cliffs, and the Path then rises to the vantage point of Goat Island, with its magnificent views. Continue across the grassy area then follow the Path as it descends through woodland to enter the strange world of the Undercliff.

This old landslip is a National Nature Reserve, being an area of virtual wildlife wilderness. The Path through the Undercliff rarely offers sea views and can feel almost claustrophobic in places. There are no escape routes inland nor safe paths to the sea shore. However, the route is well waymarked and the maps on the Natural England display boards show walkers their exact location; no one should ever feel lost and many find it an exhilarating experience.

Eventually the Path emerges on cliffs and is then waymarked down through woods to arrive adjacent to Lyme Regis's scenic harbour, the Cobb. Lyme Regis is a charming and attractive town and has all facilities.

Seaton Harbour from Axmouth Bridge

OS Maps: Landranger 193; Explorer 116

	This Walk	Cumulative	This Walk	Cumulative	Grading	Timing
Ascent	3,097ft	105,432ft	944m	32,136m	Moderate then strenuous	5.5 hours
Distance	10.0mi	554.4mi	16.1km	892.2km		

For detailed directions see our Walking Guide no. 62, Lyme Regis to West Bay.

A major feature of this Section is the large number of cliff slippages caused by a combination of wet weather and geology. This means that the route between Lyme Regis and Charmouth (approximately 3 miles/4.5km) relies on a footpath diversion. However, the remainder of this Section is a superb coastal experience, climbing as it does over the top of Golden Cap, the highest point on the entire south coast of England, with views to match as well as a challenging steep climb!

Directions

A regular bus service between Lyme Regis, Charmouth, Chideock (which is about 0.75 mile/1.25km inland of Seatown) and West Bay makes a variety of bus walks possible.

Lyme Regis to Charmouth

Major diversions have had to be put in place in this Section, especially between Lyme Regis and Charmouth to avoid the cliff falls that have occurred. A new route is planned for 2020. For up-to-date details on diversions and route changes check the Association's website **www.southwestcoastpath.org.uk**.

Lyme Regis is a charming and attractive town with all facilities. From the Cobb harbour proceed along the esplanade to the small car park at Cobb Gate and the Millennium Clock Tower: the town centre is on your left. Continue along the new sea wall, passing seaward of the Millennium Theatre for approximately 550 yards/500 metres, turn up the large flight of steps on the left that lead to Charmouth Road car park. Cross the car park to the main road (A3052), then turn right uphill past the Football Club beyond. Opposite the cemetery, go through a pedestrian gate to follow the Path across fields to a lane. Turn left and after 100 yards/90 metres turn right at a sign before the wooden gate, climbing through woods to emerge on Timber Hill.

Preferred Diversion, Lyme Regis-Charmouth

Several public footpaths are shown on the Ordnance Survey map seaward of the current Coast Path. These cross The Spittles, Black Ven and the edge of the golf course but are all impassable and closed due to active landslips, which make this a hazardous area. Since the major cliff falls of 2001, this part of the walk has been shown as a 'diversion' in the expectation that the Path could be reinstated along the cliff top. However, the ongoing instability of the cliffs has meant that this has not been possible, and so the Path will continue to be routed inland and across the golf course.

Once you've re-joined the road, turn right and follow the road uphill for 600 yards/550 metres past the entrance to the Golf Club until you reach a fingerpost pointing the route across the golf course. Follow the Path across the golf course to the woods on the far side. The Coast Path turns left at this point to run north-east through the woods to re-join the A3052. Turn right to the roundabout then take the road signposted to Charmouth and shortly after the junction take steps on the right to a stile and public footpath. Follow the waymarked direction up the field to the former Lily Farm, now holiday accommodation. Cross a stile, hidden to the right of the farm gate and pass between the buildings and the

Dutch barn on the left. After the buildings cross a field to arrive after 25 yards/23 metres at a tarmac lane (Old Lyme Hill). Turn right and after 90 yards/80 metres turn left to arrive at Old Lyme Road.

Go left along Old Lyme Road and after 80 yards/70 metres turn right into Westcliffe Road, which is a public right of way for pedestrians. Descend steeply for 330 yards/300 metres to a junction with Five Acres. Bear right here and at the end of the cul-de-sac take a footpath going forward into a narrow lane. Shortly it reaches a wider road (Higher Sea Lane). Turn right and continue ahead, ignoring various signs pointing off the lane, continuing round the bend to the west in the lane that rises for some 130 yards/120 metres to an oak signpost on the left. Here leave the lane through a metal gate to re-join the Coast Path, descending over grassy slopes to Charmouth Beach, with its toilets and refreshments.

Beach route, Lyme Regis to Charmouth

It is possible to walk along the beach between Lyme Regis and Charmouth, but this is not recommended. Mudslides midway along mean that the route is very narrow and only passable at low tide. As such IT SHOULD ONLY BE ATTEMPTED AFTER CHECKING TIDE TABLES AND ON A FALLING TIDE. Many people are cut off or get stuck trying to cross one of the innocuous looking mud flows and have to be rescued.

Coast Path, Charmouth East to Seatown (Chideock)

From the Jurassic Coast Heritage Centre on the seafront at Charmouth (well worth a visit) the route crosses a footbridge and climbs the obvious green path up to Stonebarrow. However, because of cliff falls it may be necessary to follow a diversion here that takes a route away from the coast and up Stonebarrow Lane after the village and rejoins the Path on Stonebarrow Hill. After a couple of moderate hills, the route starts the long, steep climb to Golden Cap, the highest point on England's south coast, but the climb is rewarding as the views from the top are spectacular. At the top go slightly left to the trig point which then leads to the long and steep descent. Approaching Seatown, the Coast Path detours slightly inland before it emerges at Seatown, which has toilets and a pub. A shop and other facilities are at Chideock, 0.75 mile/1.25 kilometres inland.

From Seatown, the Coast Path climbs the cliff slope on its way to the high point of Thorncombe Beacon. There is a descent to the little beach at Eype then a further climb and descent to the harbour at West Bay, which has most facilities.

Towards West Bay, Seatown

OS Maps: Landranger 193 (western half); Explorer 116 (western half)
Landranger 194 (eastern half); Explorer OL15 (eastern half)

	This Walk	Cumulative	This Walk	Cumulative	Grading	Timing
Ascent	275ft	105,707ft	84m	32,220m	Strenuous then moderate	6 hours
Distance	9.3mi	563.7mi	15.0km	907.2km		

For detailed directions see our Walking Guide no. 63, West Bay to Abbotsbury.

From West Bay a sheer red sandstone cliff rises from the sea, looking almost artificial in its straight lines. Then the coastline subsides to a low level and the Coast Path loses its ups and downs. It can still be hard work here though, as the shingle of at the far western end of Chesil Beach tests the legs.

Directions

A regular bus service links West Bay with Abbotsbury, and also calls at Burton Bradstock along the length of this Section, giving various bus-walk options. A popular circular walk based on Abbotsbury uses the Coast Path as well as the South Dorset Ridgeway.

At West Bay go round the back of the harbour, pass to the right of the church and ahead to the West Bay public house, opposite which is the Coast Path sign pointing to the surprisingly steep cliff. Arriving at Burton Freshwater, the Path runs between the caravan park and the beach and is well signed. Following major cliff falls in the summer of 2012 the Coast Path has been reopened along Burton Cliff, although a short inland diversion is necessary around the hotel leading to Burton Beach where there are refreshments and toilets. Further on, the Path passes inland of Burton Mere before coming to West Bexington, where there are toilets and seasonal refreshments.

See Section 71 for details of the alternative Inland Coast Path (South Dorset Ridgeway) between West Bexington and Osmington Mills.

The Coast Path continues along the back of the beach, later passing another car park with toilets and seasonal refreshments and some 200 yards/185 metres beyond this it turns inland to Abbotsbury. There are alternative routes either going into the village or going south and east of Chapel Hill and missing the village. A permissive path alternative leaves the Coast Path and leads direct to the famous Swannery. Abbotsbury is a beautiful stone-built village with much of historic interest and most facilities.

Sunset over Chesil Beach and the Fleet Lagoon

OS Maps: Landranger 194; Explorer OL15

	This Walk	Cumulative	This Walk	Cumulative	Grading	Timing
Ascent	955ft	106,662ft	291m	32,511m	Easy. Chesil Beach route strenuous	4 hours official route
Distance	10.9mi	574.6mi	17.5km	924.7km		

For detailed directions see our Walking Guide no. 64, Abbotsbury to Weymouth.

In the west of this Section, there is an inland rural high-level field route, giving views over the unusual feature of Chesil Beach and the landlocked Fleet behind. To the east, the Path runs along the banks of the Fleet, with pleasant views over this attractive feature, but with views of the sea largely cut off by the shingle bank of Chesil Beach.

Directions

Bus X53 connects Abbotsbury with Weymouth enabling a potential bus-walk.

It is possible to walk direct from the beach near Abbotsbury to Ferry Bridge at Wyke Regis along the length of Chesil Beach. If this is intended, start at the beach at the inland turn (Walk 63) to Abbotsbury, continuing along the beach.

However, note that: 1 It is not possible to get off the beach before Ferry Bridge. **2** It is extremely hard and slow walking. **3** It is necessary to check that firing is not scheduled at the nearby Chickerell Rifle Range; check the web page which is updated regularly – www.gov.uk/government/publications/chickerell-firing-times. Alternatively telephone the Commandant on 01305 831930. **4** The beach is closed to visitors from 1st May to 31st August for the bird nesting season.

From the village of Abbotsbury follow signs to the 'Swannery' (Chapel Lane and Grove Lane take you in the right direction). From the Swannery continue past the car park until the road bends to the right just past a barn. On the left the Coast Path crosses two stiles into a field followed by a steep climb. The Path continues over a stile in line with a thatched cottage and then crosses two more stiles. After the stile in the stone wall turn immediately right down the fields until you come to a finger post pointing left. Cross the minor road and follow the edge of a field with the hedge on your left until you reach another finger post. Go right then left and bear right round Wyke Wood.

At the bottom of the slope is a lane where the Coast Path bears left across two fields to another finger post. Walk on through the next field, eventually reaching a kissing gate and finger to join the Fleet at Rodden Hive. After Langton Hive the Path continues around the edge of the Fleet. Go right at the next finger post and cross Herbury promontory past Gore Cove to Moonfleet Manor and the sandy 'gallops' of Sea Barn Farm racing stables.

At East Fleet a footbridge crosses a small stream to East Fleet Farm camp site then the Path reaches the shore of the Fleet at Chickerell Hive Point. Soon Tidmoor Firing Range sentry box is reached. If the red flag is flying, turn left and walk inland around the range. If the range is open, turn right. After the range the two options join and head to Littlesea Caravan Park. From here the Path climbs a little then levels out. A sharp left turn follows beside a wire fence, which continues around the Wyke Regis Training Area and Bridging Camp. At the camp entrance turn right down a road to reach another path on the left. At the next cove you can cross the sand at low tide. Cliff erosion near Chesil Holiday Village mean there is an inland diversion needed to arrive at Ferry Bridge, following nearby public rights of way. Look for the path turning north east to Martleaves Stud (at grid ref SY 658 767) which then connects with a path heading south east (SY 663 770).

OS Maps: Landranger 194; Explorer OL15

	This Walk	Cumulative	This Walk	Cumulative	Grading	Timing
Ascent	1,112ft	107,774ft	339m	32,850m	Moderate	6 hours
Distance	13.0mi	587.6mi	20.9km	945.6km		

For detailed directions see our Walking Guide no. 65, The Isle of Portland.

Portland is different. Different from the rest of Dorset and from the rest of the Coast Path. An almost-island jutting out into the English Channel, joined to the mainland only by the end of Chesil Beach, it has an isolated air. Formed of limestone, it has been extensively quarried and these workings, some still operational, characterise much of the landscape. Elsewhere, former military buildings and those of Verne Prison and the Young Offenders' Institution are prominent. Portland has a rugged beauty and is well worth exploring with superb views and a rich natural and historic heritage.

Directions

Bus routes run the length of Portland in the summer season (June-September) making a variety of bus-walks possible. There is also a regular bus from Weymouth to Portland throughout the year. This Section is, in any event, a circular walk. Check on local bus information.

From Ferry Bridge cross the causeway onto Portland; this is done by simply following the shared footway/cycleway alongside the A354 road or alternatively by crossing the bridge on the A354 to beyond the boatyard. Then walking along the raised bed of the old railway on the eastern bank to near the end of the causeway at the roundabout for the access road to Osprey Quay and here returning to the footway/cycleway. At the southern of the two roundabouts at Victoria Square take the main road south and shortly turn right into Pebble Lane then left just before the public toilets. Continue and bear right up onto the promenade. About half way along, at the floodgates, cut back sharp left then right, following Coast Path signs up a steep tarmac path, past the school and up the steep path in the grass incline to the steps to the terraced path that was once the old road. Bear off right onto the signed Path running between quarry banks and the cliff face, leading to 3 miles/5km of airy cliff-top walking to Portland Bill. Two short lengths of the Coast Path above West Wears have remained closed since January 2013 following movement in the cliffs. Follow the signed diversions as you proceed along the old quarrymen's tramway. At Portland Bill, as well as the lighthouse, are refreshments, toilets and bus stops.

Continue around the end of the low headland then start northwards, seaward of the wooden chalets, to follow a winding path along the top of low cliffs to join a road above Freshwater Bay after about 1.5 miles/2.5 kilometres. Turn right on the road (use the footway on the west side of the road) for 600 yards/550 metres, past Cheyne Weares car park to a signpost on the right. Follow the zigzag path into the undercliff area and follow the waymarking through disused quarry workings to Church Ope Cove.

Ascend the stepped and signed Path up to Rufus Castle. Here the South West Coast Path also becomes the England Coast Path, the first section of which, from here to Lulworth Cove, was formally opened on 30th June 2012. The signposting now usually indicates simply "Coast Path". Some, but not all, of the improvements to the route that the Association sought on Portland can now be walked and the new route is described below. Unfortunately the major alignment around the north-east corner of Portland was not resolved because of legal complications with Portland Ports plc and security issues.

After Rufus Castle the Coast Path soon joins the track bed of the former Weymouth to Easton railway line. This is then followed northwards for some 1,585 yards/1,450 metres to a pair of signposts. Here, turn left to follow a rocky path that climbs up the cliffs to what appears to be an isolated chimney seen on the skyline above. At the top turn sharp right along the prison road northwards and through a gap in a high wall. On the right is the Old Engine Shed, soon to be converted into a visitor centre. On reaching a narrow road the official route is signed across the road and takes a route across open ground passing disused quarries to reach the perimeter fence of the Verne prison. However, the Association's preferred route here, which is all on public rights of way, can be followed thus:

At the road turn right and just over the brow of a hill turn left on an access track to compounds. Continue ahead on a grassy path towards a large pinnacle of rock (Nichodemus Knob) after which, at the "rock falls" sign, bear left steeply up onto the higher escarpment, heading for a large communications mast. At the high wire perimeter fence turn left and follow it along then round to the right, to reach the south entrance to Verne Prison. Here rejoin the route of the England Coast Path.

Take a path through a little gap to the left of the entrance, passing beside railings and down steep steps. Bear right along a path that traverses under the grassy banks.

The Path drops downhill towards houses to a waymark post. Ignore the left fork and continue on the level on a grass path which then passes through an underpass below a road. Descend steeply towards Castletown down the Merchant's Incline (a former quarry tramway), crossing two footpaths and a road. Pass under a footbridge and through another underpass to reach an access road and turn left to a roundabout.

Continue ahead for some 30 yards/27 metres and then cross to turn right down Liberty Road, signposted to Portland Castle. Go past the castle entrance to the car park and turn right towards the harbour, heading for five black posts. Here join the footway/cycleway to follow the harbour-side to the Sailing Academy, the venue of the sailing events at the 2012 Olympics. Continue on the footway/cycleway to reach the roundabout on the A354 road. From here follow the former railway trackbed to the boatyard before the bridge over the mouth of the Fleet and follow the footway alongside the road to Ferry Bridge.

Near Limekiln Cave on Portland

OS Maps: Landranger 194; Explorer OL15

	This Walk	Cumulative	This Walk	Cumulative	Grading	Timing
Ascent	2,385ft	110,159ft	727m	33,577m	Easy to moderate to strenuous	6.25 hours
Distance	14.4mi	602.0mi	23.2km	968.8km		

For detailed directions see our Walking Guide no. 66, Weymouth to Lulworth Cove.

This section is part of the first section of the England Coast Path. The signposting generally only refers to "Coast Path".

The western part of this Section is a well-trodden walk through the seaside town of Weymouth with its working harbour, sandy beach and attractive Georgian sea front. East of the town is a length of relatively low cliffs but then at White Nothe, two thirds of the way along the section, the coastal geology changes. East of here is a rollercoaster of often sheer white cliffs, the length punctuated by the iconic landmarks of Durdle Door and Lulworth Cove. Both ends of this Section are busy, but in the centre is an often quiet and remote length.

Directions

A bus service (X54) from Weymouth to Osmington (and on to Wool) enables access to the Coast Path mid-way along the Section, allowing some bus-walk options.

From Ferry Bridge the Coast Path follows the foot/cycle path on the route of the old Weymouth to Portland railway (the Rodwell Trail) and passes inland of the sailing centre. Shortly afterwards follow the Coast Path signs and bear off right and then left to walk up the road (Old Castle Road), passing Sandsfoot Gardens and café on your right. Turn right into Belle Vue Road. At the end of Belle Vue Road turn right into Redcliff View then turn left onto the signed path across a grassed area, passing to the left of the Portland Stone monument erected in memory of Thomas Fowell Buxton (1786-1845), Abolitionist & Social Reformer. Follow the Path to the right of the housing estate, cross the pedestrian bridge over Newtons Road at Newtons Cove and follow the Path to and through Nothe Gardens towards Nothe Fort. (Alternatively, for a route closer to the sea turn right down the steps just beyond the seasonal ice cream kiosk and follow the lower path, Jubilee Walk.)

Before reaching the fort take the signed path left past the public conveniences. Cross the fort access road to the foot path and follow the signed path left until you reach steps on your right heading down to Weymouth harbourside. Turn left at the foot of the steps. There is a seasonal ferry (rowing boat) which crosses the harbour by Weymouth Sailing Club. If you don't take the ferry, walk along the harbour and cross the Town Bridge (a lifting bridge which opens at set times of the day to give access to Weymouth Marina). Take the steps at the end of the bridge down to the other side of the harbour to walk towards the Pavilion Theatre. Before reaching the Pavilion turn off left to follow the Esplanade along Weymouth's sea front to reach Overcombe. Here you leave the beach behind. Walk up the minor road towards Bowleaze Cove. After passing the Spyglass Inn the route bears right to cross the crest of the grassed public open space to reach the Beachside Centre at Bowleaze Cove. Follow the signed path through the Beachside Leisure Centre. The Path passes to the right of the Riviera Hotel and then on to Redcliff Point. The Path skirts around an education and adventure centre at Osmington and then goes on to Osmington Mills

See Section 71 for details of the alternative Coast Path (South Dorset Ridgeway) between West Bexington and Osmington Mills. At Osmington Mills turn right and walk down the road to the Smugglers Inn. The Path goes through the pub garden, across a bridge in front of the pub and then round to the back of the pub where the Path crosses a field and passes through an area of scrub and then along the cliffs towards Ringstead. After walking through a wooded area, you reach Ringstead.

At Ringstead follow the track in front of some houses, then bear left on the tarmac road. Turn right just before the car park and café and toilets (both seasonal). Follow the Path towards White Nothe. Shortly after the church (St Catherine's By the Sea) at Holworth the official Path goes straight on, forming two sides of a triangle. (The former path bears off to the right and is still useable, but it can become muddy in wet weather.) At the top of a short incline turn right to continue to follow the Coast Path, signed White Nothe.

Turn left through a kissing gate into a field. Follow the Path and bear right through scrub and up a series of steps. Continue on to White Nothe where you pass in front of the former coastguard cottages. From here follow the Path along the cliffs towards Durdle Door. The route is straightforward to follow but does involve some particularly severe gradients.

Just below the car park and caravan park at Durdle Door turn right at the bridle gate and follow the Path to Lulworth Cove, descending a stone pitched path into the car park. Lulworth Cove has toilets and refreshments and most facilities are found here or at West Lulworth, a little way inland.

Walk to the left of the Visitor Centre and then right to walk round the back of the Visitor Centre. At a junction of roads take the Path leading to Stair Hole, with its spectacular upturned rock formations, and then on to the Commemorative Stone marking the inauguration of the Jurassic Coast as a World Heritage Site. Walk down a series of steps, turning left at the Boat Shed Café, to the shore of the Cove itself.

View from White Nothe looking towards Bat's Head

OS Maps: Landranger 194 (most); Landranger 195 (eastern end); Explorer OL15

	This Walk	Cumulative	This Walk	Cumulative	Grading	Timing
Ascent	2,002ft	112,161ft	610m	34,187m	Severe	4 hours
Distance	7.1mi	609.1mi	11.4km	980.2km		

For detailed directions see our Walking Guide no. 67, Lulworth to Kimmeridge.

The coast of this Section is of geological interest and importance, largely formed by lines of relatively hard limestone having been breached at intervals to form coves and bays as the sea erodes the softer rocks behind. The result is a dramatic coastline of white cliffs and darker coloured coves, some prominent headlands and a succession of extremely steep slopes. Inland, the landscape of the military ranges has been unchanged by farming for some seventy years, though it is perhaps a little too obviously military in a few places.

Directions

A bus service (X54) connects Weymouth-Lulworth Cove-Wool and a seasonal service (X30) connects Lulworth Cove-Swanage. These could provide a bus-walk option.

IMPORTANT: Note that this Section passes through the Lulworth Army Firing Ranges. Before deciding to walk this Section, check that the Ranges are open. Please be aware the official Coast Path for this section may be closed at times to the general public, during the week. However most weekends and during school holidays it is normally open, but please read the section below to check the dates when walkers are allowed access along the official Coast Path. **Please be aware that the firing times can change at the last minute from the dates published below. You can phone 01929 404819 to hear the latest fire times or visit www.gov.uk/government/publications/lulworth-access-times.**

The Lulworth Range walks, including the Coast Path between Lulworth Cove and Kimmeridge Bay, plus access to Tyneham village, are open to the public every weekend.

LULWORTH RANGE WALKS AND TYNEHAM VILLAGE ACCESS TIMES 2020

The Lulworth Range walks and Tyneham Village are open to the public every weekend **excluding** the following dates:

- 22 to 23 February 2020
- 14 to 15 March 2020
- 13 to 14 June 2020
- 19 to 20 September 2020
- 3 to 4 October 2020
- 14 to 15 November 2020

In addition, Lulworth Range walks are open every day during the following times:

Christmas: 21 December 2019 to 5 January 2020

Easter: 4 to 19 April 2020

May Day: 4 May 2020

May stand-down: 25 to 31 May 2020

Summer stand-down: 21 July to 31 August 2020

Christmas: 19 December 2020 to 3 January 2021

Please note that the exhibitions in Tyneham School and Tyneham Church are open from 10am until 4pm. When no firing is taking place the gates to the walks are opened as near as possible to 9am on the Saturday morning and remain open until 8am on the Monday morning.

Tyneham Village gate permits vehicle access. It is opened at 9am daily when no firing is taking place and is closed at dusk each evening.

For further information please phone 01929 404714.

If the Ranges are closed, it is recommended that schedules are re-arranged so that the Coast Path is walked when open. If, however, this is not possible, two alternative inland diversions are shown below. If using these routes you are strongly advised to carry OS 1:25,000 Explorer Map OL15 (Purbeck and South Dorset).

Coast Path – Lulworth Cove to Kimmeridge Bay

The eastbound Coast Path from Lulworth Cove used to leave from behind a café adjacent to the beach – both the café and the cliffs were destroyed in the storms of 2013-14. The first part of the walk is from Lulworth Cove to Pepler's Point and the gate to the firing range fence. There are two options. The easy option is to walk down to the cove from the car park (or via Stair Hole) and then around the stony beach and up the steps at the east end of the cove. This route is usable at most states of the tide. At the top of the steps from the beach turn right and climb up to Pepler's Point.

The alternative route when tides are high is from the cove to go inland for about 500 yards/460 metres through the village to reach Bindon Road on the right, just before 'Cove House', where the road forks at West Lulworth. Here a finger post points along Bindon Road 'Bindon Hill Range Walks'. Walk up Bindon Road for 90 yards/85 metres and turn right through a metal gate to reach a finger post. Bear right here and climb to reach another metal gate and then continue ahead towards the coast with a hedge on your right. Pass another finger post and then the Path follows along the cliff edge above Lulworth Cove. This path reaches the firing range fence by a kissing gate. Turn right here and descend 330 steps on the east side of the cove to meet the Path that comes up from the beach. Here go left to Pepler's Point.

The route onward is straightforward – just follow the yellow topped posts through the ranges to arrive at Kimmeridge Bay. Here are toilets and seasonal refreshments (or all year refreshments in the village 0.6 mile/1 kilometre to the north). There is a new museum in Kimmeridge which is worth visiting – www.jurassiccoast.org/discovering/the-etches-collection.

If Ranges Closed – Alternative Option 1 (13.5 miles/22.0km)

This route is safer and quieter but more strenuous than Option 2; it uses mainly rights of way plus some permissive paths. It should be noted that this route is not specifically signed or waymarked as an official alternative to the Coast Path.

Leave Lulworth Cove as described above for the Coast Path and where the revised route of the Coast Path leaves to the east, continue ahead on a footpath parallel to the B3070 road. At the end of the footpath return to the road and follow it inland, forking right, before taking the next road on the left just after a bus shelter. In 100 yards/90 metres turn right on to a footpath that heads uphill for 0.75 mile/1.2 kilometres. At the second junction of paths turn right (east) and after 100 yards/90m turn left (north) to pass Belhuish Coppice and Belhuish Farm. On reaching the B3070 road at GR835 832 cross the road and take the track opposite. Ignore the first path junction to the north-east and continue downhill to the eastern boundary of Burngate Wood (GR 845 828). Turn north-east on a permissive path (blue) past Park Lodge and go across the road at GR 855 832 onto a bridleway.

Continue along the bridleway for just over 2 miles/3.4 kilometres to GR 866 856 to join a minor road from Highwood veering north and later north-east to meet an east-west road at GR 871 861. Walk east along the road then fork right (signposted Stoborough) at GR 883 856. Go over the crossroads (seat) with the B3070 road at GR 886 855 (*Route Option 2 joins this route at this location) and walk east for a further 1.5 miles/2.5 kilometres along Holme Lane to GR 909 854 (about 330 yards/300 metres before railway underbridge) and turn southwards onto diverted Doreys Farm bridleway (see Option 1A below), which is followed for 1.25 miles/2.1 kilometres before turning right onto Creech Road.

Turn right and in 0.9 miles/1.5 kilometres after Creech Grange the road climbs steeply for 0.6 miles/1.0 kilometres to the Steeple Viewpoint car park. Just before the car park turn left at GR 905 817 on a bridleway that falls steeply southwards to re-join the same road. As the road levels out, at a left hand bend at GR 907 812, take the bridleway/access road ahead that leads south through Steeple Leaze Farm. About 200 yards/185 metres south of the farm take the narrow footpath that heads up steeply south through woods to a bridleway on the ridge. Turn left through a gate and look for a narrow path on the right raking steeply downhill and then across three fields towards the coast ahead and Kimmeridge Bay, where the Coast Path is joined at a T-junction.

Option 1A (This avoids 0.6 miles/1.0km of road walking.)

On Doreys Farm bridleway (see above), after emerging from Bridewell Plantation (GR 914 839), (where a fine house comes into view through trees on the left), go through the first field gate on the right onto the east side of Grange Heath. Initially the route is indistinct and the ground can be wet in and after inclement weather. However, head south-west across the heath and in some 160 yards/146 metres a good gravel path will be found that winds its way across Grange Heath. Although this is described as a permissive path on some maps, legal access is as shown, as this area is designated as Access Land. Follow the Path south-west across the heath to join a bridleway that runs south-east passing a farm to join Creech Road by a telephone box. Turn right on the road and in 0.3 miles/0.5 kilometres pass Creech Grange and then follow the details set out in the final paragraph of Option 1 above.

If Ranges Closed – Alternative Option 2 (12 miles/19km)

This option is mainly road walking, and care is needed on narrow bends. Leave the Cove to West Lulworth on the B3070, then turn right to East Lulworth and beyond, keeping to the B3070 for some 3 miles/5 kilometres to GR 886 855. Here turn right along Holme Lane to GR 911 854. From here, follow the route described from (*) in Option 1 above.

Dorset

OS Maps: Landranger 195; Explorer OL15

	This Walk	Cumulative	This Walk	Cumulative	Grading	Timing
Ascent	1,597ft	113,758ft	487m	34,674m	Strenuous	3.25 hours
Distance	7.1mi	616.2mi	11.4km	991.7km		

For detailed directions see our Walking Guide no. 68, Kimmeridge to Worth Matravers.

This Section mostly hugs the coast running along high cliff tops. Because of the Kimmeridge Clays that are a feature of this Section of the coast, in places the Path can be claggy and slippery after wet weather. There is a particularly steep cliff at Houns-Tout. Towards the eastern end, this length is dominated by St Aldhelm's Head, a flat-topped headland surmounted by an old chapel, which gives extensive views. This is a tough Section with a remote character.

Directions

Bus-walks are not easily undertaken on this Section. Circular walks using the Coast Path, based on inland villages such as Kimmeridge or Kingston, are possible.

The Coast Path from Kimmeridge Bay eastwards is straightforward, although care may be needed where small lengths have slipped, cracked or may be close to the cliff top. Just beyond Kimmeridge, the Clavell Tower has been relocated 27 yards/25 metres inland and an improved Coast Path installed. There is a very steep climb to Houns-Tout and the descent beyond turns inland to avoid dangerous terrain at Chapman's Pool. Look out for a unique stone block sign pointing the way to Chapman's Pool at the bottom of the descent. Beyond Chapman's Pool the route climbs out round St Aldhelm's Head, with excellent coastal views west, then descends to old quarries at Winspit. (For those aiming to end at Worth Matravers, which is about a mile/1.6 kilometres inland, a path heads inland at the valley bottom at Winspit. The village has a pub, shop and café.)

Sunset at St. Aldhelm's Head

OS Maps: Landranger 195; Explorer OL15

	This Walk	Cumulative	This Walk	Cumulative	Grading	Timing
Ascent	657ft	114,415ft	200m	34,874m	Severe then Moderate	4 hours
Distance	6.5mi	622.7mi	10.5km	1,002.1km		

For detailed directions see our Walking Guide no. 69, Worth Matravers to Swanage.

The western part of this Section is dominated by St Aldhelm's Head, a flat-topped headland of limestone surmounted by an old chapel. There are extensive views, especially along the coast to the west. Leaving the valley at Winspit the cliffs become increasingly marked by the remains of old small-scale quarrying activity. The route then passes through the Country Park at Durlston Head before rounding the headland to enter Swanage.

Directions

Numerous footpaths cross the cliffs to the Coast Path from the outskirts of Swanage and the inland village of Langton Matravers. The Poole-Swanage Breezer no.40 bus runs throughout the year and this assists in enabling bus-walks which combine these link paths with the Coast Path.

(For those starting in Worth Matravers village, walk past the cottages in London Row then follow the path over a field to the track which leads down the valley to Winspit Quarry on the Coast Path.)

From Winspit there is a fine high level walk to Durlston Head. Signing in Durlston Country Park is limited; keep on the low level path all the way round Durlston Head then, coming up on the north side take the second turning right (the first is a cul-de-sac to a quarry). Durlston Castle has now been converted to a Jurassic Coast Gateway Centre and includes refreshment facilities.

After leaving Durlston Castle follow a broad stony path north through the woods for some 760 yards/700 metres to a barrier and sign. From here there is a permanent diversion following a cliff fall. Turn left on a good path for some 125 yards/115 metres to reach Durlston Road at a gate. Turn right and in 185 yards/170 metres turn right again into Belle Vue Road. Follow the road north-eastwards to the grassed open space leading to Peveril Point. In bad weather or at high tides use the roadway and then down to the footpath at the end of the coastal buildings, otherwise use the foreshore. Continue along Swanage's sea front promenade. Swanage has all facilities.

Swanage pier

OS Maps: Landranger 195; Explorer OL15

	This Walk	Cumulative	This Walk	Cumulative	Grading	Timing
Ascent	492ft	114,907ft	150m	35,024m	Moderate	3.5 hours
Distance	7.5mi	630.2mi	12.1km	1,014.2km		

For detailed directions see our Walking Guide no. 70, Swanage to South Haven Point.

This is an excellent and scenic Section. The southern, Swanage end comprises of increasingly high cliffs, culminating in the length between Ballard Point and Handfast Point, with its offshore stacks. This is an exhilarating length with superb views over Poole Bay to Bournemouth and across the Solent to the matching cliffs of the Needles on the Isle of Wight. The northern end passes along a long sandy beach before arriving at the mouth of Poole Harbour, an enormous enclosed water area and the second largest natural harbour in the world.

Directions

A regular bus service, (Breezer 50) half hourly in summer and hourly in winter, links Swanage with South Haven Point, making a bus-walk a good option. There are also popular local circuits using the Coast Path in the Swanage-Ballard Down-Studland area. If needed check that the Sandbanks to Studland ferry is running as there is a lengthy alternative route for onward journeys to and from Poole and Bournemouth.

Swanage has all facilities. The Coast Path passes along the town's sea front, following the main road (Ulwell Road) at the north end by the telephone box where it bears left and on ahead into Redcliff Road at a one-way system. At a shop and post-box turn sharp right into Ballard Way – do not be put off by "Private Estate" signs. Continue forward into the chalet estate and follow signs for the Coast Path, to emerge on a grassed area on the cliff edge. Turn left and follow the Path to reach the footbridge and steps that come up from the beach. Except at very high tides or in severe weather it is possible to follow a beach route rather then the Ulwell Road to get to the footbridge. From the sea front continue on past the Bull & Boat restaurant, along the sand (or raised walkway) and past some beach huts. You have to scramble over some groynes until you reach some steps that go up from the beach to meet the footbridge on your left. Don't cross the footbridge but go right and up some steps.

The Path climbs out to Ballard Down, then the obvious high-level route continues out to Handfast Point and the much-photographed rocks of Old Harry before turning west towards Studland. The Path from Old Harry is flat with good views across Studland Bay. After about ¾ mile, there is a finger post pointing right to 'Alternative Coast Path South Beach'. If tidal conditions permit and this route is taken when you reach South Beach go north along the beach to reach a track just in front of the café which then leads back to the road. At the road turn right to reach the Bankes Arms.

Following the official Coast Path continues on to reach the road and toilets on your right. Turn right and follow the road up past the Bankes Arms. Just opposite the NT car park entrance (on the left) is a path on your right (next to a house) that heads towards the coast. At the coast go left and walk around the grounds of 'The Pig on the Beach' to reach Fort Henry where WW 2 leaders watched preparations for D Day. Around Fort Henry the Path leads to the car park at Middle Beach. Turning right takes you towards the beach and the slope onto Middle Beach.

The last section is on the sand and is best done when the tide is low or going out so that you walk on firm sand. Walk down the slope, and onto Middle Beach (seasonal cafe and toilets). Walk along Middle Beach, over the concrete slipway and onto Knoll Beach (at high tide there is an alternative behind the toilets and beach huts). Soon after Knoll Beach is the naturist length of Studland Beach. Finally walk round the point and into Shell Bay and South Haven Point and the ferry.

If you wish to avoid the naturist section there is a path through the Studland Nature Reserve (called the Heather Walk) from Knoll Beach to Shell Bay. However, you may still encounter naturists who use the dunes above the beach.

The ferry operates all year daily every 20 minutes, from Shell Bay (South Haven Point) from Sandbanks. If you intend to use the ferry at this time check the Association's website or the ferry company's website above. For ferry details see page 24.

Postscript

For those who have been with us all the way from Minehead, be it in one go or in bits and pieces over a period, a final few words seem appropriate. Alfred Wainwright, at the end of his work on the Pennine Way, said; "You have completed a mission and satisfied an ambition. You have walked the Pennine Way, as you have dreamed of doing. This will be a very satisfying moment in your life. You will be tired and hungry and travel stained. But you will feel great, just great." Just substitute the South West Coast Path for the Pennine Way and Wainwright's words will doubtless ring true. You will be glad and proud that you have walked and finished Britain's longest and finest footpath. As Wainwright said of the Pennine Way, it's a longer step than most take in their lifetime!

Down the hill to Osmington

OS Maps: Landranger 194; Explorer OL15

	This Walk	This Walk	Grading	Timing
Ascent	2,290ft	698m	Moderate	8 hours
Distance	17.1mi	27.5km		

For detailed directions see our South Dorset Ridgeway West Bexington to Osmington Mills Walking Guide.

This is a very scenic walk, parallel to the coast and a varying distance inland. For most of its length quite extensive coastal views are obtained beyond a green and rural foreground. Substantial lengths follow chalk ridges and these give impressive views north as well. Coastal features such as Portland and Chesil Beach are clearly seen, as are the flanks of the enormous Iron Age Maiden Castle inland. This is a quiet route, often feeling quite remote, and with usually no refreshments on its length it requires preparation. It is, nevertheless, a superb experience.

Directions

Bus services link both ends, Swyre (for West Bexington) and Osmington, with Weymouth, making a bus-walk possible, especially using Weymouth as a base.

The Dorset element of the Coast Path is unique in having an official alternative route for part of its length. This was often referred to by the apparently contradictory name of the "Inland Coast Path". It is, however, now known as the South Dorset Ridgeway (SDR) and the signposting uses that name almost throughout. The waymarking has also been replaced and incorporates the name of the South Dorset Ridgeway. The length of the Section, and the fact that the two ends may be reached by bus from Weymouth, make it an ideal long day's walk. However, be aware that other than one seasonal mobile refreshment van if the timing is right, no facilities are found anywhere along the route other than at the two ends, so it is necessary to be well prepared. A detailed route description is given below.

Leave West Bexington car park by the milestone marked "South Dorset Ridgeway Osmington Mills 17" and turn inland up the road. Where the road bears left continue forward up the stony track, signposted SDR.

Near the top of the hill take the right hand fork signed "5¾ Hardy Monument". Before reaching the layby on the B3157 road there is a bench from which there is a panoramic view of the coast. At the layby go over the stile to the left of the field gate and follow the Path to reach the Limekiln. At the Limekiln bear left following the signed path. After passing through a pedestrian gate go straight ahead (rather than bearing off to the left and up to the signpost just visible in the distance). This takes you past a footpath off to the right signed "East Bexington & Beach 1", should you wish to make a detour. If not follow the signed SDR to reach a National Trust sign for Tulk's Hill adjacent to a kissing gate and field gate alongside the B3157. This time cross the road and go over the style, signposted "Hardy Monument 4".

Follow the Path and a series of steps through the Abbotsbury Castle prehistoric hill fort, passing the trig point with superb views in all directions, including Hardy Monument in the distance. At the end of the hill fort go through a kissing gate and follow the Path down to and across a minor road. Go through a metal pedestrian gate to follow the Path in an easterly direction along the ridge of Wears Hill and the Crest of White Hill, following the signed path. Be careful not to follow any signs indicating routes down to the village of Abbotsbury in the valley below and its adjacent hilltop chapel. At the east end of White Hill bear north-east as signed and leave the field in the north-east corner through a gate on to a minor road. Continue north-east along this road for some 50 yards/46 metres and then turn right as signposted.

Follow the narrow and rough bridleway along the wire fence above the scrub to a path junction; where the bridleway bears right take the yellow waymarked footpath to the left and cross a stile. At the end of this short section take a headland path north-east. At the far side of the field the track then leads approximately 50 yards/46 metres to a further gate with a stile and waymark. Immediately adjacent to this gate is a prehistoric stone circle, a scheduled ancient monument. Continue forward on the track, leaving a small wood to the left, to reach the road between Portesham and Winterbourne Steepleton. Turn left along the road for about 60 yards/55 metres and then turn right over a stile into a field, signed "Hardy Monument". Continue eastwards through four fields. At a small wooded area before Black Down Barn (ruin) turn north at a signpost to Hardy Monument. Climb through the woods to the recently renovated monument. In the 'summer' season it may be possible to find a mobile refreshment van here.

To continue find a roadside signpost 30yards/32 metres east of the car park entrance. Cross the road and descend eastward on a narrow path. Reaching the same road again, ignore the signpost "Bridleway to Coast Path" and the track opposite and turn left along the road, then in another 30 yards/32 metres turn right, signposted "Restricted Byway" with a Jubilee Trail disc.

Now there is a good ridgeway path for some 3 miles/4.8 kilometres, with excellent views seaward. At a point some 550 yards/500 metres after passing under the second set of HV power lines take the gate north of a large tumulus to stay on the north side of the fence running along the ridge. On reaching the B3159 road, marked by the Borough of Weymouth boundary stone, continue across as signposted and towards the A354 road. Cross the bridge over the A354 and follow the signed path alongside the A354 until it bears off to the left towards Bincombe Down.

Continue eastwards, then before the farm, with its adjacent radio mast, take care to go through the gate on the right, marked with a blue arrow. After crossing the field, leaving two tumuli on the left, reach a metalled road and turn right. At the junction at the corner of Came Wood turn right at the signpost "Bridleway to Bincombe". At the end of the Path join a metalled lane and at the road junction turn left, signposted "South Dorset Ridgeway".

Drop down the road into the village of Bincombe and where the road turns right take the track forward leaving the small church on the right. Where the Path splits take the left-hand fork, marked with a blue arrow and acorn. After the overhead HV power lines, pass through a small signposted wooden gate and then proceed forward through one field, into the next to a footpath sign. Here turn left and there is a choice of routes for the next couple of hundred yards/metres.

For the best option, at a waymark post turn sharp right down a steep grassy slope to a stile at a road ahead. Cross the road to go over another stile to follow a grassy path that contours around the south and east sides of Green Hill. On reaching a road at a gate and stile turn left and in 50 yards/46 metres turn right through a gate signposted "Osmington 2¾". The Path is now easy to follow with extensive views to seaward over Weymouth and Portland. On passing a ruined building on the left the route reaches a broad track; here turn right, signposted "Osmington" and after about 200 yards/185 metres go through a gate as signposted. Shortly afterwards pass a trig point on the right and at the next field gate bear left and follow the field boundary along White Horse Hill. Just beyond the next gate fork right, signposted "For Osmington".

Descend to Osmington and follow the signs through the village. On reaching the main road (A354 to Weymouth) near the Sly Fox Inn turn left and in about 250 yards/230 metres turn right at a signpost, over a stile and footbridge. Follow the field boundary on the left through two fields – at the top look back to see the Hardy Monument in the distance and the White Horse on the hillside. Go over the stile to the footpath sign, then turn half right to cross the field at an angle to a further stile. Cross it and turn left along the hedge side to the bottom. At the end of the field there is a very short length of enclosed footpath to the road; turn right along it descending to Osmington Mills.

Jurassic Rock Pools at Osmington Mills

If you enjoy sleeping, eating or drinking at any business on the Path please suggest they join us as Business Members so that we can share their brilliance!

The businesses listed here are all supporters and members of the South West Coast Path Association. Please find more details on our website www.southwestcoastpath.org.uk

- **GR** Grid Reference
- **DP** Distance from the Path
- **N** Nearest Town/Village with facilities
- **3** Number Of Rooms
- 🐕 Dogs Welcome
- 🍴 Evening Meal Available
- 🛜 Wifi
- 🚗 Parking
- 🛒 Grocery Shop On Site

Bed & Breakfast and Hotels

NAME	OTHER INFO
Quentance Farm Bed & Breakfast Salterton Road, Exmouth, EX8 5BW ☎ 01395 442733 ✉ palleandrose@hotmail.com 🌐 www.quentancefarm.co.uk	GR: SY036820　DP: 1.75 miles N: **BUDLEIGH SALTERTON** Offers one night stays **3** 🐕 🛜 🚗　Other info:
Victoria Hotel Sidmouth, EX10 8RY ☎ 01395 512651 ✉ reservations@victoriahotel.co.uk 🌐 www.victoriahotel.co.uk	GR: SY121871　DP: 0.2 miles N: **SIDMOUTH** Offers one night stays **64** 🍴 🛜 🚗　Other info:
The Bedford Hotel The Esplanade, Sidmouth, EX10 8NR ☎ 01395 513047 ✉ reservations@bedfordhotelsidmouth.co.uk 🌐 www.bedfordhotelsidmouth.co.uk	GR: SY125872　DP: 0 miles N: **SIDMOUTH** **40** 🐕 🍴　Other info:
Southcombe Guest House Vicarage Road, Sidmouth, EX10 8UQ ☎ 01395 513861 ✉ southcombeguesthouse@gmail.com 🌐 www.southcombeguesthouse.co.uk/index.html	GR: SY127880　DP: 0 miles N: **SIDMOUTH** Offers one night stays **8** 🛜 🚗　Other info:
Higher Coxes Farm Weston, Sidmouth, EX10 0PG ☎ 01297680528 / 07976618698 ✉ burroughcoxes@btconnect.com 🌐 www.devon-bedandbreakfast-highercoxesfarm.co.uk	GR: SY175889　DP: 0.6 miles N: **BRANSCOMBE** Offers one night stays **1** 🐕 🍴　Other info:
Belmont House, Beer Dolphin Road, Beer, EX12 3EN ☎ 01297 24415 ✉ belmonthousebeer@gmail.com 🌐 www.belmonthousebedandbreakfast.com	GR: SY228892　DP: 0 miles N: **BEER** Offers one night stays **5** 🛜 🚗　Other info: Adult Only & sorry no pets. Open all year.
Colebrooke House Fore Street, Beer, EX12 3JL ☎ 01297 20308 ✉ contact@jurassiccoaststays.co.uk 🌐 book.jurassiccoaststays.co.uk/property_page.php?propertyId=39588	GR: SY228894　DP: 0 miles N: **BEER** **6** 🛜　Other info:
Stay in Beer Garlands, Stovar Long Lane, Beer, EX12 3EA ☎ ✉ beervillageuk@gmail.com 🌐 beervillage.co.uk/commercial-directory/	GR: SY229822　DP: 0 miles N: **BEER** Other info:

NAME	OTHER INFO
Westley B&B Lyme Road, Uplyme, Lyme Regis, DT7 3UY ☎ 01297 445104 ✉ westleybandb@btinternet.com 🌐 www.westleybedandbreakfast.wordpress.com	GR: SY324934 DP: 1 mile N: **LYME REGIS** Offers one night stays [3] 📶 🚗 Other info: Two double rooms, One twin room, all with en-suite or private bathroom.
Lucerne View Road, Lyme Regis, DT7 3AA ☎ 01297 443752 ✉ stay@lucernelyme.co.uk 🌐 www.lucernelyme.co.uk	GR: SY339923 DP: 0.25 miles N: **LYME REGIS** Offers one night stays [4] 📶 🚗 Other info:
Chideock House Main Street, Chideock, DT6 6JN ☎ 01297 489242 ✉ annachideockhouse@yahoo.co.uk 🌐 www.chideockhouse.co.uk	GR: SY422928 DP: 0.75 miles N: **SEATOWN** Offers one night stays [3] 🐕 📶 🚗 Other info: Grade 2 listed 15th c thatched. Family business.
Mervyn House Chideock, DT6 6JN ☎ 01297 489578 ✉ callbrig@gmail.com 🌐 www.chideockandseatown.co.uk/accommodation/mervyn-house	GR: SY422928 DP: 0.3 miles N: **SEATOWN** Offers one night stays [2] 🛒 📶 🚗 Other info: Sitting Room & Kitchenette available.
Broadlands B&B Chideock, Bridport, DT6 6HX ☎ 01297 489543 ✉ enquiries@broadlandschideock.co.uk 🌐 www.broadlandschideock.co.uk	GR: SY427927 DP: 1 mile N: **SEATOWN** Offers one night stays [1] 📶 🚗 Other info:
Eype's Mouth Country Hotel Eype, Bridport, DT6 6AL ☎ 01308 423300 ✉ info@eypesmouthhotel.co.uk 🌐 www.eypesmouthhotel.co.uk	GR: SY448913 DP: 0.25 miles N: **WEST BAY** Offers one night stays [17] 🍴 📶 🚗 Other info: Situated on the SWCP a few minutes walk from the beach.
Graston Farm Cottages Graston Farm, Annings Lane, Burton Bradstock, DT6 4NG ☎ 01308 897603 ✉ info@grastonfarm.co.uk 🌐 www.grastonfarm.co.uk	GR: SY503899 DP: 1.5 miles N: **BURTON BRADSTOCK** [18] 🐕 📶 🚗 Other info: Open all year
Cowards Lake Farmhouse B&B 13 West Street, Abbotsbury, DT3 4JT ☎ 01305 871421 / 07970 181034 ✉ cowards-lakebandb@btconnect.com 🌐 www.abbotsbury.co.uk/cowards-lake-farm-house	GR: SY571853 DP: 0.33 miles N: **ABBOTSBURY** Offers one night stays [2] 🐕 📶 🚗 Other info:
Wheelwright's Cottage 14 Rodden Row, Abbotsbury, DT3 4JL ☎ 01305 871800 ✉ suenigel@wheelwrights.co.uk 🌐 www.wheelwrights.co.uk	GR: SY578852 DP: 1 mile N: **ABBOTSBURY** Offers one night stays [1] 📶 Other info: Off-road parking available
Moonfleet Manor Hotel Fleet Road, Weymouth, DT3 4ED ☎ 01305 786948 ✉ info@moonfleetmanorhotel.co.uk 🌐 www.moonfleetmanorhotel.co.uk	GR: SY617806 DP: 0.8 miles N: **ABBOTSBURY** Offers one night stays [36] 🐕 🍴 📶 🚗 Other info: Open all year

NAME	OTHER INFO
Alessandria Hotel 71 Wakeham Road, Portland, Weymouth, DT5 1HW ☎ 01305 822270 ✉ booking@alessandriahotel.co.uk 🌐 www.alessandriahotel.co.uk	GR: SY694716 · DP: 0 miles N: **ISLE OF PORTLAND** Offers one night stays [14] 🐕 📶 🚗 · **Other info:** Dogs by arrangement. Please telephone to book.
Turnstones 6 Ventnor Road Fortuneswell, Portland, DT5 1JE ☎ 07969 040811 ✉ info@turnstones.net 🌐 www.turnstones.net	GR: SY686735 · DP: 0.5 miles N: **ISLE OF PORTLAND** Offers one night stays [3] 📶 🚗 · **Other info:** Open All Year
Harbour Lights Guest House 20 Buxton Road, Weymouth, DT4 9PJ ☎ 01305 783273 ✉ harbourlights@btconnect.com 🌐 www.harbourlightsguesthouse.com	GR: SY673779 · DP: 0.1 miles N: **WEYMOUTH** Offers one night stays [9] 📶 🚗 · **Other info:** 4 star Visit England silver award.
Kelston Guest House 1 Lennox Street, Weymouth, DT4 7HB ☎ 01305780692 ✉ karensjames@gmail.com 🌐 www.kelstonguesthouse.co.uk	GR: SY681157 · DP: 0.5 miles N: **WEYMOUTH** Offers one night stays [5] · **Other info:** Parking Permits are available f.O.C for street parking. Bike Hire is available.
1 Old Coastguard Cottages Osmington Mills, Weymouth, DT3 6HQ ☎ 01305 832663 ✉ hope.horvath68@live.co.uk 🌐 www.southwestcoastpath.org.uk/1-old-coastguardsosmington-mills	GR: SY736817 · DP: 0 miles N: **OSMINGTON MILLS** Offers one night stays [2] 📶 · **Other info:**
The Dairy House B&B Chaldon Herring, Dorchester, DT2 8DN ☎ 01305 852138 / 07968225269 ✉ joanneselfe@hotmail.com 🌐 www.southwestcoastpath.org.uk/dairy-house-bb-chaldon-herring	GR: SY795834 · DP: 2 miles N: **LULWORTH COVE** Offers one night stays [2] 🐕 📶 🚗 · **Other info:**
Chiltern Lodge 8 Newfoundland Close, Worth Matravers, BH19 3LX ☎ 01929 439337 ✉ densor@btopenworld.com 🌐 www.chilternlodge.co.uk	GR: SY975777 · DP: 1 mile N: **WORTH MATRAVERS** Offers one night stays [2] 🍴 📶 🚗 · **Other info:** Open All Year.
Kingston Country Courtyard West Street, Kingston, Wareham, BH20 5LR ☎ 01929 481066 ✉ enquiries@kingstoncountrycourtyard.com 🌐 www.kingstoncountrycourtyard.com	GR: SY962793 · DP: 2 miles N: **KINGSTON** Offers one night stays [25] 🐕 📶 🚗 · **Other info:** Packed lunches on request.
Alford House B&B 120 East Street, Corfe Castle, BH20 5EH ☎ 01929 480156 ✉ info@alfordhouse.com 🌐 www.alfordhouse.com	GR: SY962 816 · DP: 2 miles N: **KINGSTON** Offers one night stays [3] 🐕 📶 🚗 · **Other info:** There are four pubs within 10 minutes walk for an evening meal.
Knoll House Hotel Ferry Road, Studland, BH19 3AH ☎ 01929 450450 ✉ info@knollhouse.co.uk 🌐 www.knollhouse.co.uk	GR: SZ030833 · DP: 0.1 miles N: **STUDLAND** Offers one night stays [71] 🐕 🍴 📶 🚗 · **Other info:** Open Feb-Dec

Campsites and Holiday Parks

NAME	OTHER INFO	
Ladram Bay Holiday Park Ladram Road, Otterton, Budleigh Salterton, EX9 7BX ☎ 01395 568398 ✉ info@ladrambay.co.uk 🌐 www.ladrambay.co.uk	GR: SY095 852	DP: 0.1 miles
	N: **BUDLEIGH SALTERTON**	
	Offers one night stays	
	🐕 🍴 🛒 📶 🚗	**Other info:** Restaurant, Takeaway, Swimming pool, Shop, Entertainment & Activities.
Oakdown Holiday Park Gatedown Lane, Weston, Sidmouth, EX10 0PT ☎ 01297 680387 ✉ enquiries@oakdown.co.uk 🌐 www.oakdown.co.uk	GR: SY167902	DP: 2 miles
	N: **SIDMOUTH**	
	Offers one night stays	
	🐕 🍴 🛒 📶 🚗	**Other info:**
St Gabriels Golden Cap Campsite Shedbush Lane, Morcombelake, Bridport, DT6 6DR ☎ 0345 335 1296 ✉ westdorset@nationaltrust.org.uk 🌐 www.nationaltrust.org.uk/holidays/st-gabriels-campsite-golden-cap	GR: SY404936	DP: 1 mile
	N: **SEATOWN**	
	Offers one night stays	
	🐕 🚗	**Other info:** 15 pitches
Tom's Field Campsite & Shop Langton Matravers, Swanage, BH19 3HN ☎ 01929 427110 ✉ tomsfield@hotmail.com 🌐 www.tomsfieldcamping.co.uk	GR: SY995785	DP: 1 mile
	N: **SWANAGE**	
	🛒	**Other info:**

Self Catering

NAME	OTHER INFO	
The Granary, Larkbeare Grange Talaton, Exeter, EX5 2RY ☎ 01404 822069 ✉ granary@larkbeare.net 🌐 www.larkbearegranary.net	GR: SY067976	DP: 12 miles
	N: **SIDMOUTH**	
	2 🐕 📶 🚗	**Other info:** Accessible NAS level 1. Excellent drying facilities.
Higher Wiscombe Southleigh, EX24 6JF ☎ 07772 630104 ✉ info@higherwiscombe.com 🌐 www.higherwiscombe.com	GR: SY180933	DP: 3 miles
	N: **SIDMOUTH**	
	16 🐕 📶 🚗	**Other info:** Luxury Eco holiday cottages. Mid-week breaks a speciality
Forge Cottage Seaton, EX12 3DB ☎ 0345 800 2070 ✉ cottages@nationaltrust.org.uk 🌐 www.nationaltrust.org.uk/holidays/forge-cottage-devon	GR: SY197887	DP: 1 mile
	N: **SEATON**	
	2 🐕 📶 🚗	**Other info:**
Holyford Farm Cottages Holyford Lane, Colyford, Colyton, EX24 6HW ☎ 01297 552983 ✉ stay@holyfordfarm.co.uk 🌐 www.holyfordfarm.co.uk	GR: SY236923	DP: 1.5 mile
	N: **SEATON**	
	Offers one night stays	
	6 🐕 📶 🚗	**Other info:** 3 cottages sleeping 6,4,2. Open All Year.
Stone Barrow Bunkhouse Charmouth, DT6 6RA ☎ 0344 335 1296 ✉ bunkhouses@nationaltrust.org.uk 🌐 www.nationaltrust.org.uk/holidays/stone-barrow-bunkhouse-dorset	GR: SY373933	DP: 1 mile
	N: **CHARMOUTH**	
	2 🚗	**Other info:**

NAME	OTHER INFO		
Shedbush Farm House Shedbush Lane, Morcombelake, Bridport, DT6 6DR ☎ 0345 800 2070 ✉ cottages@nationaltrust.org.uk 🌐 www.nationaltrust.org.uk/holidays/shedbush-farm-house-dorset	GR: SY404936 DP: 2 miles N: **SEATOWN** Other info: 3 🐕 🛜 🚗		
Dorset Seaside Cottages Chideock and Greenwich Cottage, Bridport, DT6 6JF ☎ 01297 480882 ✉ info@dorsetseasidecottages.co.uk 🌐 www.dorsetseasidecottages.co.uk	GR: SY424927 DP: 0.75 miles N: **SEATOWN** 2 🛜 🚗 Other info: Open all year		
Ammonite Cottage 5 Seymour Place East Street, Bridport, DT6 3LR ☎ 01308 459342 ✉ emilyaltham@yahoo.co.uk 🌐 www.ammonitecottage.wordpress.com	GR: SY469928 DP: 1.5 miles N: **WEST BAY** Offers one night stays 2 🐕 Other info: Open all year		
Chesil Cottage West Bexington, DT2 9DE ☎ 0345 800 2070 ✉ cottages@nationaltrust.org.uk 🌐 www.nationaltrust.org.uk/holidays/chesil-cottage-dorset	GR: SY541862 DP: 0 miles N: **WEST BEXINGTON** 2 🐕 🛜 🚗 Other info:		
Fossil & The Cross Cottage - Dream Cottages Swyre Road, West Bexington, DT2 9DF ☎ 01305 789000 ✉ admin@dream-cottages.co.uk 🌐 www.dream-cottages.co.uk/holiday-search/south-west-dorset-cottages	GR: SY532872 DP: 1 mile N: **WEST BEXINGTON** Other info: 2 🐕 🚗		
Upton Grange Holiday Cottages Totemplant, Ringstead, Weymouth, DT4 9LH ☎ 01305 853970 ✉ info@uptongrangedorset.co.uk 🌐 www.uptongrangedorset.co.uk	GR: SY742831 DP: 1 mile N: **RINGSTEAD** 🛜 🚗 Other info:		
Portland House Weymouth, DT4 8RZ ☎ 0345 800 2070 ✉ cottages@nationaltrust.org.uk 🌐 www.nationaltrust.org.uk/holidays/portland-house-dorset	GR: SY679779 DP: 0 miles N: **WEYMOUTH** 7 🛜 🚗 Other info:		
Spyway Langton Matravers, BH19 3HG ☎ 0345 800 2070 ✉ cottages@nationaltrust.org.uk 🌐 www.nationaltrust.org.uk/holidays/spyway-cottage-dorset	GR: SY997786 DP: 0 miles N: **WEYMOUTH** 2 🐕 🛜 🚗 Other info:		
Wyke Dorset Cottages 137a, High Street, Swanage, BH19 2NB ☎ 01929 422 776 ✉ bookings@dorsetcottages.com 🌐 www.dorsetcottages.com	GR: SZ027786 DP: 0 miles N: **SWANAGE** 🐕 🛜 🚗 Other info: Open all year		
Allnatt Stop and Stay 35 Ulwell Road, Swanage, BH19 1LG ☎ 01929 421075 ✉ enquiries@stopandstay.co.uk 🌐 www.stopandstay.co.uk	GR: SY029801 DP: 0.5 miles N: **SWANAGE** Offers one night stays 9 🐕 🍴 🛜 🚗 Other info: Open All Year		

Activities

NAME	OTHER INFO	
Jurassic Coast Walking 2 Down Lodge Close, Alderholt, Fordingbridge, SP6 3JA ☎ 01425 655779 ✉ robertwestwood7@gmail.com 🌐 www.jurassiccoastwalking.co.uk	GR: 801 976	DP: 0 miles
	N: **LYME REGIS**	
	Other info: Open all year	
Beer Village Fore Street, Beer, EX12 3JH ☎ 07817934903 ✉ beervillageuk@gmail.com 🌐 www.beervillage.co.uk	GR: SY229822	DP: 0 miles
	N: **BEER**	
	Offers one night stays	
	Other info: Traditional picturesque English fishing village.	

Getting Around

NAME	OTHER INFO	
Eazy Cabs 10 Court Orchard, Bridport, DT6 5EY ☎ 01308 424242 / 07714 444017 ✉ info@eazycabs.co.uk 🌐 www.eazycabs.co.uk	GR: SY460929	DP: 0 miles
	N: **WEST BAY**	
	Other info:	
A1 Taxis 12 Sandhills Crescent, Wool, Wareham, BH20 6HB ☎ 07758 130281 ✉ alex.a1taxis@gmail.com 🌐 www.a1-taxis-wool.business.site	GR: SY831868	DP:
	N: **LULWORTH COVE**	
	Other info: Covering Purbeck area/dog friendly/baggage transfers.	

St Catherine's Chapel in Abbotsbury

The South West Coast Path Association has the support of its membership and many others who help us to champion and care for the Path.

Walking the whole of the South West Coast Path will see you cross hundreds of bridges, gates and stiles, pass more than 4,000 Coast Path signs and go up or down over 30,000 steps. All this vital infrastructure makes the stunning coastline accessible, but it takes a lot of time and money to keep it in good shape.

9 million people every year use the South West Coast Path to experience nature and adventure as well as support their mental and physical wellbeing. To some the Path represents freedom from the frenzy of modern-life, to others it is somewhere to keep fit, rehabilitate or just a much-loved gateway to the sea.

We are reliant on donations and fundraising to keep this important National Trail open and maintained.

How our members' and supporters' money helps:

- **£40** could buy the materials for four oak steps to help you safely climb cliffs or access beautiful coves

- **£75** could provide a school with an interactive workshop on the wildlife and heritage of the Coast Path

- **£250** could buy and install an oak fingerpost to help Path-users navigate between beautiful coastal towns

- **£400** could buy an interpretation panel to bring to life the amazing biodiversity of the trail

- **£500** could deliver a day of educational activities on the Coast Path for two youth groups

- **£1,000** could buy and install two wooden gates, allowing Path-users and livestock farmers to coexist in harmony

One of the ways that supporters help is to fund the 1,000 wooden steps that need to be replaced each year. There are about 20,000 along the entire route.

By providing local rangers with good quality hard wood materials, all with a standard height, their local stretch of the Coast Path is improved.

Replacing these well-known icons of Coast Path infrastructure, enables us to make the hills easier for you and importantly they reduce erosion across some of the most protected landscapes in the UK.

Our efforts to replace steps on the Coast Path is ongoing, please visit our website **www.southwestcoastpath.org.uk** or call us on **01752 896237** to give back to the trail through our latest appeals.

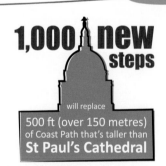

1,000 new steps

will replace

500 ft (over 150 metres) of Coast Path that's taller than **St Paul's Cathedral**

2020

25 MAY

At least **1,000** need to be **replaced** every year

Introducing Coast Path Friendly Events and Tours

The South West Coast Path plays host to many running and hiking events and tours throughout the year. You may well pass by (or be part of!) groups taking part in these sorts of activities as you make your way around the Trail, particularly at weekends.

Event and tour organisers who use the Coast Path can give back to the Trail on which they depend through our 'Coast Path Friendly' scheme. We ask organisers to make their activity 'Coast Path Friendly' by making a contribution of £1 per participant towards our work caring for the Trail, as well as adhering to the National Trails guidance for considerate event management. In return they receive a Coast Path Friendly digital badge which demonstrates their support.

Events and tours help make experiencing the freedom and beauty of our Path easy and fun for people of all ages and backgrounds. However – they do impact the Trail.

Increasing public interest in conservation and a growing belief that we all have a role to play in caring for our beautiful places mean many organisers are eager to support the initiative. The whole National Trail family is now encouraging organisers give back in a similar way across all paths that carry the acorn.

If you participate in paid-for activities on the Trail – be that charity walks, trail-running challenges, hiking holidays or similar, please look for the 'Coast Path Friendly' badge, and support organisations that display it on their website. If your favourite doesn't yet have the badge – encourage them to be 'Coast Path Friendly'! More details can be found at: **www.southwestcoastpath.org.uk/friendly-events**.

Town	Address	Phone	Website
Minehead	The Beach Hotel, The Avenue, Minehead TA24 5AP	01643 702624	www.mineheadbay.co.uk
Porlock	West End, Porlock TA24 8QD	01643 863150	www.porlock.co.uk
Lynton & Lynmouth	Town Hall, Lee Road, Lynton EX35 6BT	01598 752225	www.visitlyntonandlynmouth.com
Combe Martin	Museum, Cross Street EX34 0DH	01271 889031	www.combemartinmuseum.co.uk
Ilfracombe	Landmark Theatre, Ilfracombe EX34 9BZ	01271 863001	www.visitilfracombe.co.uk
Woolacombe	The Esplanade, Woolacombe EX34 7DL	01271 870553	www.woolacombetourism.co.uk
Braunton	Bakehouse Centre, Caen Street EX33 1AA	01271 816688	www.visitbraunton.co.uk
Barnstaple	The Square, Barnstaple EX32 8LN	01271 346747	www.staynorthdevon.co.uk
Bideford	Burton Art Gallery, Kingsley Rd EX39 2QQ	01237 477676	www.visitdevon.co.uk/northdevon
Bude	The Crescent, Bude EX23 8LE	01288 354240	www.visitbude.info
Boscastle	The Harbour, Boscastle PL35 0HD	01840 250010	www.visitboscastleandtintagel.com
Padstow	South Quay, Padstow PL28 8BL	01841 533449	www.padstowlive.com
Newquay	Marcus Hill, Newquay TR7 1BD	01637 838516	www.visitnewquay.org
Perranporth	Wheal Leisure, Perranporth TR6 0EY	01872 575254	www.perranporthinfo.co.uk
Hayle	Hayle Library, Commercial Road TR27 4DE	01736 754399	www.visitcornwall.tv/cornwall-visitor-information/tic/hayle
St Ives	The Library, Gabriel Street, TR26 2LX	01736 796297	www.stives-cornwall.co.uk
Penzance	Station Road, Penzance TR18 2NF	01736 335530	www.purelypenzance.co.uk/tourism
Falmouth	Prince of Wales Pier, Falmouth, TR11 3DF	01326 741194	www.falriver.co.uk
Mevagissey	Hurley Books, 3 Jetty St, Mevagissey PL26 6UH	01726 842200	www.visitmevagissey.co.uk
Fowey	5 South Street, Fowey PL23 1AR	01726 833616	www.fowey.co.uk
Looe	The Guildhall, Fore Street, Looe PL13 1AA	01503 262072	www.visit-southeastcornwall.co.uk
Plymouth	3-5 Plymouth Mayflower, Barbican PL1 2LR	01752 306330	www.visitplymouth.co.uk
Salcombe	Market Street, Salcombe TQ8 8DE	01548 843927	www.salcombetourism.business.site
Kingsbridge	The Quay, Kingsbridge TQ7 1HS	01548 853195	www.hellokingsbridge.co.uk
Dartmouth	The Engine House, Mayors Ave TQ6 9YY	01803 834224	www.discoverdartmouth.com
Brixham	Hobb Nobs Gift Shop, The Quay TQ5 8AW	01803 211211	www.englishriviera.co.uk
Paignton & Torquay	5 Vaughan Parade, Torquay TQ2 5JG	01803 211211	www.englishriviera.co.uk
Shaldon	Shaldon Car Park, Ness Drive TQ14 0HP	01626 873723	www.shaldon-village.co.uk
Teignmouth	Pavillions, Den Crescent, Teignmouth TQ14 8BG	01626 215665	www.visitsouthdevon.co.uk
Dawlish	The Lawn, Dawlish EX7 9PW	01626 215665	www.visitsouthdevon.co.uk
Exmouth	45A The Strand, Exmouth, EX8 1AL	01395 830550	www.visitexmouth.org
Budleigh -Salterton	Fore Street, Budleigh Salterton EX9 6NG	01395 445275	www.visitbudleigh.com
Sidmouth	Ham Lane, Sidmouth EX10 8XR	01395 516441	www.visitsidmouth.co.uk
Seaton	The Underfleet, Seaton EX12 2WD	01297 300390	www.seatontouristinformation.co.uk
Lyme Regis	Church Street, Lyme Regis DT7 3BS	01297 442138	www.lymeregis.org
Bridport	Town Hall, South Street, Bridport DT6 3LF	01308 424901	www.bridportandwestbay.co.uk
Swanage	The White House, Shore Road BH19 1LB	01929 766018	www.swanage.gov.uk
Poole	Poole Museum, 4 High Street, Poole BH15 1BW	01202 262600	www.pooletourism.com

Not on Coast Path			
Truro	30 Boscawen St, Truro TR1 2QQ	01872 274555	www.visittruro.org.uk
Weston Super Mare	The Tropicana, Marine Parade BS23 1BE	01934 888877	www.visit-westonsupermare.com
Ivybridge	The Watermark, Ivybridge PL21 0SZ	01752 897035	www.ivybridgewatermark.co.uk

9 million people use the South West Coast Path every year to experience nature and adventure, as well as support their mental and physical well-being - but most don't realise the hard work that goes into keeping the coastline accessible.

It costs at least £1,400 per mile each year just to keep the trail open. Will you challenge yourself to give back to the trail? Join the South West Coast Path Challenge fundraiser at
www.southwestcoastpath.org.uk/challenge

Shop and show your support

We have some fantastic practical publications to help you plan your adventures on the Coast Path and some beautiful gifts for you and your loved ones. All of the below are available on our online shop, along with a varied selection of guides, maps, clothing and gifts for you to purchase and show your support for the Path. Visit www.southwestcoastpath.org.uk/shop or call 01752 896237 to place your order.

FREE UK POSTAGE & PACKAGING

Reverse guide £7.00

We love our Reverse Guide, redesigned in 2019. This guide will direct you around the whole 630 miles of the Coast Path from South Haven Point to Minehead. It is the perfect companion to this Complete Guide to the South West Coast Path. Dimensions: 150mmx210mm.

'My Coast Path journey' - Pocket-sized journal £5.50

We have redesigned our 'Little yellow log-book' into this beautiful pocket-sized journal for you to record your memories as you journey along the South West Coast Path. We have broken the journal down into 70 sections along the 630 miles of the Coast Path, each section detailing the distance with room for the date, weather and notes.

Completion certificates £6.00

Completing any of the South West Coast Path is an achievement, whether it takes you a few weeks or several years. Commemorate your time on the Path with a Completion certificate. We have certificates for completing the whole 630 miles of the South West Coast Path as well as certificates for the Cornwall, South Devon, North Devon or Jurassic Coast Sections individually. All certificates also come with a badge.

Members of the South West Coast Path Association receive the Completion certificate and badge FREE of charge!

Map poster £9.50

Our Map Poster, measuring 84cm x 59.5cm (A1) comes complete with peninsula outline for marking off sections of the Path you have completed.

Thirty photos of the beautiful landscape around the Path, frame the map, which also includes place names and distances in miles and km.

Tea towel £7.00

Support the Path with this fun and colourful 100% cotton Tea Towel measuring 730mm x 430mm (with hem). Perfect as a gift or just to treat yourself.

Donate!

Walking the whole of the South West Coast Path will see you cross:

- **230 bridges**
- **880 gates, climb over**
- **436 stiles**
- **Pass more than 4,000 Coast Path signs**
- **Go up or down over 30,000 steps**

All this vital infrastructure makes the stunning coastline accessible, but it takes a lot of time and money to keep it in good shape. Help us to continue to keep the Coast Path open and well maintained for generations to come. Any amount you can give will be very appreciated. Donate online at **www.southwestcoastpath.org.uk**, by phone on **01752 896 237** or send a cheque to **Unit 11, Residence 2, Royal William Yard, Plymouth, Devon, PL1 3RP**.

Section reopened in 2019.
Photo: National Trust